Professional Lear
in Schools and Hi

Volume 6

Christopher Day • John Chi-Kin Lee
Editors

New Understandings of Teacher's Work

Emotions and Educational Change

Springer

Editors
Prof. Christopher Day
School of Education
University of Nottingham
Jubilee Campus, Wollaton Road
NG8 1BB Nottingham, UK
christopher.day@nottingham.ac.uk

Prof. John Chi-Kin Lee
Hong Kong Institute of Education
Tai Po, New Territories
Hong Kong SAR
jcklee@ied.edu.hk

DOI 10.1007/978-94-007-0545-6
Springer Dordrecht Heidelberg London New York

Printed on acid-free paper

Springer is part of Springer Science+Business Media (springer.com/mycopy)

Contents

Contributors

Mike Askew University of London, Malet Street, London, WC1E 7HU, UK

Brenda R. Beatty School of Graduate Studies in Education, University of Melbourne, Melbourne, VIC, Australia
e-mail: bbeatty@unimelb.edu.au, brendabeatty@brbconsulting.ca

Robert V. Bullough Jr. CITES (Center for the Improvement of Teacher Education and Schooling), Brigham Young University, Provo, UT, USA
e-mail: bob_bullough@byu.edu

Megan Crawford Oxford Brookes University, Oxford, UK
e-mail: mcrawford@brookes.ac.uk

Christopher Day School of Education, University of Nottingham, Jubilee Campus, Wollaton Road, NG8 1BB Nottingham, UK
e-mail: christopher.day@nottingham.ac.uk

Jeremy Hodgen Department of Education and Professional Studies, King's College London, London, UK
e-mail: jeremy.hodgen@kcl.ac.uk

Chris James Department of Education, University of Bath, Bath, UK
e-mail: cj234@bath.ac.uk

Geert Kelchtermans Catholic University of Leuven, Leuven, Belgium
e-mail: geert.kelchtermans@ped.kuleuven.be

John Chi-Kin Lee Hong Kong Institute of Education, Tai Po, New Territories, Hong Kong SAR
e-mail: jcklee@ied.edu.hk

Diane Mayer School of Education, Deakin University, Burwood, Australia
e-mail: diane.mayer@deakin.edu.au

Nel Noddings Lee Jacks Professor of Education Emerita, Stanford University, Stanford, CA, USA
e-mail: noddings@stanford.edu

Izhar Oplatka School of Education, Tel Aviv University, Tel Aviv, Israel
e-mail: oplatka@post.tau.ac.il

Thomas G. Reio Jr. Department of Leadership and Professional Studies, Florida International University, Miami, USA
e-mail: reiot@fiu.edu

Hong-Biao Yin Faculty of Education, The Chinese University of Hong Kong, Sha Tin, NT, Hong Kong, China

Michalinos Zembylas Open University of Cyprus, Nicosia, Cyprus
e-mail: m.zembylas@ouc.ac.cy

About the Authors

Mike Askew Professor of mathematics education at Kings College, University of London. His teaching and research interests span research methods and mathematics education, and his research focus is in developing theoretical perspectives on the interaction between teaching and learning, understanding how primary teachers' beliefs and knowledge interact with both their interpretation of policy and their practices, and exploring the nature of teacher and pupil change.

Brenda R. Beatty Her research, writing and keynote address the emotions of school leadership, collaborative culture building and leadership development. She has been awarded a lifetime fellowship with the Australian Council for Educational Leaders in recognition of her national and international contribution to educational leadership development and research. She is currently a faculty member of the University of Melbourne, School of Graduate Studies.

Robert V. Bullough Jr. Professor of teacher education and associate director of the Center for the Improvement of Teacher Education and Schooling (CITES), Brigham Young University, Provo, Utah. His most recent books include (with Craig Kridel), *Stories of the Eight-Year Study: Reexamining Secondary Education in America* (SUNY Press, 2007) and *Counternarratives: Studies of Teacher Education and Becoming and Being a Teacher* (SUNY Press, 2008). His professional interests are wide ranging, from studies of the history of education and teacher education to mentoring, beginning teacher development and self-study. Most recently he has completed a book addressing the various issues associated with traumatic brain injury and recovery.

Megan Crawford Reader in education at Oxford Brookes University. Previously, Megan worked at the Institute of Education, London, Warwick University and the Open University. Her background is in primary schools and she is the chair of the British Educational Leadership, Management and Administration Society (BELMAS). Her research interests include emotion and leadership and leadership preparation and development.

Christopher Day Professor of education in the University of Nottingham. He is editor in chief of *Teachers and Teaching: Theory and Practice and co-editor of the Educational Action Research International Journal*. In addition to directing a four-year nationally funded research study on variations in teachers' work, lives and effectiveness, he is currently directing an international project on successful school principalship and co-directing a national ESRC-funded seminar series on teacher resilience. His books have been published in several languages, and recent publications include *The New Lives of Teachers* (2010 London, Routledge); *Teachers Matter* (2007 Maidenhead, Open University Press); *Successful Principalship: International Perspectives* (co-edited, 2007 Dordrecht, Springer); *A Passion for Teaching* (2004 London, Routledge); and *International Handbook of the Continuing Professional Development of Teachers* (2004 Maidenhead, Open University Press).

Jeremy Hodgen Senior lecturer in mathematics education at King's College London. His research interests include mathematics teaching and learning, assessment and teachers' professional development and subject knowledge. He is a member of the Editorial Board of Research in Mathematics Education and a member of the National Centre for Excellence in the Teaching of Mathematics Higher Education group.

Chris James Professor of educational leadership and management in the Department of Education at the University of Bath. His main research interests are in the leadership and management in schools and colleges, the affective aspects of educational organisations, collaborative working in educational settings and school governing. During his career, Chris has directed a large number of educational research projects and published over 170 items including five books.

Geert Kelchtermans He studied educational sciences and philosophy at the University of Leuven (Belgium), where he now works as a full professor and chair of the Center for Educational Policy, Innovation and Teacher Education. His main research interests involve teacher development, life history and narrative research, school improvement and pedagogy of teacher education.

John Chi-Kin Lee Vice president (academic) and chair professor of curriculum and instruction of the Hong Kong Institute of Education. He was formerly dean of education and professor at the Chinese University of Hong Kong as well as guest/adjunct professor in more than twenty universities in Mainland China including the Beijing Normal University, Shanghai Jiao Tong University and Nanjing University. His recent publications include *The Changing Role of Schools in Asian Societies: Schools for the Knowledge Society* (with Kerry Kennedy, Routledge, 2008), *Schooling for Sustainable Development in Chinese Communities: Experience with Younger Children* (co-edited with Michael Williams, Springer, 2009).

Diane Mayer Head of the School of Education at Deakin University, Australia and recently associate dean for professional programs in the Graduate School of

Education at the University of California at Berkeley, USA. Her research and scholarship examines issues associated with the professionalism of teaching and what that means for the policy and practice of teacher education and the work of early career teachers.

Nel Noddings Lee Jacks Professor of Education, Emerita, Stanford University. She is past president of the National Academy of Education, the Philosophy of Education Society and the John Dewey Society. In addition to seventeen books, she is the author of more than 200 articles and chapters on topics ranging from the ethics of care to mathematical problem solving. Her latest book (2010) is *The Maternal Factor: Two Paths to Morality.*

Izhar Oplatka Associate professor and head of the executive program of educational administration and leadership in the School of Education, Tel Aviv University, Israel. His current areas of interest are the career and career development of teachers/principals, gender and educational administration, school marketing and foundations of educational administration as a field of study.

Thomas G. Reio Jr. Associate professor in the Department of Leadership and Professional Studies at Florida International University. His research interests include learning motivation-cognitive and sensory curiosity, risk-taking, teacher workplace socialization and school-to-work transition. He is editor of *Human Resource Development Review* and co-editor of *New Horizons in Adult Education and Human Resource Development.*

Hong-Biao Yin Assistant professor at the Department of Curriculum and Instruction, Faculty of Education, The Chinese University of Hong Kong. He was awarded his PhD on teacher emotion in curriculum reform at the Chinese University of Hong Kong. His main research interests include curriculum change and implementation, teacher emotion, teacher development and student motivation.

Michalinos Zembylas Assistant professor of education at the Open University of Cyprus. His research interests lie in the area of exploring how discursive, political and cultural aspects define the experience of emotion and affect in education. He is particularly interested in how affective politics intersect with issues of social justice pedagogies, intercultural and peace education and citizenship education.

Chapter 1
Emotions and Educational Change: Five Key Questions

Christopher Day and John Chi-Kin Lee

This book contains original contributions from scholars from various parts of world. Each chapter addresses five key questions which relate to the role of emotions in educational change, teaching, teacher education and leadership:

1. What are the central emotional theme(s) of teacher lives and careers in teaching and what part do they play in their work, lives, and leadership roles in the context of widespread educational reform?
2. How do working conditions, organizational structures, school/teacher cultures and individual biographies affect teachers' emotional well-being?
3. To what extent do the context-specific dynamics of reform affect teacher emotions? What is the relationship between these and the roles of teachers and leaders?
4. What are the implications of 1. to 3. for the management and leadership of educational change for school improvement? and
5. How might research on teacher emotions in education inform programmes of pre-service, in-service teacher education and school leadership?

The nature, roles and effects of emotions in teacher development, educational change and school improvement have become subjects of increasing importance in understanding the work, quality and effectiveness of teachers and school leaders. In 1996, the *Cambridge Journal of Education* published a special issue on teacher emotion in teaching while in 2005, *Teaching and Teacher Education* published another special issue on teacher emotion and educational change (van Veen and Lasky 2005). There are a small number of edited books in the area of emotions, e.g. *Handbook of the Sociology of Emotions* (edited by Stets and Turner 2006), Springer; *Emotion in Education* (Schutz and Pekrun 2007), Elsevier/Academic Press; *Emotions in the Workplace: Research, Theory, and Practice* (Ashkanasy et al. 2000) but education is not the main focus. Schutz and Zembylas' (2009) recent edited book *Advances in teacher emotion research: The impact on teachers' lives* focuses upon

C. Day (✉)
School of Education, University of Nottingham, Jubilee Campus, Wollaton Road, NG8 1BB Nottingham, UK
e-mail: christopher.day@nottingham.ac.uk

C. Day, J. C.-K. Lee (eds.), *New Understandings of Teacher's Work*, Professional Learning and Development in Schools and Higher Education 6,
DOI 10.1007/978-94-007-0545-6_1, © Springer Science+Business Media B.V. 2011

different epistemological and theoretical lenses on teacher emotions. Four major findings are identified from that book: "[T]eachers emotions are inextricably linked to teachers' well being, identity and emotion management in teaching" (p. 368); "teachers' emotions influence and are influenced by student-teacher relationships" (p. 369); "emotions constitute a key dimension in teachers' lives, especially in times of change—demographic changes; social and cultural changes; large-scale educational reforms—in which emotions are further intensified" (p. 370); and "teachers' emotions are embedded in particular social, cultural and political structures". Overall, however, there is still a dearth of authoritative works on teacher emotions in school education.

In her seminal text on emotional work and labour in organizations, Hochschild (1990, pp. 118–119) defines emotion as "an awareness of four elements that we usually experience at the same time: (a) appraisals of a situation; (b) changes in bodily sensations; (c) the free or inhibited display of expressive gestures; and (d) a cultural label applied to specific constellations of the first three elements". Her definition of emotion may be understood as an interactional model which reflects a flexible blend of organismic and social constructionist factors (Beatty 2000). Barbalet (2002, p. 4) found that emotion is "A necessary link between social structures and social actor...provoked by circumstance and...experienced as the transformation of dispositions to act. Emotions are also... 'embedded' in history, and purposeful; they include intentions about the future; and embedded in them are our hopes, expectations, and desires." (Bullough and Young 2002). As such, they often have a moral dimension. They are about our self as well as our situation, reflecting our "personal ideologies" and sense of identity in the world. Teachers may experience emotions of joy, happiness, hope, pride, love, compassion, wonder and excitement as expressions of their well being and vocational commitment and achievement (Lazarus and Cohen-Charash 2001; Samier and Schmidt 2009). They may also experience negative emotions such as guilt (Hargreaves 1994), shame (Tamara 2002), envy, jealousy, frustration, disappointment, anxiety, anger, fear, embarrassment and sadness (Little 1996; Oplatka 2007), when threatened, when they receive negative feedback or when their hard fought for professional identity is threatened by mandated reform, rather than renewal efforts. Emotion, with cognition, thus plays a key role in teachers' capacities to transform their circumstances, as well in their responses to change.

The ways in which emotions are managed by teachers often relate to the culture of teaching. In elementary schools, for example, teachers are said to display emotions related a culture of care, love, concern and affection (Oplatka 2007, p. 1377). Nonetheless, there are also mechanisms at work such as *emotional labour* and *emotional work* that may cause their expression of emotions to differ from how they actually feel. *Emotional labour* refers to "a situation in which employees are required to display particular emotional states as a part of their job (Hochschild 1983), displays for which they receive remuneration and that are controlled by others (Wharton 1993)". *Emotional work* refers to "a state in which individual is autonomous in managing his or her emotions in the workplace and is not paid for doing so, and emotion management of any kind is not enforced" (Hochschild 1983). We might relate this to a sense of identity associated with being a professional. Yet

> [identity] is culturally embedded...the broader social conditions in which teachers live and work, the emotional contexts, and the personal and professional elements of teachers' lives, experiences, beliefs and practices are integral to one another, and ... there are often tensions between these which impact to a greater or lesser extent upon teachers' sense of self or identity. (Day and Kington 2008, p. 9)

> Research suggests, also, that schools may be places of emotional 'silence' (exclusively rational) or emotional absolutism (cultural conformity to organizational rules). When teachers become leaders in their schools, they may experience alienation and disconnectedness between themselves and other teachers. (Beatty and Brew 2004, p. 334)

This book is divided into four parts: teachers and teaching; educational change; teacher education and emotions in leadership.

In the opening chapter of the first part, teachers and teaching, *Hope, Happiness, Teaching and Learning,* Robert Bullough critiques current models of educational reform as portraying teachers as incompetent, selfish and self-serving. In doing so, he suggests that recent government reforms internationally are based upon, "a punishing rather than a positive psychology, a view fixated on weaknesses and deficits rather than learning and growing". The results, he suggests, are the growth of cultures of emotional unhappiness which result in the weakening of a key virtue—hope. This critique of new public management is not new in itself. However, by placing emotions at the centre of the debate about reform, Bullough goes to the heart of conditions for successful change. Teachers' willingness and capacities to teach to their best, to be effective, he implies, are defined by the presence of hope and happiness, and these are a product of agency. Hope, Bullough argues, can be both taught and learned but the power of its presence is influenced by context. Bullough suggests that, whilst most schools are unlikely to be places of hopelessness, mandated reforms which do not take hope and happiness into account may cause this to be the case. Feelings of exhaustion, depersonalisation and reduced sense of personal achievement are well documented as features of poorly led, poorly managed reform; and there is evidence that far from, for example, raising standards of teaching, learning and achievement, such reforms may, over the longer term, not fulfil their purposes. Like Goodlad and his colleagues (2004), before him, Bullough sees the solution to problems of reform in educational "renewal" of hope through, for example, the development of professional learning communities.

In *Teaching and Teacher Emotions: A Post-structural Perspective,* Michalinos Zembylas focuses upon a discussion of one epistemological perspective and its methodological implications for research in the field of emotions. He chooses this in the belief that issues of culture, power and ideology affect the discourse about emotion, the ways in which "emotion" is framed. In doing so, he acknowledges the complexity of and the connections between micro and macro contexts which, for example, Robert Bullough and Chris James explore in this book. Thus, emotions cannot be thought of as only internal states or "personality dynamics" but must, also, be "socially or culturally constructed". Lee and Yin's chapter in Part II provides a good exemplar of this perspective. Emotion, in the sense which Zembylas uses it, is, therefore both "interactional and performative" (see also James), public and private (see also Lee and Yin), positioned in "complex webs of power relations" and, "constituted through language".

In this poststructuralist perspective, emotions are seen as interactive, performative and trans-formative. On the one hand, cultural and social phenomena are constitutive of emotions as a public, political space and on the other, emotions could become constitutive forces for (trans)forming individual, social interactions and power relations. In the context of teaching, teachers and students engage in political transactions as they relate emotionally to one another. These are influenced by their power relations as well as organisational emotional norms. Zembylas proposes three possible directions for future research on emotions in education—theoretical discussion, multiple methods of data collection and analysis and new, "more attractive" ways of representing ethnographic research so that it may better illustrate affective experience. In the final part of his chapter, Zembylas proposes that "critical emotional reflexivity" be central to educational leadership, pre-service and in-service education programmes. The chapter provides an important perspective on how we understand emotions through re-examining the efficacy, usefulness and authenticity of the ways in which research on emotions in education is conducted. Zembylas argues that by using poststructuralist thinking, teachers, teacher educators, policy makers and researchers can, "further explore…how teachers' emotions are located in particular educational histories…and challenge the prevailing social, cultural and political structures"—providing them, perhaps, with a more powerful sense of agency in contexts of change.

In the third chapter, *Uncertain Professional Identities: Managing the Emotional Contexts of Teaching,* Christopher Day draws upon data from a unique national, mixed methods four-year project on teachers' work lives and effectiveness. He finds associations between teachers' emotional states and their sense of professional identity. The findings suggest that identity is neither stable nor unstable but varies according to context and response to the context. Emotional identify is affected, positively and negatively, by socio-cultural and educational policy environments, the nature and management of mandated reforms, but also by the leadership and workplace culture of the school, by relationships with colleagues and by personal influences located in individual biographies and vulnerabilities which are rooted in life outside the school setting. Teachers' stable sense of identity is associated with their perceived and measured effectiveness in contributing to their students' progress. Teachers experience periods of stable and unstable identity and it is their capacity to manage these which influences their sense of well being, commitment, agency and, ultimately, their effectiveness in the classroom. Change, he suggests, affects not only what teachers have to do and how they do it, but also how they feel about their work. There is, therefore, an unavoidable inter-relationship between cognitive and emotional identities. The chapter identifies four identity "scenarios". The author characterises these as, "sites of struggle" in which the pressure to sustain stability varies in intensity. Through teacher cameos drawn from the larger study of 300 teachers, he points to the presence of key positive and negative influences in each site of struggle. He provides, also, examples of the strategies which teachers adopted in their efforts to manage these. Day's chapter provides a health warning for policy makers and school leaders who fail to account for this relationship in their efforts to implement new reforms.

In the final chapter in the section *Vulnerability in Teaching: The Moral and Political Roots of a Structural Condition,* Geert Kelchtermans discusses Flemish teachers' negative emotions and cognitive processes which are associated with their feelings of vulnerability. He argues that such feelings of vulnerability in the workplace have moral and political roots. The chapter provides a complementary perspective to that of Christopher Day's chapter. He argues that teachers' experience of negative feelings of, "powerlessness, frustration, disappointment, disillusion, guilt and even anger and fear", at times during their working lives, are in contrast to more positive feelings of "joy, fascination, pride, wonder and enthusiasm" which are at the heart of their motivations to teach; and that teachers' vulnerability is a condition of all their work, regardless of change. Understanding vulnerability, he argues, is thus crucial for understanding their satisfaction (or lack of it) and the quality of their performance. Drawing upon hermeneutical analysis of a case study of the biography of one teacher, Kelchtermans, like Day, identifies educational administration policy, professional relationships and classrooms as sources of vulnerability. He goes on to argue that vulnerability always has "political and moral" roots. Teachers have strong commitments to the best interests of students from both educational and development perspectives, and because they are aware that their decisions in the classroom will have consequences, then criticism and changes in policy may threaten their core values, their ethical/moral purposes. Kelchtermans thus argues that, "the social recognition of both one's technical skills and competences and one's moral integrity is a highly valued social workplace condition and that teachers are always potentially vulnerable". He concludes, with Day, that, whilst the experience of vulnerability, "is always a particular experience, in a particular context, by a particular person", nevertheless, "The basic structure in vulnerability is always one of feeling that one's professional identity and moral integrity, as part of being a 'proper teacher', are questioned…". Yet the chapter ends on a note of optimism and hope with the assertion that vulnerability is not only a condition to be endured in times of challenge but also one to be embraced for the pedagogical possibilities which it enables.

Part II focuses upon educational change. In *Teachers' Emotions in a Mandated Curriculum Reform: A Chinese Perspective,* John Chi-Kin Lee and Hong-Biao Yin observe that teachers' voices are often marginalised as decisions about change and its implementation are taken. Yet, they suggest, positive emotions are a necessary part of teachers' commitment to their work, whether in individualistic, emotionally expressive Western cultures or in the less overt emotional, more collective, interdependent mind sets which, at least until recently, have illustrated Chinese culture. This chapter is one of the first systematic investigations in mainland China to explore the emotional responses and experiences of Chinese teachers towards national curriculum reforms. The three-year project used interviews and reflective journals with 17 Chinese teachers in two senior secondary schools to elicit and analyse memories of particular incidents which caused positive or negative emotions.

The researchers found that these teachers experienced a mixture of anticipatory excitement and, like those in Reio's chapter which follows, anxiety, together with feelings of, at least temporary loss of control as they learnt to work with new text books which demanded the use of a greater range of teaching approaches. In keeping with the traditional culture of privacy, so called face (*Mianzi*) public compliancy and professionalism, on the one hand they did not share their anxieties with their students or their administrators and on the other, they did share their feelings with their school colleagues. The interview findings revealed that Chinese teachers' emotional episodes could be categorized into three levels: individual level, highlighting teachers' morality and responsibility towards the students; interactional level, emphasizing teachers' dignity and teachers' collaboration; and institutional level reflecting the respect for superior, harmony (*he*) and the examination culture in Chinese society. The authors conclude that "the Confucian quest for interpersonal and social harmony in Chinese society", may discourage rather than encourage the mediating role which teachers in other countries take in the implementation of mandated reform. Like Reio in the next chapter, they suggest increased collaborative activities as a means of increasing teachers' positive emotional responses to change.

In *Teacher Emotions and Socialization-Related Learning in the Context of Educational Change*, Thomas Reio first provides a critique of policy-led reforms in the United States which are aimed at boosting students' academic outcomes, especially in mathematics, science, reading, writing and civics. Drawing primarily on American research, he observes, with others, that more often than not, teachers are provided with insufficient time and direction and that these, together with an accompanying increase in workload, result in a range of principally negative emotions which tend to challenge existing professional identities and have adverse effects upon their motivation, learning and performance. Building on his previous work, he charts relationships between teacher emotions, learning and adaptation and proposes a range of professional learning opportunities within a notion of "socialisation-related learning", as a means of reducing the uncertainties, anxiety and stress experienced by teachers, particularly in contexts of mandated change. Such learning emphasises the importance of skilled interventions through, for example, coaching, mentoring, consultation with experienced peers and "supervisors" in contexts where leaders provide time and open cultures which build trust. Such interventions will need to be made by those who themselves are emotionally attuned to the personal, professional and organisation contexts in which they work.

In *The Importance of Affective Containment for Teacher Effectiveness and Successful Educational Change,* Chris James explores issues of emotional disturbance from the standpoint of educational institutions as places of affective intensity. Whereas Chin and Yin's work focused upon the teachers lived experiences, his chapter provides a close and detailed analysis of the nature of affective experience and its relationship with teacher effectiveness in contexts of change. He defines emotions as, "mobilisations of power" and differentiates between 'feelings' and "moods". Key to the discussion is his view of anxiety as a defence which is 'brought into play' in social settings the discussions. He discusses, largely from a psychological perspective, four particular social defences which are used for protection from primitive, personal and work-related anxieties—routines, resistance and task-related defences and splitting and projection. These are especially important as a means of enhancing the self-awareness of the individual, (understanding one's own responses to change) and for those in leadership roles. James' detailed examination of these social defences leads to a discussion of the benefits of 'affective containment' of emotions at individual and group levels in educational organisations and procedural principles for actions in support of this.

In the first chapter of the third part, "teacher education", *"But That's the Thing; Who Else Is Going to Teach Besides the Idealist?" Learning to Teach in Emotional Contexts,* Diane Mayer focuses upon the dilemmas which occur at the intersection of vision and context for teachers in their early years in urban schools. Using illustrations of four teachers in urban schools in the USA, she charts how they negotiated these dilemmas in order to establish and sustain their personal and professional identities and discusses the implications of her findings for pre-service teacher educators. The findings are important for policy makers also, given the high dropout rate of teachers in their first five years. Drawing on Lasky's (2005), Kelchtermans's (2005) and Day et al.'s (2006) concepts of identity, Mayer argues that teacher identities are constructed and reconstructed through negotiation within the space between the structure or context and an individual's agency within that context. Mayer found that three dilemmas were reported: when teachers found that in order to survive in these urban contexts they had to teach in ways which were inconsistent with their beliefs and vision; when their future career expectations were in conflict with those of others in their workplace; and when state and district mandates about what and how to teach conflicted with their vision of what was an appropriate curriculum which was defined by them as being in the best interests of their students. In negotiating these dilemmas, Mayer found that teachers need to adjust conceptions of success with an ethic of care, locate communities of support from teacher colleagues, administration and teacher education cohorts, and search for fulfilment outside the school. In a sense, this chapter mirrors the "vulnerabilities" and the "complex web of power relations" identified by Kelchtermans and Zembylas, which these new teachers had to learn to navigate. Like Nodding's chapter in this book, Mayer identifies the ethic of care and "doing the right thing" for students as a core concern of these teachers. Along with others in this book (see Day, and also Reio especially), she identifies colleagues, principals and peers, but also, importantly, "the idealism of their vision" (what Bullough refers to as "moral purpose") as key factors in teachers' motivation to continue their work in education; and she calls upon teacher educators to build the capacities required for their pre-service teachers to sustain their idealism.

In her original paper *Stories and Affect in Teacher Education,* Noddings (1996) laments that affect and emotion have been ignored or distrusted in the teaching profession and the tendency to insist on "detachment, distance, cool appraisal and systematic procedures" (p. 435). She further highlights the importance of affect in teacher education and argues that stories could be used to enhance the engagement and human relationships of both students and teachers. In a new postscript of this paper, she re-affirms the importance of stories in facilitating the development of empathy which comprises both cognitive and emotional processes and refers to both understanding and feeling. She illustrates through Bill's story that "A fully developed empathy will respond to the feeling expressed without regard to the personal history of the one suffering." This implies that we may try to learn how to understand and empathize even with negative feelings such as pain or fear. The ultimate value is to encourage empathic development that helps contribute to both social justice and world peace. Other scholars such as Kassem (2002) echo that teacher educators should discuss with student teachers Goleman's (1995) six innate emotions including fear, anger, sadness, surprise, disgust, and enjoyment. Noddings highlights the imperative of emotional "decoding" skills which "involve empathy, the ability to 'read' and to feel the social/emotional signals of others" (p. 367).

In the following chapter, *Emotion, Identity and Teacher Learning: Becoming a Primary Mathematics Teacher,* Jeremy Hodgen and Mike Askew examine the case of a primary teacher in England who developed an identity as a teacher of mathematics. Using Wenger's (1998) notion of communities of practice, they refer to a teacher identity which may encompass various identities within different communities ranging from classroom, the wider school and professional communities on the one hand and include ongoing negotiation, meaning-making and reconciliation on the other. They also make use of the notions of "positional identity" (enacted in specific communities) and "figured identity" (such as enacted through being a mathematics teacher) to analyze the case of a primary school mathematics teacher, Ursula, exploring the deep connections between emotion and identity. One interesting finding is that against the backdrop of strong disciplinary focus of the mathematics, "currently the identities most easily and readily available to primary teachers are not associated with such an expanded notion of care". The authors call for professional development that could facilitate teachers' emotional development as well as teacher development of both disciplinary intimacy and integrity.

The final part of the book focuses upon the role played by emotions in school leadership. In the first of the three chapters, *The Dynamic Nature of Emotions in Educational Leadership: Lessons from the Career Stories of Israeli Late-Career Principals,* Izhar Oplatka identifies the key responsibility of leaders to build positive psychological and social environments for effective teaching and learning (see also Reio's and James' chapters). He uses the life stories of late career principals as a lens to view how principals can help others to promote well being, happiness and achievement in their school communities (see also, Bullough) and, in doing so, counter the alienation, anxieties and sense of dislocation experienced by some colleagues as a result of working in neo-liberal reform contexts. Like others before him, this author finds associations between leadership trust, understanding and appreciation and teachers' sense of commitment, self-efficacy and professional identity. Building on the work of those who have researched emotional intelligence (EI), and emotional understanding (EU), using Salovey and Mayer's (1990) original conceptualisation of EI as his conceptual framework, Oplatka reports on life-story interviews with 15 late career elementary school principals. Their stories suggest that there had been a growth over their tenure as principals in their levels of trust in teachers, and in their patience and ability to exercise empathy (though sometimes at a cost as professional—personal boundaries were crossed). This had been accompanied by a growing sense of their own efficacy and self-confidence as they built teachers' capacity and distributed leadership more widely as their leadership became more "emotionally attuned". Whilst these are "single voice" stories, the consistency of the message of these elementary school principals suggests that emotional understanding needs to play a key role in all leadership training and continuing development programmes.

In the second chapter, *Rationality and Emotion in Education Leadership—Enhancing Our Understanding,* Megan Crawford argues persuasively for acknowledgement of and further research on rationality and emotion in leadership (a broader concept than principalship) in order to enhance understandings of teachers' careers as they move into leadership roles and in the belief that these may also enhance understandings of the part which leaders themselves take in leadership. In this chapter, Crawford argues that the biological and psychological aspects of emotion are mediated by the social settings and the lives and careers of the people involved. This resonates with Day's earlier chapter on teachers' uncertain identities in "sites of struggle". Like Oplatka, though, she is skeptical of the use of "emotional intelligence". Crawford draws upon leadership narratives with memories of the "emotional epiphanies" of English headteachers' work and personal lives, in order to "unravel the connections" between leadership, emotion and life story.

In the final chapter, *Leadership and Teacher Emotions,* Brenda Beatty extends the discussion in the previous two chapters in her autobiographical overview of the theoretical and practical implications of her own extensive research over time into the emotions of teaching, leadership and learning and her design and implementation of master's level preparation programmes for school leaders in the USA and Australia. Her credo is that leaders who are emotionally prepared and resilient are more likely than those who are not to, "create school cultures that acknowledge the inner work of emotional understanding", and thus "revitalise their own, as well as teachers' and students' learning".

Beatty affirms the positive power of an emotional connection between teachers and their leaders illustrated by respect, care and support. For leaders themselves, her findings from the International Leadership Conversations Project reveal that "... in face of the isolation and emotional constrictions on their patterned interactions with others and themselves, there is tremendous value in the emotional support of a candid collaborative connection with other leaders". In a wide ranging exposition of the broader research literature on successful school leadership in contexts of high intensity, mandated change, Beatty argues for the need to build more "humane and interpersonally connected" school cultures which are characterised by trusting, open teacher–leader relationships. In the chapter, Beatty describes her own research journey as she developed her understandings of emotional leadership and used these as a theoretical framework for the design of a master's degree programme in school leadership in which what she describes as the emotional silences in leadership were broken. The chapter ends with an evaluation by nine principal participants in Victoria, Australia, of the effects of the programme on their practices.

Concluding Remarks

The texts of each of the chapters in this book are based, either implicitly or explicitly, upon a view of good teachers and teaching at its best as requiring, in Tom Sergiovanni's words, "the head, the heart and the hand". The authors do not seek to draw a line of separation between cognition, affect and competency. Rather, they point to the crucial part played by emotion in teachers' capacities to exercise their professionalism. The contexts of change in which many of them work, as evidenced by the geographical spread of contributions in this book, consistently challenge their moral and ethical purposes, their vision, their sense of positive identity, efficacy and agency. Most of all they challenge the hope and optimism which characterise the teaching and learning of teachers and their students in the best classrooms all over the world. It is not that reforms themselves are intrinsically wrong, for the intentions of reformers are almost always to benefit society. It is that often the way they are presented, the speed of their imposed implementation and their management constrain rather than contribute to educational renewal. In their haste for implementation, policy makers often, it seems, still forget to engage teachers in dialogue and that it is the teachers in the classrooms, not they, who will make the difference to students' progress, well being and achievement through the contextually sensitive, knowledgeable decisions which they make. It is they who have the ultimate responsibility for change. Good teacher educators and school leaders recognise this by providing close up support through skilled and sustained interpersonal relations and, indirectly, through high-quality opportunities for continuing learning and development and collaboration or through accredited programmes. They also know, through their own experiences, the latent vulnerabilities (to students, parents and mandated external change), which are at the heart of the work which the best teachers carry out often in difficult psychological and social settings. Most of all, though, the chapters in this book represent an intelligent hope that the future can be better than the past and that, finally, an understanding of the importance of teachers' emotions will become central to future reform efforts, development programmes, the work of leaders in schools and teachers' own work and lives. It is our hope, as editors, that this collection will make a contribution to the realisation of this hope.

References

Ashkanasy, N. M., Hartel, C. E. J., & Zerbe, W. J. (Eds.). (2000). *Emotions in the workplace: Research, theory, and practice.* Westport: Quorum Books.

Barbalet, J. (2002). Introduction: Why emotions are crucial. In J. Barbalet (Ed.), *Emotional sociology* (pp. 1–9). London: Blackwell.

Beatty, B. R. (2000). The emotions of educational leadership: Breaking the silence. *International Journal of Leadership in Education, 3,* 331–357.

Beatty, B. R., & Brew, C. (2004). Trusting relationships and emotional epistemologies: A foundational leadership issue. *School Leadership and Management, 24*(3), 329–356.

Bullough, R. V., Jr., Bullough, D. A. M., & Mayes, P. B. (2002). Learning to teach as an intern: The emotions and the self. *Teacher Development, 6*(3), 417–431.

Day, C., & Kington, A. (2008). Identity, well-being and effectiveness: The emotional contexts of teaching. *Pedagogy, Culture & Society, 16*(1), 7–23.

Day, C., Kington, A., Stobart, G., & Sammons, P. (2006). The personal and professional selves of teachers: Stable and unstable identities. *British Educational Research Journal, 32*(4), 601–616.

Goleman, D. (1995). *Emotional intelligence.* New York: Bantam Books.

Goodlad, J. I., Mantle-Bromley, C., & Goodlad, S. J. (2004). *Education for everyone: Agenda for education in a democracy.* San Francisco: Jossey-Bass.

Hargreaves, A. (1994). *Changing teachers, changing times: Teachers' work and culture in the post modern age.* London: Cassell.

Hochschild, A. R. (1983). *The managed heart: Commercialization of human feeling.* Berkley: University of California Press.

Hochschild, A. R. (1990). Ideology and emotion management: A perspective and path for future research. In T. Kemper (Ed.), *Research agendas in the sociology of emotions* (pp. 117–134). Albany: State University of New York Press.

Kassem, C. L. (2002). Developing the teaching professional: What teacher educators need to know about emotions. *Teacher Development, 6*(3), 363–372.

Kelchtermans, G. (2005). Teachers' emotions in educational reforms: Self understanding, vulnerable commitment, and micropolitical literacy. *Teaching and Teacher Education, 21,* 995–1006.

Lasky, S. (2005). A sociocultural approach to understanding teacher identity, agency and professional vulnerability in a context of secondary school reform. *Teaching and Teacher Education, 21,* 899–916.

Lazarus, R. S., & Cohen-Charash, Y. (2001). Discrete emotions in organizational life. In R. L. Payne & C. L. Cooper (Eds.), *Emotions at work: Theory, research and applications in management* (pp. 45–81). Chichester: Wiley.

Little, J. W. (1996). The emotional contours and career trajectories of (disappointed) reform enthusiasts. *Cambridge Journal of Education, 26*(3), 345–360.

Noddings, N. (1996). Stories and affect in teacher education. *Cambridge Journal of Education, 26*(3), 435–447.

Oplatka, I. (2007). Managing emotions in teaching: Toward an understanding of emotion displays and caring as nonprescribed role elements. *Teachers College Record, 109*(6), 1374–1400.

Salovey, P., & Mayer, J. D. (1990). Emotional intelligence. *Imagination, Cognition and Personality, 9*(3), 185–211.

Samier, E. A., & Schmidt, M. (2009). Editors' introduction. In E. A. Samier & M. Schmidt (Eds.), *Emotional dimensions of educational administration and Leadership* (pp. 1–17). London: Routledge.

Schutz, P. A., & Pekrun, R. (Eds.). (2007). *Emotion in education.* Burlington: Academic Press.

Schutz, P. A., & Zembylas, M. (Eds.). (2009). *Advances in teacher emotion research: The impact on teachers' lives.* Dordrecht: Springer.

Stets, J. E., & Turner, J. H. (Eds.). (2006). *Handbook of the sociology of emotions.* The Netherlands: Springer.

Tamara, B. (2002). Shame: An emotional response to doing Mathematics as an adult and a teacher. *British Educational Research Journal, 28*(5), 705–721.

Van Veen, K., & Lasky, S. (2005). Editorial: Emotions as a lens to explore teacher identity and change: Different theoretical approaches. *Teaching and Teacher Education, 21*(8), 895–898.

Wenger, E. (1998). *Communities of practice: Learning, meaning and identity.* Cambridge: Cambridge University Press.

Wharton, A. (1993). The affective consequences of service work: Managing emotions on the job. *Work and Occupations, 20,* 205–232.

Part I
Teachers and Teaching

Chapter 2
Hope, Happiness, Teaching, and Learning

Robert V. Bullough Jr.

Introduction

The intention of this chapter is to explore *hope*, as a virtue—one of three Christian martyrs, daughters of Sophia (Wisdom)—and as an emotion, and *happiness*, an especially complex emotion, in relationship to teaching, learning, and school improvement. My desire is to broaden the conversation about teaching and learning to include greater attention to the central but underappreciated place of hope and happiness in all things educational. Being taken for granted, hope and happiness have been dismissed to the sidelines in debates of school of improvement with the result that a great deal of harm has been caused to teachers and to children. Up front it is important to mention that neither hope nor happiness can be made sense of without their opposites, hopelessness, despair, and sadness. In addition, I should mention here the perspective that underlies this chapter is a view consistent with positive psychology, of humans as self-directed and adaptive beings that, when they can, "choose behaviors that make them feel fully alive, competent, and creative" (Seligman and Csikszentmihalyi 2000, p. 9).

The Problem

Across much of the industrial world teachers are under attack as incompetent, selfish, and self-serving. Aggressive reform—not renewal—efforts are underway based on a set of generally false assumptions about teacher motivation (increased competition promises higher levels of teacher and school performance), intentions (teachers are selfish and self-serving), the nature and difficulty of the work of teaching (aims can be prescribed in advance and almost anyone can teach), evidence of performance (test scores are meaningful representations of the essential school aims),

R. V. Bullough Jr. (✉)
CITES (Center for the Improvement of Teacher Education and Schooling),
Brigham Young University, Provo, UT, USA
e-mail: bob_bullough@byu.edu

C. Day, J. C.-K. Lee (eds.), *New Understandings of Teacher's Work*, Professional Learning and Development in Schools and Higher Education 6,
DOI 10.1007/978-94-007-0545-6_2, © Springer Science+Business Media B.V. 2011

the power of schooling (that setting standards and tinkering with curricula can resolve persistent social problems), and responsibility (teachers are wholly responsible for student learning). The driving assumptions of school reform are grounded in a punishing rather than a positive psychology, a view fixated on weaknesses and deficits rather than on learning and growing. The result, as Bottery (2003) argues, may be the creation of a "culture of unhappiness" in schools, where, in the attempt to create "error-free, risk-less organisations where trust is unnecessary because everything is so controlled and micro-managed" (p. 196), hope weakens and teachers are left increasingly anxious, fraught with self-doubt, and lacking control over their work-lives.

Behind the scenes, Ball (2003) observes the rise of a modernist specter, a new managerialism supporting a narrow professionalism in education and moored to a naive and tenacious but misplaced faith in the development of a science of human engineering. On this view, as Gadamer suggests, the person of "practical wisdom" and, I would add, of deep compassion, is replaced by the "expert": "What becomes important is not the capacity to make responsible decisions on one's own but rather the willingness to adapt to decisions others have made for one, decisions that, in addition, largely follow the logic of technological imperatives…. [G]oals and purposes are…dictated by technological demands and possibilities" (Warnke 1987, p. 163). These are the origins of "best practices" in education, free floating rules of action—just the sort of rules that Dewey (1929) argued were "objectionable and destructive" of the art of education (p. 14) and that have the consequence of distancing teachers from those they teach and of undermining the sources of happiness found in teaching.

There is no doubt that the signs of "performativity" are increasingly evident across the educational landscape as are signs of teaching becoming more stressful and, for many educators, much less satisfying. When "valued for their productivity alone" authentic social relations, the sort that encourage hope and happiness, are replaced by "judgmental relations" (Ball 2003, p. 224) and "fabrications" follow—"versions of an organization (or person) which [do] not exist…. [Rather] they are produced purposefully in order 'to be accountable'" (p. 224). Judgmental relations enhance vulnerability and undermine trust by encouraging deceit. As I have written elsewhere, under such conditions a kind of schizophrenia results among teachers, a deep "double-mindedness," a "condition resulting from feeling or being compelled to work against what one believes and of being pulled in multiple directions by conflicting but always insistent claims. Under such conditions, work slowly becomes joyless" (Bullough 2008, p. 5). Being required to be other than self is clearly numbing (Bullough and Knowles 1990). Where educational ends are test-score dominated, narrow, and uninspiring, educators find investing fully in their work difficult, and aspirations lower and performance flattens (Valli and Buese 2007). Under such conditions, exceptional teachers are domesticated, and a stultifying sameness sets in yet, happily, not for all teachers (Day et al. 2006). Despite deteriorating work conditions many teachers not only avoid burning out but actually thrive, demonstrating "high levels of commitment and agency, often against the odds" (p. 314). These are teachers of hope and happiness, heroic in their resistance and resilience.

Remarkably, despite their importance to teaching and learning hope and happiness are rarely topics of discussion among educators and most especially among those who seek to influence educational practice through policy pronouncements or by legislative enactment. This is so even though, as almost every beginning teacher knows, to teach is inevitably to be in the hope and happiness business, for hope and happiness are essential conditions for life, living, and learning, and most especially for the well-being of those, like teachers, who live with and for the young (see Elbaz 1992). The centrality of hope and happiness to teachers is evident in studies of teacher motivation; mostly, teachers teach for intrinsic reasons, the "desire to make a social contribution, shape the future, and work with children/adolescents" (Richardson and Watt 2006, p. 44). Every parent knows of the importance of hope and happiness to a child's growth and development. Yet, when it comes to the hope and happiness of children and their teachers, generally there is a deafening silence when what is needed is a consistent and robust institutional commitment.

Efforts to create greater effectiveness among teachers, more learning among students, and higher performing schools that ignore the hope and happiness of children and teachers will inevitably fail. Worse, they will be harmful.

On Hope

> Hope is both the earliest and the most indispensable virtue inherent in the state of being alive. Others have called this deepest quality *confidence*.... If life is to be sustained hope must remain, even where confidence is wounded, trust impaired. (Erikson 1964, p. 115)

Surveying the results of various attempts at educational change, Fullan (1997) concluded that mostly teachers' experience was profoundly negative, leaving behind a "sense of hopelessness, either because they are on the defensive from external attack or because they have been part of small groups of reformers who have burned themselves out" (pp. 229–230). Perhaps in frustration, he urged that teachers must "stay hopeful under negative conditions" (p. 230), that "we are down to our last virtue: hope" (p. 221). Fullan did not call for increased optimism but for hope, despite the two terms often being used interchangeably (Gillham and Reivich 2004). What he seems to have noticed is that unlike optimism, which brings with it an expectation of a best outcome, at least as commonly understood, hope may be present even in the most dire of circumstances and despite recognized limits in one's ability to change a situation, a point made by Frankl (1970), among many others. Hope serves as a basis for remaining not only positive but actively engaged in life. For this reason, hope, as a virtue to be sought and practiced, like faith, may be merely a matter of tenacity, as Bertrand Russell once argued, but acting hopeful, even as a matter of stubbornness or of will, can and does encourage positive changes in life circumstances.

Typically, in Western cultures, hope is thought of as a state of mind; when understood as closely related to optimism it is thought of as a personality trait, a matter of temperament; when times are desperate, it is spoken of as a coping mechanism most clearly recognized when lost or missing; and, as previously noted, its deepest grounding is as a virtue to be cultivated and cherished, something taught first by parents and later by teachers (Bullough 2001), among others. Hope also is an emotion, or what Lazarus (1999) calls an "affective blend" (p. 655), a mixture of emotions including fear, anxiety, and happiness, each anticipating possible outcomes and all wrapped to one or another degree in a quiet but determined confidence that enables action and encourages persistence. Hope, then, has a distinctive "feel" about it, distinctive in its emotional blend even as its intensity and duration may vary. Given so many senses of hope, some sorting is required and some digging to identify its educationally important qualities and characteristics.

Lazarus (1999) provides a helpful departure point when he describes hope as involving and following from an appraisal of a situation and as being about "our well-being and the well-being of those about whom we care" (p. 658). In appraising, we seek a realistic assessment of the situation we find ourselves in which guides action and enables coping while simultaneously we seek "the most favorable spin possible on our plight in order not to undermine hope [and thereby avoid falling into the passivity of despair]" (p. 659). As a virtue hope is usually first learned in infancy and childhood and develops in maturity to become the "capacity not to panic in tight situations, to find ways and resources to address difficult problems" (Fullan 1997, p. 221). When facing a troubling situation, we desperately seek reasons to sustain hope even when or especially when to do so seems foolish. We look outside ourselves to others for help and strength, sometimes invoking Providence. Giving up or giving in may be the rational, easy, or even the expected thing to do, but to do so is to act without virtue, courage, or integrity, to be found lacking in an essential way as a human being. To be hopeful is not to *expect* a perfect outcome, yet because hoping takes us beyond our normal abilities, favorable—although often unexpected—outcomes may follow, and to receive them is in a profound sense to live in a state of grace for a time. Relief and happiness then follow; and streams of hope, faith, and gratitude flow together.

Hope is both taught and learned—or not learned—and is often conditional, dependent for its vitality on who and what is involved in the troubling situation faced. Who is involved is important for several reasons, among them that hope, like pessimism, fear, and anger, is contagious (McDermott and Hastings 2000). Remarkably, as Carter (1999) observes, the sight of persons experiencing strong emotions, like disgust, actually "turns on the observer's brain areas that are associated with [the] feeling" (p. 87). That hope is taught to children early and usually by example and through stories, has far reaching implications for those who lack hope as well as for those who care for and about the well-being of the young. As Lasch (1991) suggests:

> Hope implies a deep-seated trust in life that appears absurd to those who lack it. It rests on confidence not so much in the future as in the past. It derives from early memories—no doubt distorted, overlaid with later memories, and thus not wholly reliable as a guide to any factual construction of past events—in which the experience of order and contentment was so intense that subsequent disillusionments cannot dislodge it. (p. 81)

Hence, hope cannot be taught by those who do not possess it and in abundance. Like optimism, to a degree hopefulness is also a matter of temperament, disposition, or personality, a matter of the interaction of rearing with genetics and evolutionary biology. As a trait or disposition, hope has been extensively studied by researchers at the University of Kansas who developed the Hope Scale (Snyder et al. 1991, 2005). Deeply anchored in the assumption that humans are goal directed, the Hope Scale combines self-reports of two elements thought to capture the essential nature of hope: *agency*, a "sense of successful determination in meeting goals in the past, present and future" and of *pathways*, a "sense of being able to generate successful plans to meet goals" (p. 570). Proven valid and reliable, scores on the Hope Scale, like personality measures, remain relatively stable across time and across situations. The model emphasizes cognition, where emotions are:

> the sequelae of cognitive appraisals of goal-related activities. The quality of emotion for a particular goal-related setting depends on the person's perceived hope in that setting. More specifically, the high-hope person's analysis of sufficient agency and pathways in a given goal setting should lead to the perception of relatively high probability of goal attainment, a focus on success rather than failure, a sense of challenge, and a relatively positive emotional state as goal-related activities are conceptualized and undertaken. (p. 571)

Studies by Snyder and his colleagues point toward a wide range of differences between individuals with higher and lower hope scores, each having consequences for teachers and students. (Which side of the equation can claim causality is, of course, uncertain.) For example, individuals with higher scores reported higher self-esteem, greater optimism, less depression, tended to present themselves in a more favorable light, revealed more positive and less "negative affectivity" (p. 575), better problem-focused coping, greater sense of agency even in the face of negative feedback, more pathways to problem solution when blocked, seeking more difficult goals and, importantly, higher overall "self-reported well-being" (p. 577). Respecting the last point, higher hope individuals are reportedly happier than lower hope individuals. The authors conclude that the instrument, even when compared with measures of optimism, "contributes some unique predictive variance in relation to other cognitive- and emotion-based dispositional measures…supporting the robustness of the Hope Scale" (p. 582).

When discussing the "Future of Optimism" Peterson (2000) characterized Snyder and his colleagues' conception of hope as one of three approaches to optimism, uniting elements of the other two models: expectation of goal accomplishment and agency. For Peterson (2006), hope and optimism are nearly identical concepts; hope is "dispositional" or "big optimism." The difficulty with this conclusion, as Lazarus (1999) observes, is that hope cannot be equated to successful agency nor to positive expectations. "I consider this erroneous because we can hope even when we are helpless to affect the outcome. Self-efficacy, or a sense of competence and control, facilitates hope, and it certainly aids in mobilizing problem-focused coping actions, but it is not essential to hope" (p. 674). I agree. Implicitly *to hope* is to acknowledge one's own limitations and dependency even while longing for outcomes beyond one's own understanding, influence, or ability. Nevertheless, facilitating agency and pathways provide promising avenues for educators to encourage hope and happiness in the young and in one another. Others have criticized the agency/pathways conception of hope as reflecting "more egotistical than collective concerns" (Snyder et al. 1997, p. 107). Responding to this charge, Snyder and his colleagues point toward "how high hope individuals enjoy competition and the process of testing themselves and of interacting with others" (p. 114). Hope, they argue, is embedded in social processes; and so it is.

As an emotion, hope has some unusual features. Normally, among the distinguishing characteristics of an emotion is that it is of brief duration, comes on quickly, and has a distinctive physiology, generally including a high state of system arousal. On this view, hope may be more of a mood or an emotional attitude than an emotion. By emotional attitude, Ekman (1992) means emotions like love and hatred that are sustained and "typically involve more than one emotion" (p. 194). This said, as a positive emotion or emotional attitude, hope, like happiness and many other emotions, is more difficult to distinguish than negative emotions like anger, fear, and disgust. In contrast to such emotions, which Fisher (2002) aptly describes as the "vehement passions," hope often brings an acute awareness of others. Generally, the vehement passions tend to "extinguish the reality and claims of others while creating, as illness does, an almost painfully pressing awareness of self—to the point that only the self, and, even more, only the self as it is in its current state of panic, or grief, or rage has any reality at all" (p. 60). By implication, hopelessness is selfish; and selfish teachers are unlikely to be effective educators.

On Happiness

On the surface, the connection between hope and happiness seems obvious: "In the context of hope theory, barriers [to achievement of goals] produce negative emotions, especially when a child encounters profound blockages. However, the successful pursuit of goals tends to produce positive emotions, especially when barriers are overcome" (Snyder et al. 1997, p. 108). Hence, both hope and happiness have a great deal to do with stress, with the persistent and daily challenges of living, and how those challenges are met such that happiness or sadness follow and hope is strengthened or diminished. Arendt (1958) makes the point this way:

> There is no lasting happiness outside the prescribed cycle of painful exhaustion and pleasurable regeneration, and whatever throws this cycle out of balance—poverty and misery where exhaustion is followed by wretchedness instead of regeneration, or great riches and entirely effortless life where boredom takes the place of exhaustion and where the mills of necessity, of consumption and digestion, grind an impotent body mercilessly and barrenly to death—ruins the elemental happiness that comes from being alive. (p. 108)

Peterson (2006) argues that hope leads to happiness: the "strengths 'of the heart,'" among them gratitude, hope, and love, make humans happy because they "orient us toward others" (pp. 154–155). Peterson's point, in part, is that greater happiness follows a life of engagement, of being deeply connected to and invested in others and their well-being (see p. 74), and so hope is inevitably and ineluctably tied to happiness. From another angle, Fullan (1997) suggests that hope and the emotions share an "intimate two-way link" (p. 221). In effect, hope disciplines the passions, offering means for avoiding despair and containing fear and anger. As a coping mechanism, hope keeps open the door to the positive possibility of being, in C. S. Lewis' phrase, "surprised by joy." On this view, the hopeful are prepared for the worst yet remain open to the best of possible outcomes and proof of openness comes in their acting in ways that suggest this possibility is not fanciful but genuine.

As an emotion, happiness is understood in multiple ways, "brief events, extended moods, and stable predispositions to particular emotional states" (Bates 2000, p. 382). Such multiplicity adds to the difficulty of saying something meaningful about the relationship between hope and happiness. Nettle (2005) helps sort out the confusion by positing "three increasingly inclusive senses [of happiness]" (pp. 16–17). The first level represents the most immediate and direct sense of happiness as a feeling "brought on by a desired state being (perhaps unexpectedly) attained, and there is not much cognition involved, beyond the recognition that the desired thing has happened" (p. 17). Level 1 is all about feeling good. The second sense, Level 2, mostly centers on general or over-all well-being and arises "When people say that they are happy with their lives.... They mean that, upon reflection on the balance sheet of pleasures and pains, they feel the balance to be reasonably positive over the long term.... It concerns not so much feelings, as judgements about the balance of feelings. Thus it is a hybrid of emotion, and judgement about emotion. Its synonyms are things like contentment and life satisfaction" (p. 19). Level 3, Nettle suggests, is represented by Aristotle's ideal of the good life, *eudaimonia*, which is often translated as happiness but more nearly means flourishing, the fulfilling of ones full potential. Nettle writes: "Contemporary psychologists and philosophers have sometimes talked of happiness when they really mean the good life or *eudaimonia*.... Note that 'level three happiness' has no characteristic phenomenology since it is not an emotional state. There is no single thing that it feels like to achieve *eudaimonia*, since everyone's potential is different" (Nettle 2005, p. 20). This conclusion, however, is not fully justified as studies of the development of expertise suggest (Bereiter and Scardamalia 1993): There are moments, sometimes extended, when humans flourish and these are well-remembered and immediately recognized as possessing commonly experienced qualities. Such happiness, a kind of deep satisfaction that comes after the fact, is evident during the experience of "flow" (Csikszentmihalyi 1990), times when one is working at the very edge of one's ability and is fully and deeply invested in a valued activity such as teaching, studying physics, playing the guitar or even watching children at play.

Speaking about Level 2 happiness, what researchers frequently describe as "subjective well-being" (SWB) (Diener and Lucas 2000), Nettle raises serious questions about the widely recognized conclusion that most people report themselves as being relatively happy. The definition of happiness used in such studies, unlike the concerns of Level 3 happiness, is "simply whatever people mean when describing their lives as happy" (Myers 2000, p. 57). While not dismissing the importance of these conclusions, nor of the strong correlations between reported happiness and a range of positive behaviors—less self-absorption, less hostility, more loving, more creative and healthy (see Myers 2000, pp. 57–58)—Nettle (2005) concludes that "the finding that most people are pretty happy is in part a reflection of an endearingly unrealistic psychology with which we address the world" (p. 54). Studies of Level 2 happiness, he asserts, generally rely on the use of instruments that lack a frame of reference and are overly dependent on recent events and feelings, especially when those events are judged positive or strongly negative. For educators, that studies of subjective well-being generally lack a frame of reference is a serious criticism that goes straight to the heart of our deepest concerns, as Noddings (2003) has noted.

> Education, of all enterprises, cannot neglect…the normative aspect of happiness…. We hope that children will learn to derive some happiness from doing the right thing, from satisfying the demands of their souls. We shrink from people who are happily untroubled by the misery of those around them. There is a kind of happiness that creeps through, even in the presence of pain and misery, when we know that we have done what we can do to improve things. Thus education for happiness must include education for *un*happiness. (p. 36)

Nettle raises additional and important questions about the nature of Level 2 happiness, suggesting that "no organism should ever be completely satisfied for anything more than a short time" (pp. 57–58). In his and in Noddings' views, dissatisfaction and unhappiness have important parts to play in human motivation not so much in terms of what is felt when facing significant blocks to meeting life's goals but rather in the sense of recognizing that a situation might be *better* and not only for us. Furthermore, Nettle observes that while most persons are reportedly happy in general, when specific contextual questions are posed things often seem different. When internalized as an imaginative and positive ideal, a vision of another way of being and of being more deeply satisfied and happier inspires and invites human striving. Happiness does not only require meeting goals, but worthy goals of ever increasing significance. Else why seek happiness; why not be satisfied with physical pleasure?

Ultimately, Nettle argues we are hard wired to seek happiness; there is a drive toward happiness built into humans and into the operating systems of the brain that form a "happiness system" which keeps us moving, searching, for ever larger and enduring satisfactions and enjoyments. Nevertheless, Nettle (2005) concludes, "people will never be completely happy, whatever their external conditions" (p. 63). It is, he asserts, the striving that is most important for the future of humanity, not the achieving of happiness, and striving is sustained by hope and stands as proof of its existence.

Support for Nettle's conclusion comes from Kegan (1982) and his conception of human development and self-formation. For educators, Kegan's argument deepens the linkage between happiness Levels 2 and 3 by broadening what counts as motivating and underscoring the centrality of growth to being happy. A key to his argument is how hope and happiness are bound together in identity, the kind of person we take ourselves to be and that others take us to be (as hopeful and happy or not). Seeking to make sense of how humans develop over time, Kegan locates then describes an inherent tension within human beings of two drives both essential to the survival of the species and to the individual's well-being: a drive toward self-preservation and another toward transcendence—contentment and satisfaction on one hand (Level 2 happiness) and growth and learning on the other (Level 3 happiness). One result of this view is recognition of patterns of adaptation in every life such that what is found to produce contentment at some point comes to be experienced as flatness or staleness at another; following adaptation and feeling flat, a healthy person seeks a higher state of happiness (see Bullough and Baughman 1997).

> While this evolutionary process may be described in purely biological terms, it is as true that the same ongoing tension between self-preservation and self-transformation is descriptive of the very activity of hope itself… "a dialectic of limit and possibility." Were we "all limit" (all "assimilation"), there would be no hope; "all possibility" (all "accommodation"), no need of it. That "energy field" which to the evolutionary biologist may be about "adaptation," is as much as anything about the very exercise of hope. Might we better understand others in their predicament if we could somehow know how their way of living reflects the state of their hoping at this depth?—not the hopes they have or the hoping they do, but the hoping they are? (Kegan 1982, p. 45)

For the individual lacking hope, the tension fails and self-preservation dominates self-transformation and striving ceases. Speaking of happiness under such a condition is misleading, as other emotions come to fill life and characterize the self–boredom or perhaps sadness, fear, and anxiety. Certainly, for such a person there may be episodes of laughter and moments of pleasure and of feeling good, signs of Level 1 happiness, but it is unlikely that contentment can be sustained nor is it likely that the happiness of eudaimonia will follow (Bullough 2009). In part this is so because lower-hope compared to higher hope individuals tend to avoid complex and especially challenging goals and situations if they can while higher hope individuals pursue "stretch" goals (Snyder et al. 1997, p. 110). Stretching involves choosing enjoyment over pleasure, the "good feelings people experience…when they do something that stretches them beyond what they were" (Seligman and Csikszentmihalyi 2000, p. 12). Stretching implies a frame of reference and points toward avenues for experiencing self-transcendence and thereby the happiness of eudaimonia.

A Culture of Unhappiness

That measures of hope and happiness tend toward stability suggests external contextual differences have little influence over their formation and strength. Mostly internal over external factors determine outcomes. In part an artifact of measurement, including the tendency to focus on adults (whose life habits and personalities appear rather fixed) than children (a large body of the theory and research on hope and happiness relies on tests of undergraduate psychology students), such conclusions might lead to a kind of determinism, an acceptance that outside of gene splicing and childhood there is little that can be done to strengthen hope or increase happiness. Common sense suggests otherwise even as recognition of the power of early rearing practices sets the difficulty of the challenge. Erikson (1968) is helpful here: "The ontological source of faith and hope [is] a *sense of basic trust:* it is the first basic wholeness, for it seems to imply that the inside and the outside can be experienced as an interrelated goodness" (p. 82). Such trust forms very early in life, and tends to persist. Yet, as Peterson (2006) writes, contextual differences matter and in part because basic trust comes in degrees and fortunately is not usually wholly lacking; there is, in short, something to build upon: Most children are hopeful, at least about some things and some relationships.

Clearly, it is much easier to recognize the ways in which hope and happiness are undermined than to understand how they are built institutionally. Peterson (2006) writes (speaking of optimism but here the point holds for hope and happiness as well):

> Constant striving for control over events without the resources to achieve it can take a toll on the individual who faces an objective limit to what can be attained regardless of how hard she works. If optimism is to survive as a social virtue, then the world must have a causal texture that allows this stance to produce valued rewards. If not, people will channel their efforts into unattainable goals and become exhausted, ill, and demoralized. Or people may rechannel their inherent optimism into attainable but undesirable goals. (p. 127)

There is little doubt but that the hope and happiness generally brought by children and teachers into schools is more easily destroyed than sustained and enhanced. This is so because within and without families the enduring strength of hope and happiness depend largely on the depth, quality, and variety of human relationships, and relationships formed within schools are inevitably unstable, and, particularly in the upper grades, to a degree intentionally guarded. Goodlad (1984) observed this tendency more than 20 years ago, and his conclusion still holds: "[The picture is] of rather well-intentioned teachers going about their business somewhat detached from and not quite connecting with the 'other lives' of their students" (p. 80).

Building and Renewing School Cultures of Hope and Happiness

Most schools are not places of either hopelessness or despair, except occasionally. But, consistent with the argument made here, all schools might become more hopeful and happier places for both teachers and students. The importance of such efforts is underscored by Kelchtermans' (1999) observation: one of the more prominent coping mechanisms for teachers facing exhaustion, depersonalization, and reduced personal accomplishment, the three signs of burnout (Maslach 1999), is to leave teaching, and leaving often is not especially difficult even in harsh economic times. At some point, hope must be joined by happiness and longer-term well-being to convince a teacher to persist in teaching—there must be a positive point to teaching and continuing to teach despite what Margolis (2008) aptly describes as the "ugly stuff" (p. 179). For students there is a parallel point: there must be a positive point to staying engaged in schooling.

As means for building hope and encouraging happiness among educators, the growing interest in professional learning communities (PLCs) appears promising. Generally linked to "reform" efforts, the concept gains in power when bound to a different and competing language tradition, namely "renewal." "Reform" dilates attention on organizational and institutional features and blocks recognition of the ways in which educational improvement is most fundamentally a matter of learning and of development. Renewal offers a much more hopeful alternative, representing a way of thinking that not only recognizes but respects the historicity and humanity of those who work within schools—children and adults—and their need to learn and to grow (Goodlad et al. 2004). All change, of course, is embedded in the past, growing out of established ways of thinking and behaving, and ignoring these only assures failure.

Definitions of PLCs vary (see Cox and Richlin 2004), but the concept is generally taken to mean a group of educators who "continuously seek and share learning, and act on their learning" (Hord 1997, p. 6). A key component of the concept is that decisions are data driven (DuFour 2005) and efforts are consistently directed toward creating conditions that support continuous problem solving and inquiry. Stoll et al. (2006) describe the essential features of a PLC as including "shared beliefs and understandings; interaction and participation; interdependence; concern for individual and minority views…; and meaningful relationships" (p. 225). Such conditions, it is believed, benefit children and educators. Shade (2006), whose concern is for developing school cultures that build hope, would add an additional and generally overlooked feature: that it is likely that the most powerful and morally centered learning communities are those that explicitly develop what he terms, "habits of hope" (p. 196). Raising test scores without attending carefully to the kind and quality of life lived within schools by teachers and students and whether or not that life encourages hope and enables happiness is an empty accomplishment. Data of a different kind are called for—of teacher and student investment in learning and of hope and happiness.

Persistence, resourcefulness and courage are among the habits of hope (Shade 2006). Of these three habits, Shade writes:

> Each of hope's habits is itself a complex of other habits. Persistence requires habits of patience and self-control to maintain focus without losing commitment to a hoped-for end. Trust also proves important as an acknowledgment that other forces contribute to our ends; humility is similarly relevant in that we typically do not know all possible routes to our end.… Resourcefulness, which enables us to expand our abilities, is similarly constituted by a variety of abilities. These include habits that enable us to identify real conditions, to explore new means and abilities in a knowledgeable, skilled, and imaginative manner, and to intelligently formulate and adapt means and ends.… Realizing hope's ends involves transcending antecedent limitations.… Finally, courage also displays complexity. Hoping illuminates our limits and vulnerability and so calls for us to face weaknesses, dangers, and risks. Intelligence functions in courage as it does in other contexts to assess means and ends in the light of one another, though courage involves more than intelligent appraisal. It also indicates the willingness and ability *to act* on that appraisal. Those who are courageous must summon the energies to overcome risks and play an active role in bringing about conditions necessary to realize desired ends. (2006, pp. 196–197)

Noting that habits are developed through interaction with the environment, including with those sharing it with us, Shade calls for creation of a curriculum and a school culture characterized by experiences and human relationships that inspire and sustain hope and happiness not as afterthoughts but as a central aim of education.

Shade's "habits" relate directly to Snyder's goal of encouraging agency and pathways as means for strengthening hope. Building on Snyder's insights, McDermott and Hastings (2000) offer several promising means for encouraging greater hope in families, classrooms, and schools. Their position is framed by an important insight, that "Hopeful thinking…is more than a set of shared behaviors. Rather, it flows from core self-beliefs that the individual is capable of generating pathways and of sustaining the energy necessary to pursue goals" (p. 196). Moreover, they observe that developing hope, especially when it is weak, is a slow and demanding process, a point of importance for both teachers and children—for teachers not only because they are called upon to model hope for the young but because they too may need help becoming and being hopeful. For teachers, suggestions include learning how to guide children in setting, parsing, and prioritizing goals and helping locate and pursue alternative solutions, including learning how to get around intractable problems. Teachers must demonstrate patience and learn to be realistically encouraging, helping children learn to pool their resources and work together to realize their goals. From a content perspective, building a curriculum of hope includes use of stories about "high-hope protagonists" (p. 196) with whom children can identify and who serve as models of hopefulness. Children's own stories have a place here. Shade (2006) adds that teachers can "cultivate hope by explicitly focusing on it as a regular resource in student learning and classroom behavior" (p. 207).

Shade underscores the importance of how children are helped when facing difficult learning challenges, such as learning to read and write. Failure, as I have written elsewhere (Bullough 2006), must become "smart". The point here is that failure can be an opportunity to celebrate honest effort and clever but not wholly satisfying solutions to nagging problems. Rather than scorn those who try and fail, failure presents the opportunity to learn about and develop some of the most significant qualities of hopefulness. Stories of failure and triumph such as biographies of Churchill, Lincoln, Gandhi, Mother Teresa, and Barack Obama are particularly dramatic and compelling. The happiness of eudaimonia is the promise of activities of these kinds, where with the help of skilled and strongly invested and hopeful teachers children confront their limitations and are supported in their effort to move beyond present capabilities and emotional habits. This said, classrooms and schools ought to also evidence Level 1 and Level 2 happiness—lots of laughter, feelings of well-being produced by living within a safe environment and being valued and trusted. But challenge is as important as support if transcendence is to follow.

Fullan's (1997) argument, noted previously, that hope is crucially important to educational renewal, raises a difficult question: Under current social, economic, and work conditions, how are teachers to be helped to avoid disenchantment and to remain or become more hopeful themselves? In most respects the principles for building hope among teachers are the same as those for the young. To build hope and to maximize teacher happiness necessitates work conditions that enhance agency and pathways and, importantly, encourage engagement and invite and inspire self-transcendence. Teachers need to be encouraged to do what they believe is best for children and build to their strengths. Respecting agency, Nettle (2005) makes a particularly telling point, that "Personal control is a much better predictor of happiness than income is (in statistical terms, it accounts for twenty times more of the variation)" (p. 74). Moreover, he observes that autonomy—which is closely related to agency—is related to health and well-being. Looking at the available data, he concludes, "People really don't like being told what to do, whatever the material inducements" (p. 75). For teachers facing ever greater and mean-spirited accountability measures, the point is perhaps obvious: Happiness is dependent on having a relatively high degree of control over one's own work life, rich and loving relationships with those they teach and those with whom they work, and being supported in pursuing highly valued ethical goals. Moreover, happiness, most especially Level 3 happiness, like hope, is related to increasing competence and, importantly, teacher as well as student learning. Surely, such aims are within the reach of most schools.

When hope is lacking, both children and teachers need help developing explanatory styles that strengthen agency and blunt the threat of helplessness. Teachers, like students, may need help to recognize the place of prior beliefs in the judgments they make about experience and that guide their actions. As Gillham and Reivich (2004) suggest, hopefulness is promoted by understanding that there are multiple takes on reality, not just one, and that our sense of the world might be distorted, even wrong. Such insight is a first step toward recognizing that changing beliefs also can and often does change how we understand problems and shape the outcome of our efforts to improve our situations. Greater hope and happiness likely follow, and resiliency may grow. The goal is not to exchange positive for negative attributions, however, but to learn to think more deeply, accurately, and realistically about situations and resources and thereby to locate genuine points of action where agency holds most promise. Importantly, where hope is concerned, the goals set and plans made are most promising when widely shared and inspiring, and when realizing goals requires reaching beyond one's own capability and inevitable shortcomings. The point here is supported by studies of distributed cognition (Moore 2007). In effect, in a classroom or within a faculty, the thinking that takes place is greater than the total of the individuals' cognition and thereby hope becomes realistic and powerful not quaint or fanciful.

This said, temperaments differ. Some teachers and some children are not naturally hopeful while others seem always to have an inner strength, the confidence noted by Erikson, that lightens even the darkest disappointment. In varying degrees temperament forms the boundaries of emotionality, yet what emotions are activated and expressed and how they are expressed is influenced by learning and by the social and economic contexts within which we live. Institutions are characterized by different ways of living, thinking and acting and they support certain preferred ways of feeling, as Zembylas (2002) has suggested. As institutional cultures form and evolve, intentionally or unintentionally, they come to embody "structures of feeling" that shape emotion and normalize experience. Some schools embody cultures of hope and happiness, and from such schools a great deal can be learned. As noted, hope and happiness, like hopelessness and despair, are infectious. If the work of school renewal is to produce higher achievement among the young and increase the quality of teaching there is probably no better long-term strategy than to work to create conditions that invite and inspire greater levels of hope and happiness at each of the three Levels discussed by Nettle. Noddings (2003) underscores what is at stake in such efforts: "Children (and adults, too) learn best when they are happy" (p. 2). But, there is no lasting happiness without hope.

References

Arendt, H. (1958). *The human condition.* Chicago: University of Chicago Press.
Ball, S. J. (2003). The teachers' soul and the terrors of performativity. *Journal of Education Policy, 18*(2), 215–228.
Bates, J. E. (2000). Temperament as an emotional construct: Theoretical and practical issues. In M. Lewis & J. M. H. Haviland-Jones (Eds.), *Handbook of emotions* (2nd ed., pp. 382–396). New York: Guilford.
Bereiter, C., & Scardamalia, M. (1993). *Surpassing ourselves: An inquiry into the nature and implications of expertise.* Chicago: Open Court.
Bottery, M. (2003). The leadership of learning communities in a culture of unhappiness. *School Leadership & Management, 23*(2), 187–207.
Bullough, R. V., Jr. (2001). *Uncertain lives: Children of promise, teachers of hope*. New York: Teachers College.
Bullough, R. V., Jr. (2006). Developing scientifically-based researchers: Inter-disciplinarity and whatever happened to the humanities and education? *Educational Researcher, 35*(8), 3–10.
Bullough, R. V., Jr. (2008). *Counternarratives: Studies of teacher education and becoming and being a teacher*. Albany: State University of New York Press.
Bullough, R. V., Jr. (2009). Seeking eudaimonia: The emotions in learning to teach and to mentor. In P. Schutz & M. Zembylas (Eds.), *Teacher emotion research: The impact on teachers' lives* (pp. 33–53). New York: Springer.
Bullough, R. V., Jr., & Baughman, K. (1997). *First-year teacher, eight years later: An inquiry into teacher development.* New York: Teachers College.
Bullough, R. V., Jr., & Knowles, J. G. (1990). Becoming a teacher: Struggles of a second-career beginning teacher. *Qualitative Studies in Education, 3*(2), 101–112.
Carter, R. (1999). *Mapping the brain.* Berkley: University of California Press.
Cox, M. D., & Richlin, L. (Eds.). (2004). *Building faculty learning communities: New directions for teaching and learning*. San Francisco: Jossey-Bass.
Csikszentmihalyi, M. (1990). *Flow: The psychology of optimal experience.* New York: Harper and Row.
Day, C., Kington, A., Stobart, G., & Sammons, P. (2006). The personal and professional selves of teachers: Stable and unstable identities. *British Educational Research Journal, 32*(4), 601–616.
Dewey, J. (1929). *The sources of a science of education.* New York: Horace Liveright.
Diener, E., & Lucas, R. E. (2000). Subjective emotional well-being. In M. Lewis & J. M. Haviland-Jones (Eds.), *Handbook of emotions* (pp. 325–337). New York: Guildford.
DuFour, R. (2005). What is a professional learning community? In R. DuFour, R. Eaker, & R. DuFour (Eds.), *On common ground* (pp. 31–43). Bloomington: Solution Tree.
Ekman, P. (1992). An argument for basic emotions. *Cognition and Emotion, 6*(3/4), 169–200.
Elbaz, F. (1992). Hope, attentiveness, and caring for difference: The moral voice in teaching. *Teaching & Teacher Education, 8*(5/6), 412–432.

Erikson, E. H. (1964). *Insight and responsibility*. New York: W. W. Norton.
Erikson, E. H. (1968). *Identity, youth and crisis*. New York: W. W. Norton.
Fisher, P. (2002). *The vehement passions*. Princeton: Princeton University Press.
Frankl, V. (1970). *Man's search for meaning*. New York: Touchstone Books.
Fullan, M. (1997). Emotion and hope: Constructive conceptions for complex times. In A. Hargreaves (Ed.), *Rethinking educational change with heart and mind* (pp. 216–233). Washington: Association for Supervision and Curriculum Development.
Gillham, J., & Reivich, K. (2004). Cultivating optimism in childhood and adolescence. *Annals of the American Academy of Political and Social Science, 591,* 146–163.
Goodlad, J. I. (1984). *A place called school*. New York: McGraw-Hill.
Goodlad, J. I., Mantle-Bromley, C., & Goodlad, S. J. (2004). *Education for everyone: Agenda for education in a democracy.* San Francisco: Jossey-Bass.
Hord, S. M. (1997). *Professional learning communities: Communities of continuous inquiry and improvement*. Austin: Southwest Educational Development Laboratory.
Kegan, R. (1982). *The evolving self.* Cambridge: Harvard University Press.
Kelchtermans, G. (1999). Teaching career: Between burnout and fading away? Reflections from a narrative and biographical perspective. In R. Vanderberghe & A. M. Huberman (Eds.), *Understanding and preventing teacher burnout* (pp. 176–191). Cambridge: Cambridge University Press.
Lasch, C. (1991). *The true and only heaven: Progress and its critics*. New York: W. W. Norton.
Lazarus, R. S. (1999). Hope: An emotion and a vital coping resource against despair. *Social Research, 66*(2), 653–678.
Margolis, J. (2008). What will keep today's teachers teaching? Looking for a hook as a new career cycle emerges. *Teachers College Record, 110*(1), 160–194.
Maslach, C. (1999). Progress in understanding teacher burnout. In R. Vandenberghe & A. M. Huberman (Eds.), *Understanding and preventing teacher burnout* (pp. 211–222). Cambridge: Cambridge University Press.
McDermott, D., & Hastings, S. (2000). Children: Raising future hopes. In C. R. Snyder (Ed.), *Handbook of hope: Theory, measures and applications* (pp. 185–199). San Diego: Academic.
Moore, D. T. (2007). Analyzing learning at work: An interdisciplinary framework. *Learning Inquiry, 1,* 175–188.
Myers, D. G. (2000). The funds, friends, and faith of happy people. *American Psychologist, 55*(1), 56–67.
Nettle, D. (2005). *Happiness: The science behind your smile.* New York: Oxford University Press.
Noddings, N. (2003). *Happiness and education.* New York: Cambridge University Press.
Peterson, C. (2000). The future of optimism. *American Psychologist, 55*(1), 44–55.
Peterson, C. (2006). *A primer in positive psychology.* New York: Oxford University Press.
Richardson, P. W., & Watt, H. M. G. (2006). Who chooses teaching and why? Profiling characteristics and motivations across three Australian universities. *Asia-Pacific Journal of Teacher Education, 34*(1), 27–56.
Seligman, M. E. P., & Csikszentmihalyi, M. (2000). Positive psychology. *American Psychologist, 55*(1), 5–14.
Shade, P. (2006). Educating hopes. *Studies in Philosophy and Education, 25,* 191–225.
Snyder, C. R., Harris, C., Anderson, J. R., Holleran, S. A., Irving, L. M., Sigmon, S. T., et al. (1991). The will and the ways: Development and validation of an individual-differences measure of hope. *Journal of Personality and Social Psychology, 60*(4), 570–585.
Snyder, C. R., Cheavens, J., & Sympson, S. C. (1997). Hope: An individual motive for social commerce. *Group Dynamics: Theory, Research, and Practice, 1*(2), 107–118.
Snyder, C. R., Rand, K. L., & Sigmon, D. R. (2005). Hope theory: A member of the positive psychology family. In C. R. Snyder & S. J. Lopez (Eds.), *Handbook of positive psychology* (pp. 257–312). New York: Oxford University Press.
Stoll, L., Bolam, R., McMahon, A., Wallace, M., & Thomas, S. (2006). Professional learning communities: A review of the literature. *Journal of Educational Change, 7,* 221–258.

Valli, L., & Buese, D. (2007). The changing roles of teachers in an era of high-stakes accountability. *American Educational Research Journal, 44*(3), 519–558.
Warnke, G. (1987). *Gadamer: Hermeneutics, tradition and reason.* Stanford: Stanford University Press.
Zembylas, M. (2002). 'Structures of feeling' in curriculum and teaching: Theorizing the emotional rules. *Educational Theory, 52*(2), 187–208.

Chapter 3
Teaching and Teacher Emotions: A Post-structural Perspective

Michalinos Zembylas

Emotions in education are increasingly the focus of a variety of investigations from different methodological and epistemological perspectives (Schutz and Pekrun 2007; Schutz and Zembylas 2009). These investigations highlight the impact of emotions on teachers' and students' lives, showing that emotions have significant implications for teaching and learning. The findings of research in this field suggest that emotions are important to pedagogical practices, to student–teacher relationships, to issues of reform efforts and processes of change, and to an understanding of power relations and social structures in schools and the society. Despite these recent developments, as both Pekrun and Schutz (2007) and Zembylas and Schutz (2009) point out, there is need for further enrichment of this work, especially in terms of employing new epistemological and methodological perspectives.

The purpose of this chapter is to highlight one epistemological perspective and its methodological implications that has not been fully explored in the past but which is valuable to consider in future research in the field of emotions in education. This epistemological perspective is grounded in *post-structuralist* views on emotions in education. By post-structuralist views, I refer to ideas that problematize issues of culture, power, and ideology and the ways such issues create certain discourses about emotion and engage teachers and students to adopt or resist those discourses (Boler 1999; Zembylas 2003a, b, 2005a, b, 2007a, b). An important contribution of post-structuralist perspectives on emotion in education is that they pay attention to the link between microscopic perspectives focused at the level of the "teacher self" and the macroscopic level of social, cultural, and political structures of schooling. Admittedly, this is an idea that is often put aside in research efforts to investigate how teachers' emotions are embedded in teachers' lives (Zembylas and Schutz 2009). Therefore, this chapter aims at discussing a point of view that not only acknowledges the complexities of the link between micro- and macro-level perspectives but also puts forward a "response" that creates openings to address these complexities with effectiveness.

M. Zembylas (✉)
Open University of Cyprus, Nicosia, Cyprus
e-mail: m.zembylas@ouc.ac.cy

C. Day, J. C.-K. Lee (eds.), *New Understandings of Teacher's Work*, Professional Learning and Development in Schools and Higher Education 6,
DOI 10.1007/978-94-007-0545-6_3, © Springer Science+Business Media B.V. 2011

The first part of this chapter describes how post-structuralist views of emotion inform the study of teaching and teacher emotions. The next part analyzes the methodological implications of grounding research on teaching and teacher emotions in a post-structuralist perspective. The final part discusses how research on teacher emotions that is grounded in a post-structuralist perspective might inform educational leadership as well as pre-service and in-service teacher education.

Post-structural Views of Emotion: Implications for Teaching and Teachers

Different understandings of emotions have produced conceptually and methodologically different approaches to the study of emotions in teaching. For instance, many studies of teacher emotion are inspired by psychological and sociological perspectives (see Zembylas 2005b, for a comprehensive review of such perspectives). From the psychological perspective, emotions are primarily conceptualized as private components of the personality structure of an individual. Consequently, psychological research focuses on the internal, individual (intrapersonal) characteristics of a teacher's emotional responses (e.g. see Sutton and Wheatley 2003). This perspective frequently reduces emotions to little more than internal personality dynamics most often divorced from social and cultural contexts. In contrast, the sociological perspective conceptualizes emotions as socially or culturally constructed. Sociologically based studies, then, focus on how teachers' emotions are socially constructed in the group dynamics of social situations and how those situations uni-directionally shape teachers' emotional experiences and expressions (e.g. see Hargreaves 2001). Often ignored in this perspective are both the individual aspects of emotion and the reciprocally shaping interactions of emotion and socialization (Zembylas 2003b).

While both the psychological and the sociological perspectives offer important insights, claiming that emotions are simply a matter of the individual or the group does not sufficiently address the complex role of emotions in teaching (Chubbuck and Zembylas 2008; Zembylas and Chubbuck 2009). Rather, a more useful approach locates emotions in the liminal space between individual and social constructivist approaches, challenging the divisions between individual vs. social, private vs. public, and emphasizing that emotion operates as a constitutively reciprocal component in the interaction/transaction of the *individual* and the *social* (Leavitt 1996).

Support for this approach is found by applying post-structuralist perspectives, that is, views which examine the role of culture, power, and ideology in creating emotion discourses and highlight how teachers and students participate in this process by adopting or resisting these discourses; these perspectives emphasize the role of language and social practices and avoid privileging self-consciousness or sociality as essentialist phenomena, that is, they reject the dichotomy between "individual" and "social" life. In adopting post-structuralist thinking, the central argument is that emotion is *interactional* and *performative*. By that it is meant that the words used to describe emotions are not simply names for "emotion entities", preexisting situations with coherent characteristics; rather, these words are themselves practices performed to serve specific purposes in the process of negotiating reality (Lutz 1988). Therefore, post-structuralist thinking emphasizes the role that language and culture play in constituting the experience of emotion.

In particular, it is argued that cultural and social phenomena are constitutive of emotions, and affect the ways in which people feel, perceive and conceptualize life events (Lutz and Abu-Lughod 1990). On this perspective, emotions are public, not exclusively private, objects of inquiry that are interactively embedded in power relations; thus this perspective historicizes the ways in which emotions are constituted, their organization into discourses and technologies of power, and their importance as a site of social and spatial control through surveillance and self-policing (Ahmed 2004; Barbalet 1998; Lupton 1998). As power relations are inherent in cultural processes (for example, in terms of age, gender, kinship, class, or ethnicity), domination, resistance, and sociality are at the core of emotional processes (Svasek 2008).

Post-structuralist views, then, challenge an ahistorical conception of the subject and analyze the transaction between larger social forces and the internal psychic terrain of the individual, highlighting the ways this historicization can draw out changeable aspects of reality, thus allowing the possibility of ruptures and discontinuities of power differentials in the future (Boler 1999; Zembylas 2005a, 2007a, 2009a). Within this transactional process emotions are not private; neither are they merely the effects of outside social structures. Rather, drawing on post-structuralist thinking helps us theorize emotions as *trans-formative* (Chubbuck and Zembylas 2008; Zembylas and Chubbuck 2009).

Post-structuralist thinking acknowledges that emotion discourses position individuals as socially and culturally specific persons engaged in complex webs of power relations. Those power relations and the social norms embedded in them allow or disallow the constitution of certain emotions; for example, anger expressed by men may seem acceptable while women's anger is often considered an *outlaw emotion* (Barrows 1996; Bartky 1990). As Abu-Lughod and Lutz (1990) write, "Power relations determine what can, cannot, or must be said about self and emotion, what is taken to be true or false about them, and what only some individuals can say about them. [...] [E]motion discourses establish, assert, challenge, or reinforce power or status differences" (p. 14).

Consequently, emotions are trans-formative in that they are not peripheral by-products of events, but rather they are constitutive forces for (trans) forming individuals, social interactions and power relations. As such, emotions are constitutive of the power relationships of political and cultural exchange among individuals. For example, in his last published work, *Pedagogy of Indignation*, Freire (2004) emphasized the role of emotions (e.g. indignation) as transformative forces in the fight for social justice. Emotions in the classroom, then, are not only a private matter but also a political space in which students and teachers interact with implications in larger political and cultural struggles (Albrecht-Crane and Slack 2003; Zembylas 2005b).

The notion of *political space* as applied to emotions here refers to "a process of determining who must repress as illegitimate, who must foreground as valuable, the feelings and desires that come up for them in given contexts and relationships" (Reddy 1997, p. 335). The allocation of power is manifested in who gets to express and who must repress various emotions (Campbell 1997), as seen in the earlier example with anger and who gets to express/repress it. In other words, there is a reciprocal transaction between the individual and the social where emotions also contribute to the formation of particular relationships and power dynamics. As post-structuralist thinking emphasizes, emotion practices are not simply sites of social control but may, in fact, constitute spaces for transforming existing power relations—such as re-claiming anger as a site of struggling for recognition and re-distribution of power relations (Holmes 2004).

Post-structuralist thinking, then, enables a *politicized* (Holmes 2004) analysis of emotions, and interrogates the traditionally held cultural and historical norms about emotion such as what emotions are, how they are expressed, and who gets to express them and under what circumstances. From this perspective, teachers and students are always engaged in political transactions as they relate emotionally to one another across classroom and school spaces, because power relations inherent in and expressed through emotional norms are essentially unavoidable; emotional rules constantly influence emotion discourses and emotional expressions (Zembylas 2006). For example, teachers may feel insecure about expressing their opposing views to the zero tolerance policy followed in their school because it is a highly politicized issue in their community; or white teachers may feel anxious asking students of colour to discuss issues of racial injustice. A politicized analysis of emotions helps educators analyze and sort through various discourses about emotion, and understand how those discourses operate to fabricate particular meanings for emotion that are circulated through educational practices.

In summary, post-structuralist thinking of emotion in teaching and teachers rests on two important assumptions: First, emotions are not private or universal and are not impulses that simply happen to passive sufferers (the Aristotelian view). Instead, emotions are constituted through language and refer to a wider social life. This view challenges any sharp distinction between the "private" domain (the existentialist and the psychoanalytic concern) and the "public" domain (the structuralist concern).

Second, power relations are inherent in "emotion talk" and shape the expression of emotions by permitting us to feel some emotions while prohibiting us from experiencing others (for example, through moral norms and explicit social values, e.g. efficiency, objectivity, neutrality). Unavoidably, then, resistance is a part of this process and power is productive, that is, power is not (only) repressive but produces knowledge and truth.

The preceding set of assumptions have important implications in the study of teaching and teacher emotions, because they allow researchers to move beyond theories that psychologize emotions and treat them as internalized (such as psychoanalysis) or structural theories that emphasize how "structures" shape the individual (such as Marxism). On this conception of emotion, teacher emotions are not private, nor merely the effects of outside structures, nor simply language-laden, but are performative—that is, the ways in which teachers and students understand, experience, perform, and talk about emotions are highly related to their sense of identity. Thus, teaching and teacher emotions can be studied in the classroom and other school settings where teachers are emotionally engaged in how their selves come to be constituted.

Methodological Implications of Studying Teaching and Teacher Emotions Through a Post-structuralist Perspective

In terms of research methodologies grounded in a post-structuralist perspective, in-depth ethnographic investigations become the forefront of examining issues of power relations, socialization practices and emotion (e.g. see Denzin 1997; Holstein and Gubrium 2000). The use of ethnographic methodologies creates spaces for the voices of those studied and describes—through photographs, documents, transcribed interviews, and videotapes—multiple aspects of their emotional experiences. In education, the context of inquiry in which ethnographic methodologies are discussed has been primarily qualitative research and interpretive methodologies (e.g. deMarrais and Tisdale 2002; Gilbert 2001).

In general, post-structuralist thinking has not received much attention in investigations of emotions in education (Zembylas 2007a). However, there have been some attempts to understand emotions as both individual and socio-cultural experiences, focusing on the role of culture, body, power, subjectivity and ideology in creating particular discourses in education that privilege some teaching and learning practices while preventing others (e.g. Boler 1999; Boler and Zembylas 2003; Estola and Elbaz-Luwisch 2003; O'Farrell et al. 2000; Zembylas 2003a, b, 2005a, b). The studies conducted from a post-structuralist perspective emphasize the seamlessness of thinking and feeling through exploring the role of language, body, and social practices. Researchers focus on various sets of discourses embedded in curricula, classrooms and learning environments to show how the individual and the social may be studied simultaneously without undermining their unity in teaching and learning. The methodologies of doing this vary from historical to philosophical to ethnographic work.

Historical methodologies (e.g. Reddy 2001; Stearns and Lewis 1998) remind us how individuals and groups shape their lives, sometimes conforming to prevailing emotional norms, other times resisting, but always negotiating between experience and expression, in the processes within which historical events are lived. Philosophical methodologies (Calhoun and Solomon 1984; Terada 2001) make visible the discourses and ideologies of emotion throughout philosophical thought, and describe emotion as an experience in relation to its difference with other constructs (e.g. cognition, mind). Finally, ethnographic work (e.g. Lutz 1988; Lutz and Abu-Lughod 1990) situates emotional experience in different cultures and tells stories that record the deeply felt emotions of love, suffering, pride, pain, and respect.

Researchers in education can learn a lot from these methodologies when they study emotion in schools.

In the remainder of this section, I propose three possible directions for future research on emotions in education that attempt to ground investigation in post-structuralist thinking and thus move beyond the prevailing individual/social and mind/body dichotomies. The first direction is to consider more seriously the theoretical alternatives to such dichotomies proposed by post-structuralist thinking. The second is to utilize multiple methods of data collection and analysis. And the third is to seek better and most attractive ways of presenting ethnographic writing for the translation of affective experience in practice (Leavitt 1996).

The first direction suggests the utilization of theoretical tools that have not been used as much in education such as a post-structuralist perspective. In view of such a perspective, emotions may be theorized for their embodied and performative force, and their political implications for school leaders, teachers, and students. Much writing about teaching and learning refuses to problematize the body, out of fear for getting into the sexual dynamics of the classroom; however, bodies and emotions inevitably produce pedagogy and learning as they produce subjects, that is, the political consequences are unavoidable (Zembylas 2007a). A post-structuralist analysis of emotions and bodies offers new perspectives because it focuses not on what emotions or bodies *mean* but on what they *do*: what connections they do (or not) permit, what enable teachers and students to feel, and to engage in particular emotional practices that may be empowering in some ways and constraining in others.

My own work (see e.g. Zembylas 2005a, b), for example, constitutes an example of research grounded in post-structuralist theory and examines how a teacher's emotions are embodied, enacted and performed within the power relations of a school over three years. This work shows how affective connections in the classroom are formed and trans-formed over time through resistance and transformation. It also critically analyzes the discursive practices that underlie the flow of emotions in the ways that a teacher and her students' identities come to be constituted and assigned to them through classroom and school discourses, practices, and performances. As a body of literature, this study emphasizes that emotions play an important political role in enabling resistance and transformation, two aspects that are currently missing from many accounts of emotions in education. Along these lines, my most recent ethnographic work (see e.g. Zembylas 2008, 2009b; Zembylas et al. 2010) builds on a variety of methodological and theoretical tools to explore how mourning traumatic loss in conflict-ridden societies intersects with emotional politics in education.

Leavitt (1996) urges us to study emotions in renewed theoretical and methodological perspectives that transcend previous views that have forced us to think in dichotomous ways. He writes:

> We would have to see emotions as primarily neither meanings nor feelings, but as experiences learned and expressed in the body, in social interactions through the mediation of systems of signs, verbal and nonverbal. [...] But we would equally recognize in theory what we all assume in our everyday lives: that emotions are *felt* in bodily experience, not just known or thought or appraised. (p. 526, author's emphasis)

New conceptualizations of bodies and emotions "open affective territories that promise passionate educational exploration not yet colonized in the economies of mind ... away from stagnant habits and towards collaborative affective inquiry" (Boler 1997, pp. 268–269). These new conceptualizations will have to see emotions as moving beyond the *both/and* conceptual schema, that is, the claim that emotions are *both* individual *and* social, because such a schema perpetuates the assumed boundaries between the individual and the social by affirming their territorialization.

The second direction of future research on emotions in education is the need for using multiple methods—for example, a combination of quantitative and qualitative methods—and alternative research practices that may allow a deeper exploration of emotions. Critical post-structuralism, for example, proposes the need for a new set of criteria, divorced from the positivist and post-positivist traditions; these criteria stress subjectivity, emotionality, and verisimilitude (Denzin 1997). Thus, the study of emotions in education may be more appropriately treated in an interpretive rather than a causal manner. This research program may be grounded in a perspective which combines previously polarized individual and social aspects and is based on a holistic, not a reductionist vision. Some examples of possible methodological innovations that transcend the boundaries between the individual and the social include interdisciplinary models of research, post-modern ethnography (Lofland and Lofland 1995), and journalism-as-ethnography (Charity 1995).

Researchers also should feel free to seek interpretations in a great range of material: in childhood memories, current life situations, cultural expectations, myths, definitions, observed emotions, bodily movement and so on (Leavitt 1996). With the above notion in mind, educators may begin to pursue lines of research that could lead to more exciting interpretations of the role of emotions in education. Rethinking the theoretical and methodological dimensions of research helps to reveal the interrelations between what is called cognition and emotion, mind and body, individual and social, and the significance of finding ways to further explore them. Using such ideas as analytic tools and inspirations, educators can explore how emotions are "located" in bodies *and* educational histories (of institutions and individuals) in visible or invisible ways, and challenge the prevailing normalizing tendencies.

The final direction of future research on emotions in education has to do with the question of "producing a new concept of writing" (Derrida 1981, p. 26) and reading about emotions. Theory, writing and methodology are inseparable practices. Together they create the conditions, evocations and resonances that produce powerful effects beyond the semantic (Leavitt 1996). This implies that researchers of emotions "must work on their own feelings, modifying them to model the emotional experiences of people" (Leavitt 1996, p. 530) in various contexts. This brings us to the issue of empathy and the strategies for dealing with a researcher's emotional engagement (Gilbert 2001; Kleinman and Copp 1993). Traditionally, academic research emphasized objectivity and rationality and the feelings of the researcher were to be controlled as a nuisance to his or her exploration (Savage 2004). However, post-structuralist researchers argue for an approach that makes uses rather than denies the researcher's feelings. In fact, in ethnography and oral history, as Harding and Pribram (2004) write, "the investigator's ability to *feel with* the subject enables conversation and the re-telling of experiences and confidences that constitute the data and direct its interpretation, analysis, and writing up" (p. 878, authors' emphasis). Harding and Pribram continue by arguing that "Emotions are always in play in any inquiry but to differing extents. That is, research operates through relations of closeness and difference (between investigator and investigated whether human or non-human) where these are context specific" (Harding and Pribram 2004). Thus, some researchers emphasize the significance of empathy, a feeling-with the participants of the research study based on common or similar experiences. Empathy is particularly found in the new anthropologies of the body (Leavitt 1996). According to this approach, we cannot fully grasp what people are at, without having experienced something similar; emotional connection with what is studied is deemed essential.

It may be argued, then, that the ethnography of emotion is "a moral, allegorical and therapeutic project" (Denzin 1997, p. xiv). Like literature, ethnography is more than a record of human experience; it is concerned with providing a sense of possible ways of feeling and moving people to action. The narrative told is a means for readers to discover moral truths about themselves. Consequently, accounts of emotions in education could escape the limits of the written word, and "display the nonverbal signs of emotions along with the verbal ones" (Leavitt 1996, p. 531). Research reports are representations that are themselves embodied representations of experience; thus, these texts use evoked emotion as a method for establishing its claims to authority (Denzin 1997). This implies writing a report that persuades and moves the reader. To achieve these emotional effects, language is used in ways that "evoke senses of motion, ambience, taste, smell, colour, local landscape, and voice" (p. 211), creating a context in which the writer and the reader are engaged in a shared experience. Some examples of innovation in writing, for example, include narratives of the self, performance texts, autobiographies, narrative collages, diaries, and memoirs (see Denzin 1997).

Implications for Educational Leadership and Pre-service/ In-service Teacher Education

In this final part of the chapter I engage with the question: How might research on teacher emotions grounded in a post-structuralist perspective inform educational leadership as well as pre-service and in-service teacher education? Research on teacher emotions grounded in a post-structuralist perspective highlights the ways in which teachers' and principals' emotional struggles are socially and politically relevant (Chubbuck and Zembylas 2008). The contribution of this research is that it provides a particular manifestation of the resistance developed by teachers and school leaders to sustain educational change and a school improvement agenda.

In particular, *critical emotional reflexivity* (Zembylas 2008; Zembylas and Chubbuck 2009) constitutes an important aspect of leadership practice and teacher preparation in school improvement efforts. By learning how to develop practices of critical emotional reflexivity in their teaching and leadership, teachers and school leaders can learn how to create spaces for interrogating unjust and exclusionary school practices and policies (Chubbuck and Zembylas 2008) and appreciate the importance of adding this to their skill repertoire. Preparation programs for school teachers and leaders often focus their attention primarily on the effectiveness and efficiency of schools. This narrow emphasis fails to prepare school teachers and leaders to engage in the difficult emotional work that requires a shift in values, attitudes, and practices and limits their ability to address the political aspects educational change.

Pre-service and in-service teachers and school leaders need to be provided with opportunities to engage in critical emotional reflection on their values and practices as well as their impact on the community. Future (or practicing) school leaders and teachers need to address the significance of critical emotional reflexivity as a tool of sustaining their emotional resistance against unjust policies and teaching practices. In preparation programs that aim at preparing a new type of school teacher and leader who is strongly committed to achieving social justice (Cambron-McCabe and McCarthy 2005; Theoharis 2007), taking a deeper look at the emotional politics of teaching and leadership is very valuable. For instance, preparation programs would benefit from including an analysis of case studies that focus on the emotional politics of teaching and leadership and their implications.

At the personal level, it is important for school teachers and leaders to keep in mind that critical emotional reflexivity helps to identify the emotional impact of their actions on students and the wider community. Critical emotional reflexivity calls on school teachers and leaders to constantly interrogate their values and beliefs and recognize in what ways emotions "colour" their decisions and practices. Developing the skills and knowledge to analyze how various practices teach people to *feel* the world through an ideological lens is an important step in identifying effectively strategies to respond.

School teachers and leaders can challenge and expand the possibilities of educational change and school improvement by investigating the role of emotions from a post-structuralist perspective. Scholars in the field of educational leadership and teacher education often emphasize the effectiveness and efficiency dimensions of educational change and school improvement, failing to connect those dimensions to emotional processes. Emotional work is important in teaching and school leadership, thus future preparation programs could involve an exploration of the ways in which the affective politics of educational change intersect with the emotionality of teaching and leadership practices.

Understanding emotions from a post-structuralist perspective, then, informs educational leadership and teacher preparation programs in three ways. First, emotional control and emotional labour in teaching and school leadership can be historicized. By understanding how emotional rules and expectations are historically contingent, for example, teachers and school leaders begin to deconstruct the power relations that normalize their professional lives in schools (Zembylas 2010). As I have shown, post-structuralist theory tells us that professional identity is produced and constrained through disciplinary power and local emotional rules (Zembylas 2005b).

Second, post-structuralist thinking offers a fresh way of understanding the relation between self-discipline and emotional rules in teaching and school leadership. For instance, an analysis of power as a process and not a possession forces us to look beyond emotional control mechanisms and structures as immanent and uncontested. Emotional control is something that is continually constructed and reproduced through interactions of domination and resistance. Particularly, from a Foucauldian point of view, there is no pure "freedom" from the influence of emotional rules, because such rules will always be present in discursive practices (Zembylas 2003b, 2005a). Freedom, then, is an act of refusing to submit to emotional rules that discipline and normalize individuals. The practice of freedom relies upon a refusal to base one's actions in the ability to occupy an "enlightened" place or a fixed identity (Pignatelli 2002)—that is, nobody can claim that he/she is really "free" of all power relations and emotional rules. However, there is always the potential of subverting the rules and contesting the forms of identity imposed on us.

Finally, using post-structuralist perspectives, teacher educators can problematize appeals to emotional well-being tied to rationalizations and instrumental goals of the teaching profession and the school improvement agenda. Such appeals to emotional well-being tied to rationalizations need to be identified as technologies of the self that shape the meaning and drive the direction, goals, and emotional conduct in the context of educational change and school improvement efforts. Consequently, inventing opposing actions in which oppressive emotional rules are identified entails breaking with these technologies of power.

Conclusion

In this chapter, I have argued that a post-structuralist perspective has important implications for the way emotion is studied in teaching, influencing both school leaders and teachers and the methodology of investigating emotion. The educational researcher's response to the question of whether emotion is private *and/or* social will be influenced by his or her assumptions about emotions, whether those are stated explicitly or not. I have suggested that we should look closer at varying contexts in educational settings and investigate the emotional practices of school leaders, teachers and students as well as what these practices *do* on those individuals. Developing theoretical and methodological frameworks and practices that affirm a holistic look at school leaders, teachers and students' lives will provide a new sense of exploring the ways through which emotions are constituted in educational arenas.

The analysis in this chapter raises new questions that make us re-examine our assumptions about studying emotions in education: How do we understand emotional experiences of school leadership, teaching and learning, and what are the origins and consequences of such understandings? What are the implications of experimenting with new methodological and theoretical understandings of exploring emotions in education (e.g. in terms of how instruction is planned and evaluated more successfully)? I have discussed how post-structuralist thinking conceptualizes emotion in different ways. However, there is still a lot of potential in further developing ways in which this perspective enriches the study of emotion in teaching. This task is complex and has implications for research methodology as well as for teaching and leadership practice.

The contribution of post-structuralist thinking regarding emotion in education amounts to an intervention in a much larger debate about teacher subjectivity, in which our concepts of affective elements of consciousness and relations, school community, and educational change are slowly being re-examined. That is why a focus on the emotion work of teachers through post-structuralist ideas leads to more recognition of the social and political character of teacher emotion. This sociopolitical character of teacher emotion creates the difference between possible and real transformation, and it is this difference that constitutes the power of emotional knowing as a tool to subvert existing conditions. Therefore, from a post-structuralist point of view, teachers come to understand their identity through acts of resistance and consent to emotional labour. Resistances function both as defences against vulnerability and as assertions of power in the face of impositions (Boler 1999).

Using post-structuralist thinking, teachers, teacher educators, policymakers, and researchers can further explore in the future how teachers' emotions are "located" in particular educational histories (of institutions and individuals) in visible or invisible ways, and challenge the prevailing social, cultural, and political structures. Analyzing and critically reflecting on one's emotions represents a considerable risk of vulnerability yet teachers are constantly challenged in the professional lives to deal with visible of invisible pain and powerlessness. Teachers can be vastly empowered in their lives by developing accounts that recognize emotion as a site of personal transformation, professional development, and political resistance.

References

Abu-Lughod, L., & Lutz, C. A. (1990). Introduction: Emotion, discourse, and the politics of everyday life. In C. Lutz & L. Abu-Lughod (Eds.), *Language and the politics of emotion* (pp. 1–23). Cambridge: Cambridge University Press.

Ahmed, S. (2004). *The cultural politics of emotion.* Edinburgh: Edinburgh University Press.

Albrecht-Crane, C., & Slack, J. (2003). Toward a pedagogy of affect. In J. D. Slack (Ed.), *Animations (of Deleuze and Guattari)* (pp. 191–216). New York: Lang.

Barbalet, J. (1998). *Emotion, social theory and social structure.* Cambridge: Cambridge University Press.

Barrows, A. (1996). *The light of outrage: Women, anger, and Buddhist women on the edge.* Berkeley: North Atlantic Books.

Bartky, S. (1990). *Femininity and domination.* New York: Routledge.

Boler, M. (1997). Taming the labile other: Disciplined emotions in popular and academic discourses. In S. Laird (Ed.), *Philosophy of education* (pp. 416–425). Urbana: Philosophy of Education Society.

Boler, M. (1999). *Feeling power: Emotions and education.* New York: Routledge.

Boler, M., & Zembylas, M. (2003). Discomforting truths: The emotional terrain of understanding differences. In P. Tryfonas (Ed.), *Pedagogies of difference: Rethinking education for social justice* (pp. 110–136). New York: Routledge.

Calhoun, C., & Solomon, R. C. (1984). *What is an emotion: Classic readings in philosophical psychology.* New York: Oxford University Press.
Cambron-McCabe, N., & McCarthy, M. (2005). Educating leaders for social justice. *Educational Policy, 19*(1), 201–222.
Campbell, S. (1997). *Interpreting the personal: Expression and the formation of feelings.* Ithaca: Cornell University Press.
Charity, A. (1995). *Doing public journalism.* New York: Guilford.
Chubbuck, S., & Zembylas, M. (2008). The emotional ambivalence of socially just teaching: A case study of a novice urban schoolteacher. *American Educational Research Journal, 45*(2), 274–318.
deMarrais, K., & Tisdale, K. (2002). What happens when researchers inquire into difficult emotions?: Reflections on studying women's anger through qualitative interviews. *Educational Psychologist, 37,* 115–123.
Denzin, N. (1997). *Interpretive ethnography: Ethnographic practices for the 21st century.* Thousand Oaks: Sage.
Derrida, J. (1981). *Positions.* Chicago: Chicago University Press.
Estola, E., & Elbaz-Luwisch, F. (2003). Teaching bodies at work. *Journal of Curriculum Studies, 35,* 697–719.
Freire, P. (2004). *Pedagogy of indignation.* Boulder: Paradigm.
Gilbert, K. R. (Ed.). (2001). *The emotional nature of qualitative research.* Boca Raton: CRC Press LLC.
Harding, J., & Pribram, E. D. (2004). Losing our cool? Following Williams and Grossberg on emotions. *Cultural Studies, 18,* 863–883.
Hargreaves, A. (2001). The emotional geographies of teaching. *Teachers College Record, 103,* 1056–1080.
Holmes, M. (2004). Feeling beyond rules: Politicizing the sociology of emotion and anger in feminist politics. *European Journal of Social Theory, 7,* 209–227.
Holstein, J., & Gubrium, J. (2000). *The self that we live by: Narrative identity in the postmodern world.* New York: Oxford University Press.
Kleinman, S., & Copp, M. A. (1993). *Emotions and fieldwork.* Newbury Park: Sage.
Leavitt, J. (1996). Meaning and feeling in the anthropology of emotions. *American Ethnologist, 23,* 514–539.
Lofland, J., & Lofland, L. H. (1995). *Analyzing social settings.* Belmont: Wadsworth.
Lupton, D. (1998). *The emotional self: A sociocultural exploration.* London: Sage.
Lutz, C. (1988). *Unnatural emotions: Everyday sentiments on a Micronesian atoll and their challenge to Western theory.* Chicago: University of Chicago Press.
Lutz, C., & Abu-Lughod, L. (Eds.). (1990). *Language and the politics of emotion.* Cambridge: Cambridge University Press.
O'Farrell, C., Meadmore, D., McWilliam, E., & Symes, C. (Eds.). (2000). *Taught bodies.* New York: Lang.
Pekrun, R., & Schutz, P. (2007). Where do we go from here? Implications and future directions for inquiry on emotions in education. In P. Schutz & R. Pekrun (Eds.), *Emotion in education* (pp. 313–331). Boston: Academic Press.
Pignatelli, F. (2002). Mapping the terrain of a Foucauldian ethics: A response to the surveillance of schooling. *Studies in Philosophy and Education, 21,* 157–180.
Reddy, W. M. (1997). Against constructionist: The historical ethnography of emotions. *Current Anthropology, 38,* 327–340.
Reddy, W. M. (2001). *The navigation of feeling: A framework for the history of emotions.* Cambridge: Cambridge University Press.
Savage, J. (2004). Researching emotion: The need for coherence between focus, theory and methodology. *Nursing Inquiry, 11*(1), 25–34.
Schutz, P., & Pekrun, R. (Eds.). (2007). *Emotion in education.* Boston: Academic Press.
Schutz, P., & Zembylas, M. (Eds.). (2009). *Advances in teacher emotion research: The impact on teachers' lives.* Dordrecht: Springer.

Stearns, P., & Lewis, J. (Eds.). (1998). *An emotional history of the United States.* New York: New York University Press.

Sutton, R., & Wheatley, K. (2003). Teachers' emotions and teaching: A review of the literature and directions for future research. *Educational Psychology Review, 15,* 327–358.

Svasek, M. (Ed.). (2008). *Postsocialism: Politics and emotions in central and eastern Europe.* New York: Berghahn.

Terada, R. (2001). *Feeling in theory: Emotion after the 'death of the subject'.* Cambridge: Harvard University Press.

Theoharis, G. (2007). Social justice educational leaders and resistance: Toward a theory of social justice leadership. *Educational Administration Quarterly, 43*(2), 221–258.

Zembylas, M. (2003a). Caring for teacher emotion: Reflections on teacher self-development. *Studies in Philosophy and Education, 22,* 103–125.

Zembylas, M. (2003b). Emotions and teacher identity: A poststructural perspective. *Teachers and Teaching: Theory and Practice, 9,* 213–238.

Zembylas, M. (2005a). Discursive practices, genealogies and emotional rules: A poststructuralist view on emotion and identity in teaching. *Teaching and Teacher Education, 21*(8), 935–948 (Special Issue).

Zembylas, M. (2005b). *Teaching with emotion: A postmodern enactment.* Greenwich: Information Age.

Zembylas, M. (2006). Witnessing in the classroom: The ethics and politics of affect. *Educational Theory, 56,* 305–324.

Zembylas, M. (2007a). Theory and methodology in researching emotions in education. *International Journal of Research & Method in Education, 30,* 57–72.

Zembylas, M. (2007b). The power and politics of emotions in teaching. In P. A. Schutz & R. Pekrun (Eds.), *Emotions in education* (pp. 293–309). New York: Academic.

Zembylas, M. (2008). *The politics of trauma in education.* New York: Palgrave.

Zembylas, M. (2009a). The politics of emotions in education: Affective economies, ambivalence and transformation. In E. Samier & M. Schmidt (Eds.), *Emotional dimensions of educational administration and leadership* (pp. 97–108). New York: Routledge.

Zembylas, M. (2009b). Making sense of traumatic events. Towards a politics of aporetic mourning in educational theory and pedagogy. *Educational Theory, 59*(1), 85–104.

Zembylas, M. (2010). The emotional aspects of leadership for social justice: Implications for leadership preparation programs. *Journal of Educational Administration, 48*(5), 611–625.

Zembylas, M., & Chubbuck, S. (2009). Emotions and social inequalities: Mobilizing emotions for social justice education. In P. Schutz & M. Zembylas (Eds.), *Advances in teacher emotion research: The impact on teachers' lives.* Dordrecht: Springer.

Zembylas, M., & Schutz, P. (2009). Research on teachers' emotions in education: Findings, practical implications and future agenda. In P. Schutz & M. Zembylas (Eds.), *Advances in teacher emotion research: The impact on teachers' lives.* Dordrecht: Springer.

Zembylas, M., Bekerman, Z., Haj-Yahia, M., & Schaade, N. (2010). The politics of mourning in Cyprus and Israel: Educational implications. *Compare, 40*(5), 561–574.

Chapter 4
Uncertain Professional Identities: Managing the Emotional Contexts of Teaching

Christopher Day

Introduction

This chapter draws on findings from a four-year longitudinal research project, commissioned by the Department for Education and Skills (DfES), which investigated Variations in Teachers' Work, Lives and Effectiveness (VITAE). Drawing on data gathered from 300 teachers working in 100 primary and secondary schools in England, the research identified qualitative and statistically significant associations between commitment and effectiveness (perceived and in terms of pupil attainment) and found that there were more, and less, effective teachers in each of six professional life phases which were identified. It found that teachers in each of these phases experience a number of different scenarios that challenge their capacities to sustain their commitment. The chapter discusses associations between teacher commitment and professional identity. It finds that teacher identities are neither intrinsically stable nor intrinsically fragmented, but that they can be more or less stable and more or less fragmented at different times and in different ways according to the relative positive or negative impact of a number of personal, socio-cultural/policy and workplace influences; and that a positive, stable sense of professional identity is associated with teachers' ability to manage the emotional contexts of teaching.

Previous research on teachers' work and lives has tended to have been conducted over a short period of time and limited to small-scale qualitative studies or large-scale surveys. It has not, therefore, been able to provide a holistic view of the variations in the different contexts of teaching that are inevitable within teachers' professional and personal lives over the course of their teaching career, the ways they do (or do

---

This chapter is a revised, reconceptualised and retitled version of Day and Kington (2008).

C. Day (✉)
School of Education, University of Nottingham, Jubilee Campus, Wollaton Road,
NG8 1BB Nottingham, UK
e-mail: christopher.day@nottingham.ac.uk

C. Day, J. C.-K. Lee (eds.), *New Understandings of Teacher's Work,* Professional Learning and Development in Schools and Higher Education 6,
DOI 10.1007/978-94-007-0545-6_4,

not) manage these and their effects upon their sense of professional identity. The VITAE study found significant associations between professional life phases,[1] commitment, resilience, effectiveness and teacher identity (Day et al. 2006a, b, 2007).

Over the last 20 years in England, there have been a number of key educational policy changes aimed at improving standards of school governance, teaching, learning and achievement that have had an influence on the contexts in which teachers work. Starting in 1988 with the Education Reform Act, successive governments have introduced a range of initiatives aimed at raising standards of literacy, numeracy and overall student results. A national curriculum was introduced by the Conservative government of the time, involving a structured national assessment at the end of Key Stages, which were associated with both primary and secondary phases of schooling. The assessment occurs when children reach the end of Key Stage 1 (7 years of age), 2 (11 years of age) and 3 (14 years of age). In 1993, the Office for Standards in Education (Ofsted) was created to monitor and evaluate the quality of teaching in all subject areas in schools through independent, external, regular inspections. This led to the identification of some schools which, according to the Ofsted inspection criteria, were "failing". In other words, schools have become subject to demands for more transparency and accountability. These have led to an increase in bureaucracy such that teachers' work has become more intensified and their roles more diverse (Osborn et al. 1996; Ball 1994). To this standards agenda was added a concern for social justice. This became a major focus for the incoming Labour government, in 1997, especially in relation to inclusion of students from disadvantaged backgrounds. However, this emphasis on equity in schooling was adopted alongside previously implemented policies on national assessment, local management of schools and published national results. In 1998/1999, National Literacy and Numeracy strategies were introduced in primary and secondary schools (Key Stages 1, 2 and 3) in order to raise student achievement in these areas. Although positively received by the teaching profession in general, one of the criticisms of this and the previous initiatives is that they have led to increased workload pressures on teachers and have continued to focus on raising standards rather than giving consideration to the changing conditions in which teachers work (Day et al. 2007).

Change affects not only teachers' work, but also how teachers feel about their work. There is an unavoidable interrelationship between cognitive and emotional identities, if only because the overwhelming evidence is that teaching demands significant personal investment of these:

> [T]he ways in which teachers form their professional identities are influenced both by how they feel about themselves and how they feel about their students. This professional identity helps them to position or situate themselves in relation to their students and to make appropriate and effective adjustments in their practice and their beliefs about and engagement with students. (James-Wilson 2001, p. 29)

---

[1] Teachers were divided into six professional life phases according to total number of years in teaching. The phases were defined as 0–3, 4–7, 8–15, 16–23, 24–30 and 31+.

Several researchers (Nias 1989, 1996; Hargreaves 1994; Sumsion 2002) have noted that teacher identities are constructed not only from technical and emotional aspects of teaching (i.e. classroom management, subject knowledge and pupil test results) and their personal lives, but also "as the result of an interaction between the personal experiences of teachers and the social, cultural, and institutional environment in which they function on a daily basis" (Sleegers and Kelchtermans 1999, p. 579).

Emotions play a key role in the construction of identity (Zembylas 2003). They are the necessary link between the social structures in which teachers work and the ways they act:

> [E]motion is a necessary link between social structures and social actor. The connection is never mechanical because emotions are normally not compelling but inclining. But without the emotions category, accounts of situated actions would be fragmentary and incomplete. Emotion is provoked by circumstance and is experienced as transformation of dispositions to act. It is through the subject's active exchange with others that emotional experience is both stimulated in the actor and orienting of their conduct. Emotion is directly implicated in the actor's transformation of their circumstances, as well as the circumstances' transformation of the actor's disposition to act. (Barbalet 2002, p. 4)

Teachers (and their students) experience an array of sometimes contrasting emotions in the classroom. In a review of empirical research, Sutton (2000) found that love (as a social relationship) and care, surprise and joy, anger, sadness and fear, excitement and pleasure in students' progress and achievements are among the most commonly cited emotions. Thus it is not surprising that, because of their emotional investments, teachers can experience instabilities or vulnerabilities when control of long-held principles and practices is challenged by policy changes or new expectations for standards, when their moral integrity is questioned or when trust and respect from parents, the public and their students is eroded (Kelchtermans 1996). Indeed, it has been claimed that vulnerability is a structural condition of teaching (see Chap. 5 by Kelchtermans). Instabilities, whether the result of personal, socio-cultural/policy or workplace nature or a combination of these, create stresses in the emotional fabric of identity. Teachers need to be resilient and to be supported emotionally during these periods in order that these may be managed in ways that build or sustain positive identities and existing effectiveness.[2]

Research, then, into teachers' professional identities is important as a means of furthering understandings of the job of teaching and what it means to be a teacher striving to be effective in changing policy, workplace and personal contexts. It is also important to consider how teachers' emotional commitments to their work may be influenced by the extent to which changes in such contexts challenge existing identities. In other words, existing identities may become what MacLure (1993, p. 312) has described as "a continuing site of struggle". The chapter focuses upon the identification of different scenarios with which teachers are likely to engage in each phase of their working lives. Importantly, building upon a hypothesis of relationships between variations in teachers' work and lives, their identities and their

[2] For a more detailed discussion of teachers' resilience, see Gu and Day (2007).

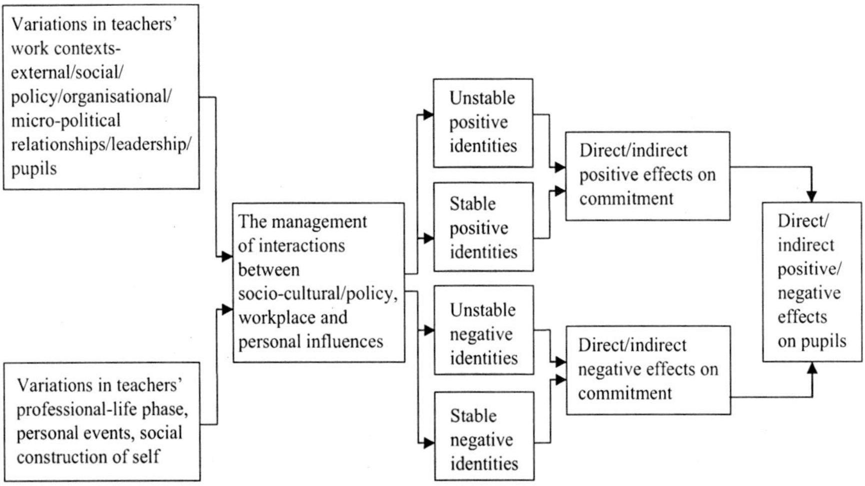

Fig. 4.1 Relationships between identity, commitment and effectiveness

commitment and effectiveness (Fig. 4.1), it finds empirical associations between teachers' positive and negative sense of professional identity, the ways in which these impact upon their sense of efficacy, agency, well-being and job satisfaction, and their perceptions of effects on pupils.

Professional identity should not be confused with role. Identity is the way we make sense of ourselves to ourselves and the image of ourselves that we present to others. It is culturally embedded. There is an unavoidable interrelationship, also, between the professional and the personal. In much educational literature it is recognised that the broader cultural, policy and social structures in which teachers live and work, the emotional contexts and the personal and professional elements of teachers' lives, experiences, beliefs and practices are integral to one another, and that there are often tensions between these which impact to a greater or lesser extent upon teachers' sense of agency (the ability and resolve to pursue one's goals) which in turn affects their sense of professional identity. Previous research has either suggested that identity is stable (Nias 1989), affected by work contexts (Beijaard 1995) or fragmented (MacLure 1993). The research reported in this chapter found that identities are neither intrinsically stable nor intrinsically fragmented, but that they can be more or less stable depending upon the capacities of teachers to manage a number of influences within a number of scenarios or sites of struggle.

It has been suggested in previous small-scale, short-term, snapshot studies of teachers, usually experiencing extreme circumstances (for example, Troman and Woods 2001; Stronach et al. 2002) that they lead lives of stability and instability at the same time. However, in analysing teachers' responses to different scenarios over a three-year period, it became apparent that teachers themselves did not perceive this to be the case; and that, whilst there were undoubtedly tensions caused by the relative dominance of one or more key influences, many teachers were able to manage these and thus maintain stability within what from the outside seemed to be, and were, vulnerable, unstable environments.[3] Their existing professional identities were, therefore, more or less vulnerable at different times and in different ways according to their management of the interaction of a number of socio-cultural/policy, workplace and personal influences, and teachers' ability to manage these (Fig. 4.1).

Research Design

The data presented in this chapter were generated via two in-depth interviews with a total of 295 primary and secondary teachers in each of three years of data collection (autumn 2002 to summer 2005), as well as teacher-generated "effectiveness" histories collected by means of a "critical incident" work line. The primary school sample comprised 143 female teachers (90%) and 16 male teachers (10%). They were fairly equally distributed between the four free school meal groups of schools. Pupils' free school meals (FSM) were used as indicators of the relative advantage/disadvantage of school teaching and learning contexts.[4] The highest proportion of teachers (28%) was in the 8–15 professional life phase (that is, they had been teaching for between 8 and 15 years), followed by 20% of teachers in both the 4–7 and 24–30 phases. The secondary teacher sample comprised 86 female teachers (63%) and 50 male teachers (37%). One third of these teachers were working in FSM 2 schools and only 17% worked in FSM 3 schools. Half of the secondary teachers in the sample were in the 4–7 (27%) or 8–15 (23%) professional life phases.

Individual profiles created for each teacher were used to identify relevant data regarding teacher motivation, commitment, self-efficacy and well-being. These data, in addition to the various policy, workplace and personal influences reported by teachers as having a positive or negative influence on their effectiveness, were classified and placed into a data matrix (Miles and Huberman 1994). At individual teacher level, this matrix qualitatively displayed policy, personal and school influences (i.e. professional life phase, gender, school phase, etc.), as well as data and analysis regarding dominant influences and scenarios. In addition, further judgements[5] were made regarding the level of resilience or vulnerability teachers were demonstrating within the scenarios. This approach of a combined analysis on statistical and descriptive data allowed connections and patterns to be identified and explored.

Once compiled, judgements were made for each teacher, based on the interview data, as to which influence or influences demanded a greater amount of time and attention from the teacher at a given time. The influences identified, based on the

[3] These dimensions—professional, situated and personal—will be discussed later in this chapter.

[4] Eligibility for free school meals is divided into four categories. FSM 1 describes schools with 0–8% of pupils eligible for free school meals. This percentage rises to 9–20% for FSM 2 schools, 21–35% for FSM 3 schools and over 35% for FSM 4 schools.

[5] Inter-rater reliability of 90%.

degree of dominance, were the primary indicators for which scenario a teacher was experiencing. Teacher interviews were also analysed and coded, at document level, using NVivo.[6] This allowed the identification of influences, dominant influences and possible scenarios. This process allowed an inter-rating level to be established on the individual teacher judgements,[7] and also gave useful insights into how the development of the data matrix could be improved so as not to lose focus of the "whole teacher" in the need to reduce data into positives and negatives. Once research judgements had been made, teachers were asked to place themselves in a scenario as a means of teacher verification of researcher judgements. The research found that teachers experience a number of positive and negative life and work scenarios that interact and which potentially may disturb the equilibrium of three clusters of influence on their professional identities—the policy, workplace and personal—and thus impact upon the teachers' resilience/vulnerability and their ability to sustain commitment.

Professional Identities: Sites of Struggle

Our research suggests that identity itself is a composite of three clusters of influences: the socio-cultural/policy, workplace and personal. Each of these influences is itself made up of interactions between a range of sometimes competing factors which have to be managed in the staffroom and classroom. How a teacher manages these will determine his/her professional identity:

1. Socio-cultural/policy. This cluster of influences reflects cultural, social and policy expectations of teachers and teaching, and the educational ideals, ethical and moral purposes of the teacher. It is open to the influence of changing policy and social trends as to what constitutes a good teacher, classroom practitioner, etc., and may contain a number of competing and conflicting elements such as local or national policy, continuing professional development (CPD), workload, roles and responsibilities, etc.
2. Workplace or socially located influences. These are located in the micropolitics and social relationships of specific school, department or classroom, contexts and are affected by local conditions, i.e. pupil behaviour, the quality of leadership, support and feedback in teachers' immediate work context.
3. Personal influences. These are located in life outside school and are associated with personal histories, present lives, family, social relationships and personal sense of efficacy and vulnerability.

Teachers may experience tensions within and between these three clusters of influence at any given time and each cluster is itself subject to a number of positive and negative influences. The strength of teachers' job satisfaction, well-being, self-

[6] NVivo is a Computer-Aided Qualitative Data Analysis Software (CAQDAS) program.

[7] Inter-rater reliability of 95%.

efficacy and vulnerability, commitment and resilience, and their ability to exercise agency will be affected but not necessarily determined by these influences, for each of these may be mediated by teachers' cultural traditions, sense of vocation/moral purpose/values and agency and the interaction between these and their working environment. Any one (or more) of these three clusters of influence may, however, at a particular time, become dominant, thus challenging the relative stability of the other two and influencing teachers' existing sense of professional identity. Managing such new (or persisting) negative instabilities and tensions will require additional time and emotional energy from the teacher, and this may affect their capacity to sustain their positive sense of professional identity.

Like "vulnerability" (see Chap. 5 by Kelchtermans), instability is not necessarily negative. It can stimulate a re-evaluation of current thinking and practices that may no longer be the most effective in new work situations. For example, a teacher who moves schools or takes a new role will inevitably experience a period of instability, as will a teacher who has to learn new knowledge about teaching or adopt new teaching, monitoring and/or assessment strategies. Indeed, as Kelchtermans (see Chap. 5) argues, it may be that their vulnerability is a structural condition of teaching. However, the longer a sense of negative instability persists, as a result of the dominance of one or more clusters of influence, the more unlikely it is what the teacher will be able to manage the others.

Sites of Struggle: Scenarios That Challenge Professional Identity

Four scenarios were identified: influences in *relative balance*, *one dominant influence*, *two dominant influences* and *three conflicting influences*. These were identified by the reported challenges that each exercised on teachers' existing professional identities. Teachers were able to be grouped into one of four stable positive or negative and unstable positive or negative "states". The extent to which the scenarios were managed depended in part upon the level of disturbance or fluctuation and in part upon the combination of internal influences (e.g. strength of personal values) and external influences (e.g. school leadership, teacher–pupil relationships, pupil behaviour, colleague support, home circumstances). We were able to plot variations between teachers and begin to identify "resilient" and "vulnerable" teachers based on their self-reported self-efficacy, motivation, job satisfaction and commitment, which in turn related to teachers' values, experiences, school and policy/socio-cultural and personal lives.

Professional Identity Scenarios: Key Characteristics and Influences

Teachers were grouped into one of the four scenarios on the basis of the degree of dominance of a particular influence cluster (or combination of these). Table 4.1 shows the number of teachers in each of the four scenario groups. Analyses of

Table 4.1 Number of teachers in each scenario

Scenario	Influence cluster	Subgroups			Total
Scenario 1	Influence in balance				102
Scenario 2	One dominant influence	Professional (n=46)	Workplace (n=57)	Personal (n=28)	131
Scenario 3	Two dominant influences	Professional + workplace (n=15)	Professional + personal (n=16)	Workplace + personal (n=13)	44
Scenario 4	Three conflicting influences				18
					295

the key features of teachers' professional life phases, school context, perceived effectiveness, motivation, commitment and self-efficacy revealed dominant patterns that characterised each scenario. Each scenario comprised teachers who were resilient (i.e. were sustaining their commitment) and those who were vulnerable (i.e. were either sustaining their commitment despite the scenario, or failing to sustain it).

For the purposes of this chapter, only the dominant features in each scenario are summarised. Excerpts from teacher stories, including a combination of data from the teacher questionnaire, teacher interviews and "worklines", are used to illustrate key aspects of each scenario group.

Scenario 1

Figure 4.2 shows a professional identity that is relatively stable, with the three influence clusters being held in balance. Thus, although there will be mild fluctuations within and between these from time to time, no action would need to be taken unless such stability resulted in negative outcomes: for example, if professional complacency was resulting in lack of commitment and continuing ineffectiveness. Professional identity becomes unstable when one or more influence cluster is disturbed by internal or external events (such as unanticipated personal crises, policy, staff, pupil, school or life changes). Then additional effort needs to be made by the individual in order to manage the imbalance, if possible restore it, or construct a new sense of professional identity.

Thirty-five per cent (n=102) of all teachers were in this scenario. Primary school teachers made up over half of this group (58%). The largest proportion of teachers were from FSM 1 and FSM 2 schools (62%) with pupils from the most socio-economically advantaged communities, and the smallest (38%) from FSM 3 and FSM 4 schools, with pupils form the most socio-economically disadvantaged communities.

One of the main characteristic of this group of teachers was their high level of motivation and commitment:

> I feel that I'm more committed and motivated than ever now that I have more time to spend on my work. Before, I had to split my time between work and children. (Brenda)

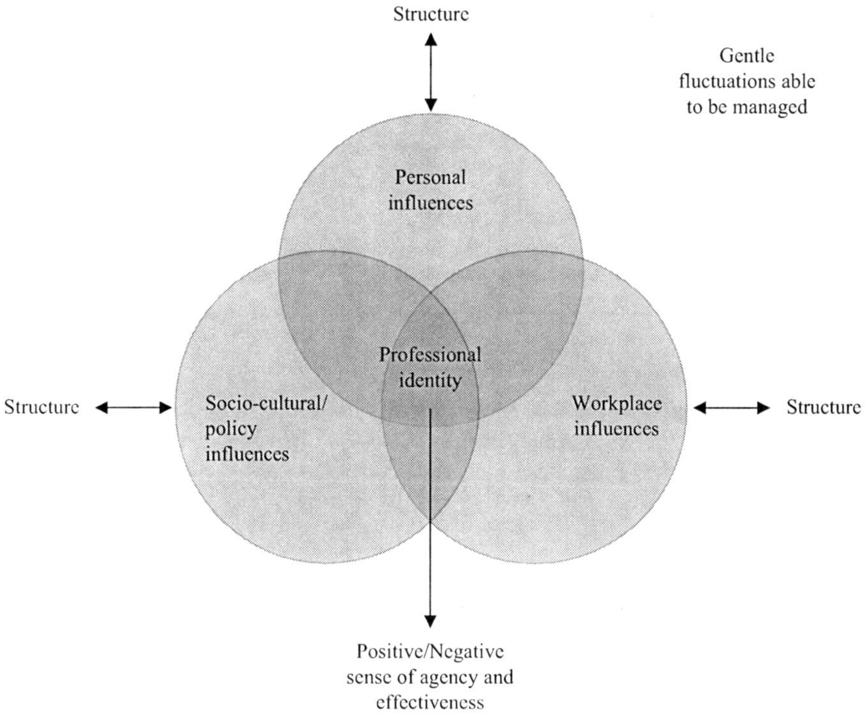

Fig. 4.2 Scenario 1: Influence clusters in relative balance

> I love working with children now as much as I did when I first started teaching. I can't imagine doing anything else. (Martin)

Teachers experiencing Scenario 1 were also more likely to be positive about their well-being and work–life balance, as Anna's story illustrates:

Anna's Story: Positive Well-Being and Work-Life Balance Anna was in her 20s and a Year 9 maths teacher. She had taught for four years, all in the same school—an urban moderate socioeconomic status (FSM 2) 11–16 mixed comprehensive school of 750 pupils. She was originally attracted to teaching because she thought it was "a valuable career" (teacher interview). According to the OFSTED report (2002), this is "an excellent school, in which very good teaching and first-rate leadership and management enable pupils to make very good progress".

Anna's husband had recently become a qualified teacher. She thought that this enabled him to fully understand what she experienced at work—"it really helps when I've had a hard day" (teacher interview). This had a major impact on her sense of well-being and work–life balance because, together, they developed a routine, separating work and home time, in order for them to

Table 4.2 Key features of Scenario 1

Scenario 1	Positive	Negative
Socio-cultural/ policy influences	• Promotion • Continued professional development	• Policy changes • Workload
Workplace influences	• Supportive leadership • Supportive colleagues • Teamwork • Pupil relationships	• Pupil behaviour (lack of respect) • Unsupportive leadership from senior management team • Inadequate discipline procedures
Personal influences	• Family/friend support • Few home commitments • Life events	• Personal/family illness • No family support

have time together and not be working every night of the week once they left school. Anna reported that they both kept certain nights and weekends free of work and this had helped her to improve her organisation both at school and in her personal life.

In common with 86% (n=91) of teachers in this scenario, Anna demonstrated a strong sense of well-being and agency and so, emotionally, was not at risk of leaving her post. Moreover, she envisaged herself teaching for many more years. However, 21 (21% of 102) teachers experiencing Scenario 1 were emotionally vulnerable and at risk of leaving the teaching profession because they were unwilling or unable to manage change. These teachers were less likely than their resilient colleagues to be positive regarding their well-being and the balance they managed to achieve between the pressures of work and personal lives. Table 4.2 shows the key positive and negative influences which teachers in this scenario identified.

Scenario 2

This scenario comprised teachers where one of the three clusters of influence dominated. In this situation, fluctuations are able to be managed in the short term, though this will depend upon the level of teachers' motivation, commitment, self-efficacy, support from colleagues and leadership (Fig. 4.3).

Forty-four per cent (n=74) of all primary teachers, and 40% (n=57) of all secondary teachers were in this group. Over one-third of teachers (35%, n=46) experiencing this scenario taught in FSM 2 schools, whilst nearly one quarter (23%, n=31) of teachers taught in FSM 4 schools. There were a number of policy, workplace and personal influences reported (Table 4.3).

Although 52% (n=68) of the teachers in this group were more likely to be negative regarding their well-being and management of work–life tensions, as in Scenario 1, teachers in Scenario 2 tended to be highly motivated, as Carmelle's story demonstrates.

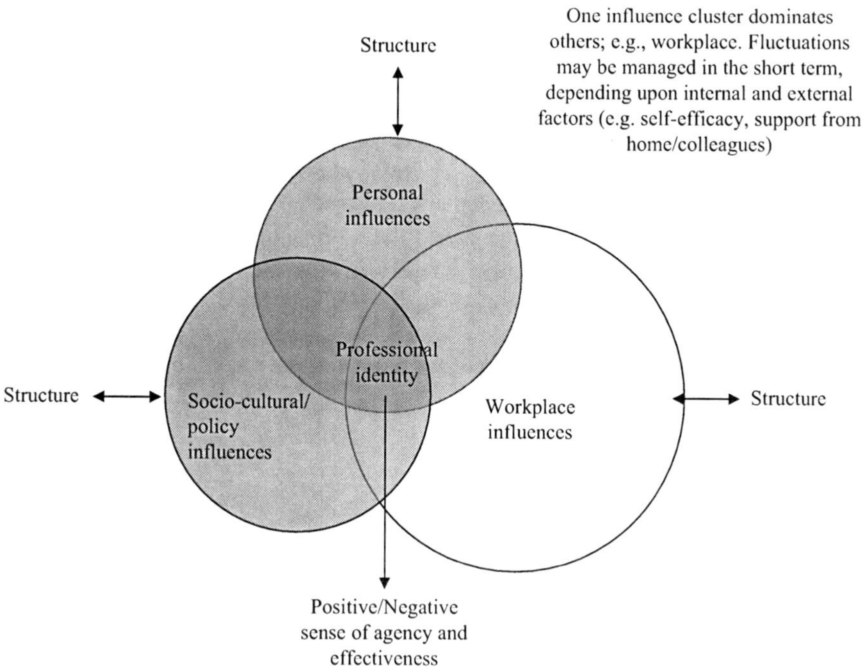

Fig. 4.3 Scenario 2: One dominant influence clusters

Table 4.3 Key features of Scenario 2

Scenario 2	Positive	Negative
Socio-cultural/policy influences	• Promotion/additional role • Departmental/school support • Motivated colleagues/pupils	• Increased workload • External policies (assessment/marking) • Pupil behaviour (lack of respect)
Workplace influences	• Teamwork • Pupil behaviour	• Lack of parental support • Poor in-school communication
Personal influences	• Life events (relationships/health)	• Live events (illness/relationships)

Carmelle's Story: Highly Motivated (Dominant Workplace Dimension) Carmelle was 51 years old and had been teaching for 29 years. In addition to being a Year 2 teacher in a village school, she was also the coordinator for maths, assessment and Key Stage One. There were nearly 250 pupils on roll, drawn from a wide range of backgrounds. An average proportion of pupils were eligible for free school meals (FSM2). She was originally attracted to teaching because of the opportunity to work with children and to help to make a difference in their lives.

Carmelle reported that the former head teacher of the school had not been supportive and the way he spoke to the staff had been "dreadful" (teacher interview). Carmelle had not been happy with the amount of pressure the previous head teacher had put onto her and, as a result, her level of motivation had started to decrease (workplace). However, the school had recently gained a new head teacher, which Carmelle saw as a positive influence on her work. She said that this had allowed her to reintroduce play into the KS1 curriculum and she felt that the new, positive interaction with the leadership was very important to her. Carmelle reported that, as a result of this change in the working context, staff had started to work more collaboratively and relationships between members of staff had become more supportive, restoring her high level of motivation for her work.

Scenario 3

This scenario included teachers where two of the three clusters of influence dominated (Fig. 4.4).

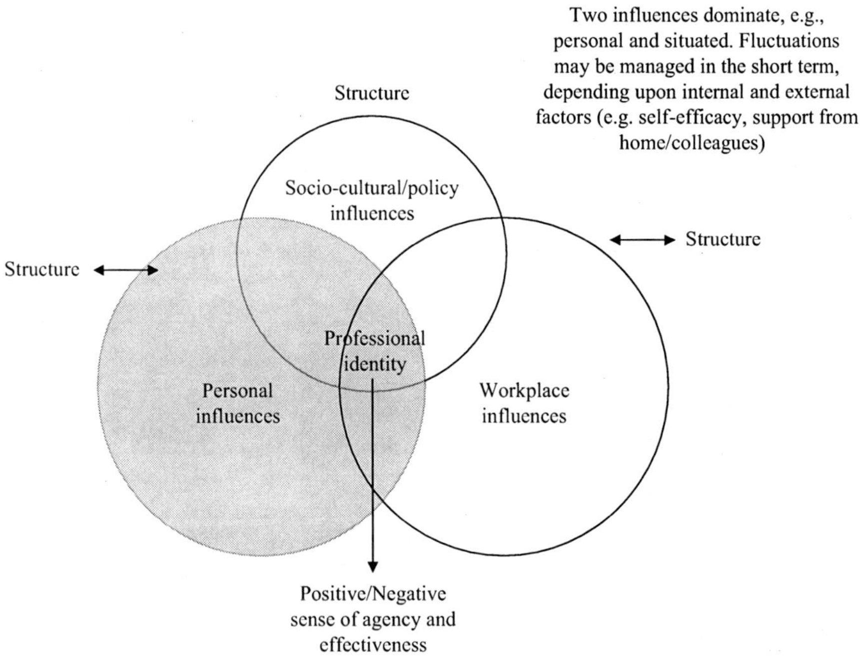

Fig. 4.4 Scenario 3: Two dominant influences

There were 44 (15% of 295) teachers in this group. Of these, the majority were female (75%, n=33). Secondary teachers made up over half of the numbers in this scenario (59%) and, as a proportion of the total number of teachers, represented 18% as against 11% primary. In terms of FSM, there was an even spread. Charlie was a teacher who was experiencing negative workplace influences.

Charlie's Story: Negative Work-Life Balance (Dominant Policy and Workplace Dimensions) Charlie was 31 years old with eight years' teaching experience, some of which had been in secondary and adult education. He achieved his first primary headship in April 2003—"It's my first headship and I'm finding it really difficult" (teacher interview). In spite of enjoying the new challenge of headship, Charlie was frustrated by the fact that his leadership/management role was distracting him from his teaching. He described this time as the lowest point in his career.

In addition, the school roll was falling, and several established members of staff were showing resentment towards changes Charlie was implementing in the school (workplace). Both of these issues were having a negative influence on his personal life, as he was having little time to spend with his wife and children.

During the project, the workplace influences began to become more positive as he established himself in the school, especially in relation to staff relationships. However, these influences remained dominant as he continued to focus his efforts on establishing his identity in the school.

Table 4.4 shows the teachers in experiencing Scenario 3 cited considerable more negative influences than those experiencing Scenarios 1 and 2. Like Charlie, 70% (n=31) of teachers in this group, unsurprisingly given the fluctuations, were more likely to be negative with regard to their well-being and work–life balance:

Table 4.4 Key features of Scenario 3

Scenario 3	Positive	Negative
Socio-cultural/policy influences	• Ambition • Career advancement • New role	• Unsuccessful promotion • Tension between roles • Increased workload
Workplace influences	• Teamwork • Staff morale • Support from leadership • Pupil motivation • Pupil relationships • Pupil self-esteem	• Drop in school roll • Lack of teamwork • Building work • Lack of enthusiasm • Challenging behaviour • Disaffected attitude • New leadership
Personal influences	• Becoming a parent • New relationship • Buying a house	• Personal illness • Family illness • Bereavement • Financial worries • Breakdown of relationship

> I've had to take some time off because it got too much; the teaching, workload, marking and my management role. (Mary)

> Work does hinder my home life because I end up working most weekends and several nights in the week. I have no energy to do other things. (Michelle)

Unlike the majority of teachers in this Scenario, who were emotionally vulnerable (52%; n=23), others demonstrated a strong sense of agency and emotional resilience. In spite of the increasing pressures on well-being, he and other teachers in this scenario were sustaining their levels of motivation (76%; n=16), commitment (90%; n=19) and self-efficacy (62%; n=13). Jeremy's story illustrates this:

Jeremy's Story: High Motivation, Commitment and Self-Efficacy (Dominant Workplace and Personal Dimensions) Jeremy was 54 years old and had been teaching for 33 years. He enjoyed teaching because of the success he had with the pupils and the department. Jeremy was committed to working with children from impoverished home environments and identified himself strongly with them, having high expectations. He had been diagnosed with high blood pressure and had tried to cut down on the amount of time he spent working "after hours". However, he continued to work on Saturdays and even sometimes on Sundays.

Despite his ill-health in the final phase of his career, Jeremy had remained highly motivated and committed to teaching and to his pupils. He was supported positively by the head teacher and by the local authority, and felt that they had helped him in making improvements to the maths department as well as to the school more generally. He had recently been invited to take on additional responsibility (and, therefore, workload) as a member of the senior management team (workplace). Jeremy found that staff morale had had the biggest positive impact on his work.

However, his strategy was one of adjusting one or more dimensions to the needs of the others, whereas other resilient teachers in this group were more likely to maintain a balance between the socio-cultural/policy, situated and/or personal dimensions by engaging with one or more influence clusters (with full commitment) and/or separating one part of work or life from another.

Scenario 4

This Scenario, where all three of the influences (policy, workplace and personal) were conflicting (Fig. 4.5), caused extreme fluctuations in teachers' professional identities. It comprised of relatively few teachers (18, 6% of 295) and considerable internal and external support to manage the conflicting negative influences of workload, leadership, pupil behaviour, family responsibilities and personal ill-health was needed (Table 4.5).

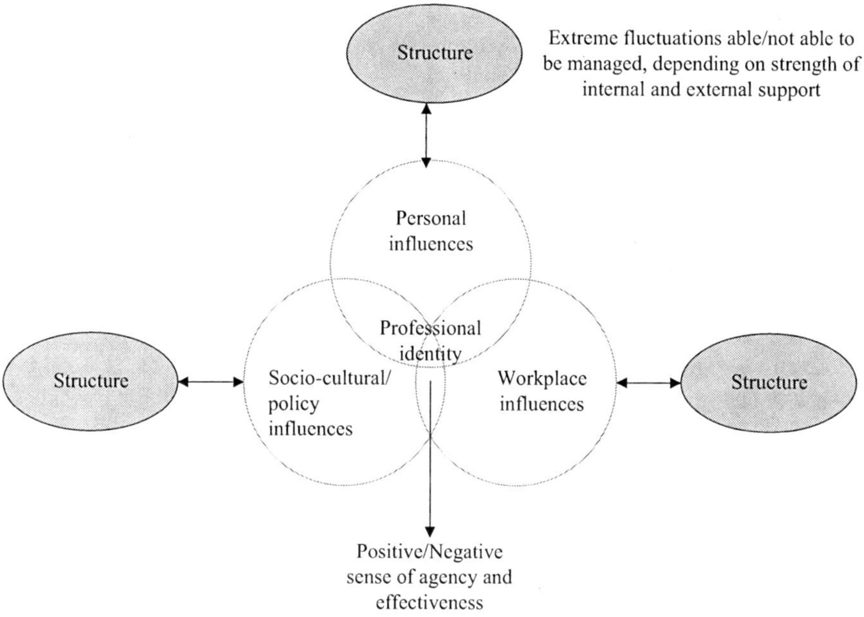

Fig. 4.5 Scenario 4: Three conflicting influences

Table 4.5 Key features in Scenario 4

Scenario 4	Positive	Negative
Socio-cultural/policy	–	• Workload
Workplace influences	–	• Leadership • Pupil behaviour
Personal influences	–	• Family responsibilities • Ill-health

Over one third (39%) of the 18 teachers in this scenario were in the 8–15 professional life phase and nearly three quarters (72%; n=13) taught pupils from more socio-economically disadvantaged communities (FSM 3 and FSM 4) schools. This suggests that the experience of conflicting pressures may be greater in more challenging contexts and during previous professional life phases. One example of a teacher experiencing these conflicts is Eva who, in spite of working in a school in such circumstances, managed to remain committed to teaching.

Eva's Story: Highly Committed (Three Conflicting Dimensions) Eva was in her 40s and had taught for nearly 25 years. She was a Year 6 teacher in an urban moderate socioeconomic status (FSM3) primary school of 255 pupils. She was assistant head teacher and maths coordinator. Eva had a difficult boy in her class in Year 1 of the project, who played a "dynamic" role in class. She was very dissatisfied with the amount of time she gave to behaviour management.

Eva felt that policies, either internally or externally developed, had negative influence on her work, her effectiveness and her values. This was particularly the case in her early career phase. But she added that her attitude towards policies had changed. Seven years ago, Eva had thought about leaving teaching because she felt that she had had enough with the national policy overload.

Eva felt that her work encroached into her personal time. She wanted to spend more time looking after her four children, but paperwork at home had taken time away from her own family and she felt guilty about this. Eva's health had suffered since Year 1 of the project, and she was on anti-depressant tablets. This was a major consequence of the pace and weight of her job, particularly the workload accrued from her multiple roles.

In spite of all this, Eva felt that teaching was part of who she was. Although she was worried that her motivation had decreased over the years as "the job has become harder over the course of the year" and the "pressures are too great" (teacher interview), she knew that her commitment towards the job and the pupils had remained high.

The majority of teachers in this scenario were judged to be emotionally vulnerable or at risk and were likely to be less motivated than those experiencing other Scenarios.

Discussion

It is clear that individual teachers' lives can be dominated (to varying degrees) by clusters of socio-cultural/policy, workplace and personal influences and that they play a significant role on how they manage variations in their work and lives and affect their sense of professional identity. The analyses revealed that the interaction between these influences contributed to teachers' sense of agency and that there was a relationship between this and their professional identity as expressed through their commitment, well-being and job satisfaction (sense of fulfilment and achievement), and resilience (the ability of an individual to withstand or recover quickly from difficult conditions related to self-efficacy). Their professional life phases, resilience and in-school support are key mediating factors in their ability to manage these influences.

Professional Life Phase

The evidence here supports the claim that teachers' initial professional identities may change over time as they are challenged by different life and work experiences and school contexts. Although the sites of struggle (scenarios) themselves cannot be attributed to specific professional life phases, there are particular points when certain policy and personal changes are more likely to occur, such as starting a family (4–7 and 8–15), taking on additional school or departmental responsibilities (4–7, 8–15 and 16–23), etc. These events can be paralleled by work-related factors such as disruptive pupil behaviour, change of leadership or relations with colleagues. Thus, identities may be more or less stable and more or less fragmented at different times and in different ways according to the capacities of teachers to manage the different scenarios that they experience within each professional life phase which they experience.

Resilience and School Socio-Economic Contexts

The vast majority of teachers in the study (79% of 295; n=233) were experiencing either Scenario 1 (relative balance) or Scenario 2 (one dominant dimension), whereas only 21% (n=62) of the 295 teachers were experiencing Scenario 3 or 4. Teachers in Scenarios 1 and 2 were more likely to be primary teachers (58% of 233; n=135), whereas in Scenario 3, teachers were more likely to teach secondary phase (59% of 44; n=26). Teachers in Scenario 1 were also more likely to teach in FSM 1 and FSM 2 schools (62% of 133; n=144). This was also the case for those teachers in Scenario 2 (56% of 131; n=73). Conversely, teachers in Scenario 4 were more likely to teach in FSM 3/4 schools (72% of 18; n=13).

Resilient teachers in Scenarios 1 and 2 were more likely to teach in FSM 1/2 schools. The difference, it seems, was in the relative intensity of the presence of a greater combination of negative influences in FSM 3/4 schools, which made "managing" the scenarios and sustaining a stable, positive sense of identity more challenging. For these teachers, the presence of positive life and work influences was more critical to sustaining their commitment. The analyses also revealed that there were associations between teachers' resilience and their perceived effectiveness and effectiveness as assessed by their pupils' test scores. Teachers who were judged to have demonstrated resilience were more likely to have pupil value-added results of "above expectations" or "as expected". Likewise, with few exceptions, those teachers who were judged and judged themselves to have demonstrated a lack of resilience (or vulnerability) were more likely to have pupil value-added results of "below expectations" or "as expected".

In-School and Personal Support

The key factors that contributed among the 198 (67%) of teachers with a positive sense of identity in all scenarios were:

School/departmental leadership	63%
Supportive colleagues	58%
Family	52%

These teachers (except for those in Scenario 4) were also more likely to demonstrate high motivation, commitment and self-efficacy. Key negative factors among the 97 (33%) of teachers judged to be "vulnerable" were:

Pupil behaviour	87%
Workload	70%

This group of teachers experienced their levels of motivation and self-efficacy decrease as the number of dominant influences increased. They were also more likely to have a negative sense of agency and well-being. Unsurprisingly, a higher proportion of teachers in Scenario 1 were positive about their well-being (73% of 98 who commented; n=72). This was not the case for teachers in Scenario 2, who found it more difficult to maintain a healthy work–life balance and felt negative about their well-being (77% of 131; n=101). Interestingly, more teachers in FSM 4 schools were resilient than those in FSM 3 schools.

Conclusions

The impact of each particular scenario upon teachers motivation, self-efficacy, commitment, resilience, well-being, job satisfaction and effectiveness related to a greater or lesser extent to (a) whether the negative dominant influences had to be managed over a short, medium or long term (e.g. unsatisfactory relationships in the classroom, staffroom or home); (b) individual biography (i.e. the strength of their values and aspirations, their emotional resilience/vulnerability to stress of different kinds and physical health); (c) personal and professional support (e.g. leadership, colleagues, friends, etc.) and (d) sense of agency.

In all scenarios, there was a dynamic relationship between structure and agency. Agency, in relation to each identity scenario, was concerned with teachers' belief in their ability to (a) manage each of the three clusters of influence and the interaction between them; (b) reconfigure themselves within them where necessary; (c) manage critical events that threatened their stability or which needed to be managed and (d) live with the vulnerabilities caused by the tensions and conflicts within and between these various clusters of influence, while continuing to be efficacious in their workplace (i.e. maintain their commitment and resilience).

In order to manage the balance (stability) or imbalance (instability) of different identity in the different scenarios, one or a combination of a number of the following strategies were adopted:

1. Accommodating by adjusting one or more component to the needs of the others
2. Tolerating the imbalance to the system caused by the new circumstances
3. Subjugating one or more component to accommodate the needs of the other(s)
4. Resisting any change

5. Reevaluating the nature of the existing composite identity
6. Accepting the imbalance positively
7. Separating one part of work or life from another
8. Engaging with one or more components with full commitment
9. Refocusing from one component to another
10. Adapting to the new situation in a positive way

There are implications from the findings of this research reported in this chapter for policy-makers and school leaders. It is not possible to control for fluctuations in scenarios caused by the dominance of one or more clusters of influence. However, teachers need to be committed and resilient in order to sustain their sense of effectiveness in what are emotionally as well as intellectually demanding and often changing work contexts. These are associated with their sense of positive or negative professional identity. This research suggests to be effective, and remain committed over a career, teachers need to have a sense of agency about who they are and what they do and that their sense of professional identity relates closely to this. Where negative influences dominate the threat to existing positive professional identities increases. It is important, then, for policy-makers and school leaders, if they really want the implementation of system-wide school and curriculum change and improvement agendas to succeed, to factor into their planning their potential positive and negative destabilising effects upon teachers' sense of agency and stable, positive professional identities.

References

Ball, S. J. (1994). *Education reform: A critical and post-structural approach.* Buckingham: Open University Press.

Barbalet, J. (2002). Introduction: Why emotions are crucial. In J. Barbalet (Ed.), *Emotional sociology* (pp. 1–9). London: Blackwell.

Beijaard, D. (1995). Teachers' prior experiences and actual perceptions of professional identity. *Teachers and Teaching, 1*(2), 281–294.

Day, C., & Kington, A. (2008). Identity, well-being and effectiveness: The emotional contexts of teaching. *Pedagogy, Culture and Society, 16*(1), 7–23.

Day, C. W., Kington, A., Stobart, G., & Sammons, P. (2006a). The personal and professional selves of teachers: Stable and unstable identities. *British Educational Research Journal, 32*(4), 601–616.

Day, C. W., Stobart, G., Sammons, P., Kington, A., Gu, Q., Smees, R., & Mujtaba, T. (2006b). *Variations in teachers' work, lives and effectiveness.* DfES Research Report, p. 743. London: HMSO.

Day, C. W., Sammons, P., Stobart, G., Kington, A., & Gu, Q. (2007). *Teachers matter.* Maidenhead: Open University Press.

Gu, Q., & Day, C. W. (2007). Teachers' resilience: A necessary condition for effectiveness. *Teaching and Teacher Education, 23*(8), 1302–1316.

Hargreaves, A. (1994). *Changing teachers, changing times.* London: Falmer.

James-Wilson, S. (2001). *The influence of ethnocultural identity on emotions and teaching.* Paper presented at the Annual Meeting of the American Educational Research Association, New Orleans.

Kelchtermans, G. (1996). Teacher vulnerability: Understanding its moral and political roots. *Cambridge Journal of Education, 26*(3), 307–324.

MacLure, M. (1993). Arguing for your self: Identity as an organising principle in teachers' jobs and lives. *British Educational Research Journal, 19*(4), 311–322.

Miles, M. B., & Huberman, A. M. (1994). *Qualitative data analysis: An expanded sourcebook* (2nd ed.). Thousand Oaks: Sage.

Nias, J. (1989). *Primary teachers talking: A study of teaching as work.* London: Routledge.

Nias, J. (1996). Thinking about feeling: The emotions in teaching. *Cambridge Journal of Education, 26*(3), 293–306.

Osborn, M., Abbot, D., Broadfoot, P., Croll, P., Pollard, A., Chawla-Duggan, R., & Pole, C. J. (1996). Teachers' professional perspectives: Continuity and change. In R. Chawla-Duggan & C. J. Pole (Eds.), *Reshaping education in the 1990s: Perspectives on primary schooling* (pp. 137–153). London: Falmer.

Sleegers, P., & Kelchtermans, G. (1999). Inleiding op het themanummer: professionele identiteit van leraren [Professional identity of teachers]. *Pedagogisch Tijdschrift, 24,* 369–374.

Stronach, I., Corbin, B., McNamara, O., Stark, S., & Warne, T. (2002). Towards an uncertain politics of professionalism: Teacher and nurse identities in flux. *Journal of Education Policy, 27*(2), 109–138.

Sumsion, J. (2002). Becoming, being and unbecoming an early childhood educator: A phenomenological case study of teacher attrition. *Teaching and Teacher Education, 18,* 869–885.

Sutton, R. E. (2000). *The emotional experiences of teachers.* Paper presented at the Annual Meeting of the American Educational Research Association, New Orleans.

Troman, G., & Woods, P. (2001). *Primary teachers' stress.* London: RoutledgeFalmer.

Zembylas, M. (2003). Emotions and teacher identity: A post-structural perspective. *Teachers and Teaching: Theory and Practice, 9*(3), 213–238.

Chapter 5
Vulnerability in Teaching: The Moral and Political Roots of a Structural Condition

Geert Kelchtermans

There is more to teaching than thorough subject knowledge and technical teaching skills. When teachers are asked about what they find motivating or satisfying in their jobs, they often spontaneously refer to feelings of joy, fascination, pride, wonder and enthusiasm, resulting from the fact that they work with "human material", as they often call it. Teachers' talk about their work immediately reveals that emotions are at the heart of teaching.

This emotional dimension, however, also has another side. Teachers do not experience only positive feelings. Teaching also implies feelings of powerlessness, frustration, disappointment, disillusion, guilt and even anger and fear. In this article I will explore teachers' feelings of vulnerability. This vulnerability refers to one way in which teachers experience their interactions with other actors in the school and the community. It thus encompasses not only emotions (feelings), but also cognitive processes (perception, interpretation).

Although I will argue that for teachers vulnerability constitutes a significant experience, I want to stress that this is only one way in which teachers can live in their job situation. When I discussed this theme with teachers, they often expressed embarrassment, because they felt that it was as if they, as teachers, were seen as pitiful victims, looking for compassion. This is not the idea I want to present in this chapter, neither do I want to reinforce the negative image of teachers that has recently been promoted by certain media. However, vulnerability in teaching is real and profoundly affects teachers' job satisfaction and the quality of their professional performance. Understanding this vulnerability is crucial for a proper understanding of teachers and the development of their teaching. It is to this understanding that I hope to contribute.

The first part of this chapter was originally published as "Teacher Vulnerability: Understanding its Moral and Political Roots", in the Cambridge Journal of Education, Vol. 26, No. 3 (1996): 307–324.

G. Kelchtermans (✉)
Catholic University of Leuven, Leuven, Belgium
e-mail: geert.kelchtermans@ped.kuleuven.be

C. Day, J. C.-K. Lee (eds.), *New Understandings of Teacher's Work,* Professional Learning and Development in Schools and Higher Education 6,
DOI 10.1007/978-94-007-0545-6_5, © Springer Science+Business Media B.V. 2011

After briefly describing the research context that provides the empirical basis of my argument, I will present the different sources of teacher vulnerability, as identified in my study of teachers' professional biographies. Using one teacher's case, I will move the analysis a step further and argue that the feeling of vulnerability has moral and political roots in the workplace conditions of the teacher. In order to reduce the negative effects of teacher vulnerability and to open up perspectives for the development of successful coping strategies, it is essential to acknowledge and understand this moral and political dimension in teachers' emotional experience of their work.

Vulnerability: A Theme in Teachers' Professional Biographies

Vulnerability turned out to be one of the recurring themes in the narrative, retrospective accounts experienced Flemish primary school teachers gave of their careers. I collected these professional biographies in a study on teachers' professional development, using a narrative biographical approach.[1] One of the major aims of this study was the reconstruction of teachers' personal interpretive frameworks as the mental sediment of their career experiences. Throughout their career experiences teachers develop a subjective "lens" through which they perceive their job situation, give meaning to it and act in it. In other words, I used teachers' career stories to understand their way of thinking about teaching and themselves as teachers. Within this personal interpretive framework, I could distinguish two important, interwoven domains: the professional self-understanding (a teacher's conceptions about her/himself as a teacher) and the subjective educational theory (the personal system of a teacher's knowledge and beliefs about teaching).[2] The professional self-understanding could be further differentiated conceptually into five components: self-image (descriptive component), self-esteem (evaluative component), job motivation (conative component), task perception (normative component) and future perspective (Kelchtermans 1993, 2009).

[1] The data were collected in 1990 and 1991 in four Flemish primary schools from ten teachers, with 15–25 years of teaching experience. From every school at least two teachers were included in the research group in order to get triangulated information about the school context. The procedure for data collection included a cumulative cycle of semi-structured biographical interviews, enriched with data from school and classroom observations and interviews with key informants (inspector, principal). Qualitative within-case and between-case analyses were used to interpret the data. For a detailed description of the research methodology see Kelchtermans (1994). The conceptual framework and major outcomes are presented extensively in Kelchtermans (1993).

[2] The concept of "self-understanding" refers to teachers' sense of identity. I have, however, purposefully avoided the notion of "identity" because of its association with a static essence, implicitly ignoring or denying its dynamic and biographical nature (development over time). Instead, I have used the word "self-understanding". The term refers to both the understanding one has of one's "self" at a certain moment in time (*product*), as well as to the fact that this product results from an ongoing *process* of making sense of one's experiences and their impact on the "self".

The teachers' sense of vulnerability became particularly clear in the narrative accounts of so-called "critical incidents" (Measor 1985): events in teachers' careers that were experienced as "turning points" or "key experiences", having a significant personal meaning for the teacher. Critical incidents question the status quo, the normal daily routine and force teachers to rethink and to reconsider it. As such, critical incidents always provoke emotions of distress, unease, doubt and uncertainty.[3]

For the purpose of this article, I "revisited" the career stories in a second, hermeneutical analysis. This took the form of different cycles of "close interpretive reading", guided by three questions:

- What are the sources of vulnerability in teachers' stories?
- What does the experience of vulnerability mean to the teachers in terms of their personal interpretive frameworks?
- How do teachers cope with it in their specific job situations?

Sources of Teachers' Vulnerability

The analysis of the professional biographies showed that a sense of vulnerability can be provoked by a wide variety of causes or sources. Three major categories of sources, at different levels of the educational system, could be distinguished. At the micro-level (the classroom), teachers experience vulnerability in their struggle with the limits of their teaching impact on pupils' learning. Principal, colleagues and parents constitute a second potential source of vulnerability at the level of the school. Beyond the school, (local) educational policy makers are a third source of vulnerability. I will discuss these three sources now in more detail, starting with the last one.

Educational Administration/Policy

Policy decisions by (local) educational administrators (e.g. school board) were an important source of teacher vulnerability. This was best illustrated from the biographical accounts of teachers' lifelong assignment (tenure). When starting their career, getting a tenured position in a school was a high-priority concern to almost all the teachers (Kelchtermans 1993, p. 452). Once they had this assignment their job situation was secure (statutory civil servant). However, to get their assignment teachers often had to do more than just good classroom teaching: taking up commitments in the local community (e.g. involvement in the local youth movement;

[3] In the German psychological "Kritische Ereignisforschung" (research on critical incidents) this "emotional non-indifference" ("emotionale Nicht-Gleichgültigkeit") is considered as a constitutive and distinctive characteristic that makes these events appear as pregnant and striking in the ongoing stream of daily experiences (Filipp 1990, p. 24).

directing the youth choir) and using mediation and (kinship) relations. This is clearly illustrated in the career story of Chris, a first-grade teacher. He recalls how he worked like hell after he got his first job. Since the school wanted to attract more pupils, extra services were provided to the parents (e.g. sport activities on Wednesday afternoon, when schools were normally closed). Chris took on all these jobs, together with the organisation of fundraising activities for the school.

> Those were the days of "pressure to perform". One always had to be prepared and willing. Always working, taking up responsibilities. … All because of that tenure. I wanted that tenure at all cost. (Chris)

He even went to do small jobs of repair and maintenance at the houses of the principal and the school board's president. In exchange for those efforts, he not only got his own tenure, but also managed to get his wife, a nursery school teacher, a tenured contract in the same school.

As long as they are not tenured, teachers are objectively vulnerable to the decisional power of the school board (e.g. forced changes in grade and job insecurity; see also Blase 1988, pp. 133–134). This is a kind of formal, statutory vulnerability. When, however, teachers start doubting their own professional qualities, because their tenure keeps being postponed, or if they feel that tenure is purposefully denied for whatever reasons, then this formal fact becomes subjectively meaningful. Individuals wonder what they are doing wrong or in what respect they are not meeting the never-explicitly-stated expectations of the school board. Nadine, a fourth-grade teacher, had to wait for several years before she got her tenure:

> Yes, I did have to wait quite long. I didn't get any support from the principal. We didn't seem to fit. … I saw my colleagues getting along well with her, but I never managed to develop that kind of relation with her. Well, yes, then you start asking yourself: "What am I doing wrong?" and that really put a damper on my enthusiasm as a young teacher.

This uncertainty, the lack of clear reasons and norms, makes teachers feel very vulnerable. They find themselves at the mercy of others, whose decisions they cannot control.

Another clear example of vulnerability stemmed from the experiences with school merger, especially when teachers were denied a voice in these decisions and their implementation. School merger processes are often regarded by the administrators (i.e. school board members) as strictly technical, organisational matters. They more or less consciously overlook what these processes mean to the people working in the school, in terms of changing interpersonal relations, professional culture (values and norms), workplace conditions, etc. Because these changes heavily affect teachers' daily workplace context and conditions, they feel personally and emotionally involved. When decisions with such impact on themselves and their work lives are taken "over their heads", it provokes intense feelings of disappointment and vulnerability. Teachers realise that they lack control over important workplace conditions and at the same time feel depreciated personally and professionally. Moni, a teacher who had been working for her entire career in the same school, is deeply shocked by the board's decision to merge with the boys' school.

Not so much the fact of the merger, however, upsets her, but the fact that she—and her colleagues—had no say at all in it:

> We were treated as if we were nobody. Just a number on the pay roll. And, I mean, I have been working in this school for so long. I really hold to that school. I would have gone through fire and water for that school and then. ... That decision. ... that treatment, it really sticks in my throat. ... Things will never be the same again.

This example reveals more than just the absence of participation structures or the consciousness of one's lack of control over workplace conditions. It is not only a matter of feeling ignored or depreciated as a professional member of the organisation. The emotions clearly reflect the experience of having lost something of professional value. In Moni's case, this is the loss of what Strike calls "goods of relationships", namely "those that human beings experience through their relationships with one another, such as caring, love, friendship, and community" (Strike 1990, p. 216). Moni believes that the cherished collegial school climate of the girls' school will disappear because of the merger and "it will never be the same...".

Policy decisions at the macro-level were not systematically included in my study. The recent policy of the Flemish Ministry of Education is characterised by a strong move towards decentralisation and giving more financial responsibility to the local level. This is, however, accompanied by the implementation of new procedures for quality control (i.e. by the inspectorate), prescribed educational basic goals (minimal curriculum) and financial cutbacks which threaten jobs. Although further research is needed, it seems plausible that these policy measures also contribute to teachers' feelings of vulnerability at the local level (see Kelchtermans 2007a).

Professional Relationships in the School

A second source of vulnerability concerns teachers' relationships in the school with the principal, parents and, to a lesser degree, with colleagues. The micro-political perspective on schools (e.g. Ball 1987, 1994; Blase 1991) criticises the dominant systems theory approach in organisational theory, because it holds unrealistic assumptions on rational efficiency and overestimates the importance of structural variables and goal consensus among the members of an organisation. Schools are much more characterised by disagreement over goals. Principals, teachers and occasionally parents do not necessarily all act from the same, commonly held vision of what "good education" is (see below: Nicole's case). Very often team members have different opinions about the best way to "be a school". This lack of consensus is further enhanced by the "whole set of often contradictory demands and expectations from outside audiences and agencies" (Ball 1987, p. 13). In other words, teachers find themselves in a micropolitical organisational reality in which individuals and/or (sub)groups "seek to use their resources of power and influence to further their interests" (Hoyle 1982, p. 88).

These interests can be thought of in terms of desired workplace conditions. Different members of the school strive for or try to maintain different workplace conditions (Kelchtermans 2007a; Kelchtermans and Ballet 2002a). These workplace conditions include material needs (e.g. decisions about which new teaching handbook should be used) or resources (time, information, funds, infrastructure facilities) and organisational and social interests (e.g. procedures, roles and positions in the organisation, types of interpersonal relations). Another group of workplace conditions that are always at stake, include what Ball calls "self interests" (Ball 1987, pp. 16–17), referring to the teacher's professional self (task perception, self-esteem, social recognition, etc.) and its place in the social network. A final, but very important, workplace condition concerns the "definition of the organisation", i.e. the processes of social construction determining what norms and goals get acknowledged as legitimate within the school. Because of the intrinsically value-laden nature of educational practices, control over these definition processes is decisive for the "cultural" workplace context in the school (Schein 1985, p. 6; Staessens 1993).

Vulnerability occurs when teachers feel powerless or politically ineffective in the micro-political struggles about their desired workplace conditions (Kelchtermans 2007a). An extreme example of this is recalled by Kurt about a Catholic school where he worked during his first year as a teacher. Life and teaching in that school were authoritarian, very strictly organised and managed by an extensive set of rules and prescriptions. Colleagues who were teaching the same grades had to move through the curriculum in perfect parallel, making sure all pupils were literally "on the same page" all the time.

> It was awful. I hated working there. That was a school with military discipline, for pupils and for teachers. I simply had to teach the lessons my colleague gave me. He photocopied his preparations and I could start. No creativity was allowed, no personal style. Nothing, just do as you're told. I still can't believe that such a school existed.

The demands about teaching methodology and treatment of the pupils were almost completely the opposite of what Kurt believed in as a beginning teacher. However, as an individual he felt powerless to change things and he was very happy when he "got rescued" by a job offer from another school.

Other respondents mentioned their powerlessness in the face of gossip or envy from colleagues (e.g. because of their commitment to innovative teaching methods). Criticism from parents can also provoke vulnerability (see below: Nicole's case).

Teachers' vulnerability was further enhanced by the high visibility of their professional activities. In spite of teachers' relative isolation in classrooms, they could be observed in action by their colleagues, principal and/or parents, especially when they also lived in the village in which their school was located. Their job situation could be characterised as "living in a fishbowl" (Blase 1988, p. 135). This is one reason why the teachers in our study spontaneously and frequently mentioned order, discipline and authority over the pupils (e.g. keeping order and discipline, making pupils be silent), especially when moving from playground to classroom (or vice versa) or on extra-mural activities.[4]

> Kurt (Grade 5): We have had quite some discussions about discipline recently. The principal accused me of having no authority with my pupils. But I don't agree with that. In my classroom they're silent. If not, I couldn't teach those 11 year olds. So, when I am teaching I see to it that they're quiet and that is no problem. But on the playground or in the corridor. ... Well, and she (the principal) would say: "What do you do to those kids that they become so naughty when in your class. Rascals always turn out to be pupils from the fifth ...". But she doesn't realize that kids change around the age of eleven, when they enter puberty ...

In other words, Kurt is held responsible by the principal for the "naughty" behaviour of his pupils. The principal argues that kids become naughty from the moment they come to the fifth grade, so the teacher of that grade should, at least in part, be held responsible and thus be seen as professionally in default. Kurt defends himself by referring to developmental psychological arguments. What upsets him is that he, as a teacher, is blamed and accused of lacking professionalism because of his pupils' misbehaviour in school.

Disciplinary efficacy is especially visible to others. Teachers feel that judgements about their professional competence by these "others" often rely too heavily on this visible part of their job. They experience this as unjust, because this is only one part of the job and as such too limited as a basis for assessing their professional quality, especially when compared with the full demands and responsibilities teachers actually have.

Limits to Teachers' Efficacy

The third source of vulnerability that could be identified in teachers' career stories is at the classroom level. One of the major professional realities teachers have to come to terms with are the limits of their professional efficacy: students' learning outcomes are only partly determined by teachers' actions. Many other factors, over which they have little or no control, determine pupils' learning. Several teachers recalled their sense of disappointment and powerlessness, especially at the beginning of their careers, towards pupils who did not manage to master the curriculum and whom they could not help properly. Leo refers to this "helplessness", recalling problems with one pupil during his first year of teaching:

> This kid in second grade could not write at all. He could only make some curls on paper. That was all. And his parents absolutely didn't want to send him to a school for special education. I sweated blood in trying to help him. But it was no use. ... I don't know what further happened to the kid. But I didn't manage to teach him any writing. It made me feel pretty frustrated, helpless.

---

[4] This finding was later corroborated and further developed in a study on the micro-politics in new teachers' work lives (see Kelchtermans and Ballet 2002a, b).

In their pupils' failures, these teachers felt that they were falling short themselves. In spite of their efforts, they had not been able to make the difference. The more committed beginning teachers are, the bigger the risk of this disappointment. Dealing with this professional reality implies learning to balance job commitment and personal distance. Unrealistic expectations about their influence can lead individuals to disappointment, demotivation or even burnout. Equally, unwitted cynicism ("You can't make a difference") may lead to reduced commitment, lack of job satisfaction and negative feelings about one's own professional competence (see also Kelchtermans 1999).

A variant of these stories concerns pupils with whom the teacher did not really succeed in "making contact" or "building a relationship". This variant is especially prominent among teachers with a strong caring ethic, who place high value on a trustful, positive relation with the children as a major condition for successful development and good learning.

> Marc: You know, a terrible thing is kids who don't let you get into personal contact. I mean, who close themselves for you. It's "you're there and I am here". You can't get any closer. Well, if I can't get to them, can't develop a relationship, things just don't work as they should. That is very frustrating. You remain a stranger, an outsider.

This experience often leads to feelings of guilt (see Hargreaves 1994, p. 141 ff.) and personal failure. Here too, teachers have to learn to cope with the limits of their efficacy.[5]

In these experiences, teachers are confronted not only with the limits of their impact, but also with the limits of their professional knowledge and skills. In other words, they realise that their professional competences (knowledge, skills), never provide a technical guarantee for success. Teaching and educating children is a complex process that is only partly affected and determined by intentional educational interventions. Whatever effort and good intentions teachers put into their work, successful outcomes remain uncertain.

In this "vulnerability to inefficacy" one also sees the specific nature of teachers' professional knowledge base (subjective educational theory) exemplified. This subjective educational theory is a personally organised set of knowledge and beliefs that guides teachers' professional behaviour. For the teacher his/her subjective educational theory has a subjective truth and legitimacy because these knowledge and beliefs have proved to work in practice (practicality ethic, Doyle and Ponder 1977–1978). This "knowledge" is further strongly affected by the task perception (teachers' personal, normative professional programme, their value choices and ethics). However, as experiential and value-laden knowledge, it constitutes a weak basis from which to defend practice, if this is attacked or questioned by others.

---

[5] Our findings confirm those of Hargreaves in his study of teachers' feeling of guilt. Hargreaves identified "guilt traps" in teaching as a job that are "socially located at the intersection of four specific paths of determination and job motivation in teachers' work: the commitment to goals of care and nurturance, the open-ended nature of the job, the pressures of accountability and intensification, and the persona of perfectionism" (Hargreaves 1994, 145 ff.).

The Moral and Political Roots of Vulnerability

The different sources of vulnerability that were identified from an analysis of the career stories remain very close to the content of these stories. However, moving the analysis one step further and getting beyond the direct events or interactions that caused the feelings of vulnerability, I came to understand that within this apparent diversity and variety, a common pattern can be discerned. Vulnerability for teachers always has political and moral roots. In other words, the emotions in teaching are linked to matters of interests and values. In order to argue this I will first present a more extended fragment of one teacher's career story. It concerns a critical incident in the career story of Nicole, a sixth-grade teacher, in which the interplay of the different sources of vulnerability becomes clear. Nicole's case will be used as an illustrative exemplar to explain the moral and political roots of teacher vulnerability.

A Fragment of Nicole's Story

Nicole had been teaching the sixth grade in the Nightingale, a suburban Catholic primary school, for about 20 years when she experienced a very frustrating conflict with the mother of a pupil. On the day of the Regional Testing[6] one pupil did not show up. She was said to be ill. Afterwards it emerged that the girl's mother had forbidden her to take the test, because Nicole had not completely finished the exercise book for mathematics. The mother had judged that her daughter was not well prepared for the test, although the girl was quite a good student. At the same time and without ever mentioning the matter directly to Nicole, the mother informed the inspectorate and even contacted the Ministry of Education about Nicole's professional shortcoming. Further, she launched it as a gossip-rumour in the parents' committee and in the local community. The incident happened just after a new principal, a former colleague in the Nightingale, was appointed. He reacted with a "wait-and-see" attitude. Yet, this hesitation in showing his explicit and unconditional support for her was perceived by Nicole as a form of distrust. She felt that her reputation as a teacher was threatened, but at the same time found herself unable to defend her case.

Nevertheless, Nicole had a clear professional justification for the situation. That year she had spent more time than usual on some geometrical subject topics (calculation of scale, volume, area). By a rich variety of hands-on learning activities,

[6] Regional Testing refers to a testing in which all the sixth-grade pupils of the different elementary schools in a certain region are invited to participate, yet without obligation and without consequences for either school or pupil. This cross-school test constitutes a basis for comparison of pupil results among the different schools. For sixth-grade teachers in Flanders, these tests are an important concern because they often feel evaluated themselves in their pupils' results. School teams and principals often put some pressure on the sixth-grade teachers to prepare the pupils as well as possible in order to get a good result for the school (public relations).

like building maquettes and calculating the amount of carpet necessary to cover the classroom floor, etc. Nicole had tried to give her pupils better opportunities to really learn and understand this curriculum topic. From her experience she knew that every year these curriculum elements caused trouble for several pupils.

Her husband was very angry about the incident and insisted that she should put a complaint for defamation against the woman. Nicole did not want to go that far, but still, she felt "deeply unhappy" at the incident.

> … my self-esteem was very low. It really hurt me to find myself working on gaining back my professional confidence after all these years of experience […]. I started doubting about myself. Was I wrong in deciding to spend more time on these difficult calculation problems? Was I really the proper teacher I believed myself to be?

The experience left her upset and troubled for months, even after the principal and the inspector had explicitly expressed their support for and confidence in Nicole's qualities as a teacher.

> For several years afterwards, I experienced the Regional Testing as an evaluation of my professional competence. It always was a relief to see my pupils getting good results. Also their results in secondary school became very important to me.

The intensity of this incident and the experienced vulnerability were very well illustrated by one of Nicole's "countering" activities (counter incidents, see Measor 1985).

> You know, one year later, a pupil from that girl's class passed by to show me the fine marks he got in his Secondary School. I took his mark-book, made an enlarged photocopy and hung it in the front window of my class, so that everybody passing by could see it.

For a long time Nicole felt the need to "prove herself" as a competent teacher in the eyes of others (parents, colleagues, principal, inspectorate).

The Moral Behind the Emotional

This critical incident from Nicole's career story illustrates how the different sources of vulnerability often work together and reinforce each other. The school board had just appointed a new principal who hesitated to back up Nicole in the conflict. The mother made the incident expand into the local community. She also informed the regional inspector and even the Ministry of Education. Her personal disagreement with Nicole was thus made very public.

However, all these elements do not explain why the incident made Nicole feel so vulnerable, uncertain, full of self-doubts. After all, she had a tenured position, so her job security was not in danger. No sanctions were taken against her. Her colleagues sympathised with her. After a while, also, the principal and the inspector backed her up. Furthermore, Nicole could provide thoughtful, rational justifications for her decisions on the lesson form and content. Notwithstanding that, the deep emotional effect was real. As she recalled the incident during the interview—about five years later—Nicole lived through the emotions again (tears in her eyes, choking voice). It had really been a significant, deeply disturbing experience.

So the question remains: why did the incident have such a profound and disturbing effect on this experienced and highly committed teacher? In order to answer this question we must understand what the experience meant to the teacher. What was at stake for her? This implies carefully listening to and interpreting the narrative account, in the context of the entire professional biography. "Giving trust and being trusted" was a recurring theme in Nicole's career story and an important element in her personal interpretive framework. Several fragments of her life history exemplify this (e.g. from childhood, from her induction period as a beginning teacher). From this background we come to see that the lack of trust by the mother constituted the heart of the experience for Nicole. In essence, this lack of trust meant to her that her professional self-understanding and personal integrity were put to question. The girl's mother questioned Nicole's professional decisions and thus publicly challenged her reputation as a proper teacher. It is this attack that caused the feelings of vulnerability and turned the conflict into a critical incident.

Was Nicole right in spending more time on the geometrical subjects with which a significant number of the pupils had problems? Did her decision harm the individual pupil's chances of good results on the Regional Test? (Remember, however, that the results of that Test had no effect on the girl's possible choice of study career in secondary education.) And if so, should Nicole have made another decision? At first sight these appear to be straightforward, even rather banal, questions about technical matters (decisions about teaching time and curriculum priorities). However, this technical discussion conceals a *moral issue*. The crucial question in the incident was: did Nicole's decision to offer the entire class extra learning opportunities do injustice to the educational needs of the individual pupil? Put this way, the incident reveals its moral dimension: it is a conflict between two competing ideas (values, norms) about the nature of "good teaching". Or, in Greenfield's words, between two "moral orientations", a moral orientation being "a point of view or reference point for action, influence, or decision that is rooted in an understanding of and a commitment to what is in the best interests of children from an educational and developmental perspective" (Greenfield 1991, p. 161).

From her moral orientation, Nicole accepts her responsibility as a teacher and makes a choice. Her guiding principle is that all pupils should get optimal learning opportunities and thus extra efforts have to be made in favour of the weaker students. The mother, however, challenges this equity norm by insisting on her daughter's individual rights. As Hoyle and John argue in their analysis of teachers' professionality: "The teacher's commitment to equity, difficult though it may be to achieve in practice, is in conflict with the parent's understandable desire for preferential treatment" (Hoyle and John 1995, p. 119).

Teachers find themselves permanently forced to make decisions with moral consequences in their dealing with the multiple, diffuse and even contradictory demands by their different clients (pupils, parents, community) (Hoyle and John 1995, p. 113; Hargreaves 1995, p. 15). Hargreaves aptly characterises the complexity of teachers' moral choices: "Attending to the moral dimensions of teaching usually involves distinguishing between better and worse courses of action, rather than right and wrong ones. There are no clear rules of thumb, no useful universal principles for deciding what to do. [...] They (the teachers) must live their moral lives in the swamp, [...] especially when moral certainties grounded in tradition or science are collapsing and people must rely on their own reflective resources as a basis for moral judgment" (Hargreaves 1995, p. 15).

In the reality of classroom and school, teachers thus have no choice but to act: to decide on what to do and then do it (Loewenberg-Ball and Wilson 1996, p. 187). In short, although teaching demands daily decisions with moral consequences, teachers can seldom rely on commonly held and acknowledged ethical principles. And even when these seem to exist, teachers themselves have to make the transfer from the abstract principle to the demands of concrete "real life" situations.

In fact, for responsible decisions in these moral matters, teachers can rely only on their task perception, the subjective, normative professional programme of basic goals and commitments that is part of their professional self-understanding. This also means that teachers' professional self-understanding, including their self-esteem and the moral "correctness" of their task perception, are at stake in discussions about being "a proper teacher". "Proper teaching", and its social recognition include not only the mastery and skilful application of knowledge and skills, but also the capacity to make sound judgements. Hoyle and John rightly state that "despite a general agreement on the basic skills and knowledge which teachers need, there remain important areas in which teachers have to decide between a range of pedagogical options" (Hoyle and John 1995, pp. 122–123). It is clear that teachers' basic value positions and choices (task perception) guide the decisions between different alternatives in concrete situations. To Nicole, for example, "giving trust and being trusted" ranks highly in her task perception, and as such constitutes an important guideline for her professional behaviour and decisions. Teachers' choices between pedagogical options are thus not merely technical. Rather, they are moral in character, because they involve the need to do justice to children's educational needs. It is not hard to see that this moral dimension in teaching contributes a great deal to teachers' vulnerability. This is especially the case because even in technical matters about effective teaching strategies and pupils' learning conditions, teachers often lack a solid technical or scientific knowledge base on which to ground their decisions and their accounts of their practice.

Thus, when a teacher feels attacked about "being a proper teacher", as is the case in Nicole's story, s/he has little solid ground from which to mount an effective defence. Yet, because threats to "being a proper teacher" are so closely connected to one's personal and professional identity, they arouse intense emotional reactions. This moral base to teachers' vulnerability and its accompanying feelings were present in all the accounts in our study, whatever the source of the vulnerability.

The Political in the Moral: Politics of Identity

"Being a proper teacher" implies the social recognition of both one's technical skills and competences and one's moral integrity. It is a very crucial element in teachers' professional self-understanding (self-esteem and task perception). At the same time, this recognition by colleagues and principal, but also by pupils, parents and administrators, constitutes a highly valued, non-material, social workplace condition. Teachers strive to establish and maintain it and as such it is a professional interest to them. Blasé and Anderson also observe that "the development of a political perspective in teachers stemmed primarily from a sense of vulnerability to criticism and threat from others. [...] A political perspective is developed to *influence* students and parents on substantive issues and to *protect* the teacher from student and parental criticism" (Blase and Anderson 1995, pp. 50–51; their italics).

However, because this recognition depends on others' perceptions, it is very vulnerable to contestation. It can be questioned by others and possibly withdrawn. This is what happened to Nicole and in this light we can come to understand why the emotional impact of the incident was so high, as well as her intense reaction to it. The way in which Nicole copes with the situation can thus be understood as a form of *politics of identity*, a struggle for recognition by others and for self-recognition (Calhoun 1994, p. 20). She engaged in intentional actions or strategies to regain the recognition and moral appreciation of herself as a teacher by others. This recognition was a necessary condition, if she was to perform her job duties both effectively and with feelings of satisfaction, joy and personal fulfillment. These feelings are themselves important because good teaching always involves commitment as a person. In teaching there cannot be a strict separation between the professional and the personal self (Nias 1989, pp. 202–203).

Put more generally, the experience of vulnerability has not only moral roots, but also political consequences. The threat, or actual loss, of valued workplace conditions (like e.g. social recognition as "good teacher") engages teachers in struggles for their maintenance or (re)establishment. Nicole's symbolic "counter-attack", by hanging out the mark book, is an example of such a struggle. As Blasé concludes in his study on the micro-politics of schools: "Issues and processes that challenge basic educational and professional values [...] are likely to provoke significant levels of political activity in schools" (Blase 1991, p. 244). Teachers' vulnerability can be understood in micro-political terms. The experience of vulnerability includes feelings of powerlessness or political inefficacy, i.e. of an inability to create the workplace conditions one considers necessary for good job performance and job satisfaction (Kelchtermans 2007a; Kelchtermans and Ballet 2002a). These workplace conditions, whether material, organisational, social or cultural, always affect teachers' professional self-understanding. So, teachers' political actions always to some extent involve the politics of identity.

A Perspective Beyond Vulnerability

In this chapter I have focused on teachers' experience of vulnerability. After describing the different sources of that vulnerability, as they were identified in the career stories of experienced Flemish primary school teachers, I used one exemplary case to explore this vulnerability in greater depth. The analysis of Nicole's case shows how trivial incidents can provoke intense feelings for teachers. The same is true for all the different sources of vulnerability that were identified above. The basic structure in vulnerability is always one of feeling that one's professional identity and moral integrity, as part of being "a proper teacher", are questioned and that valued workplace conditions are thereby threatened or lost. Coping with this vulnerability therefore implies political actions, aimed at (re)gaining the social recognition of one's professional self-understanding and restoring the necessary workplace conditions for good job performance.

Because of its link to the professional self-understanding of individual teachers, vulnerability is inherent in the teaching job and as such never completely avoidable. I think that it is necessary to acknowledge this and to try to reduce its effects. From the experience of collecting and working with teachers' autobiographical accounts of their careers I have come to believe that more systematic forms of autobiographical reflection and storytelling can effectively contribute to successful coping. Through autobiographical reflection teachers can come to understand how particular events and experiences are situated in the "story" of their careers. The experience of vulnerability is always a particular experience, in a particular context, by a particular person. This person has his/her own biography and an individual interpretive framework, resulting from his/her meaningful dealing with the events and experiences of his/her personal and professional life. Understanding vulnerability in the context of one's professional life implies taking seriously one's own career story and the particularities of context. In other words, whether or in what circumstances the potential sources of vulnerability actually provoke this feeling is heavily determined by the social, historical and biographical context, as well as by the perceptions of the person involved (personal interpretive framework).

From my work with teachers (as an interviewer, a supervisor and an in-service trainer) I have learnt that teachers are very willing to tell their career stories and to share them, as long as a psychologically safe and inviting context is created (see also Kelchtermans 2010). This collaborative sharing of stories could become exemplars of the "genealogy of contexts" that Goodson argues for as an essential complement to the "narratives of action", which still dominate most research and development work from a narrative–biographical perspective (Goodson 1992, p. 240). During and by means of autobiographical reflection and the transformation of these reflections into a narrative whole (that is their career "story"), teachers come to grips with their experiences and the meaning that these have in their lives. Narrative reconstruction and teachers' willingness to tell their stories have a great potential for empowering teacher or staff development, because they provide "meaningful intellectual, social, and emotional engagement with ideas, with materials, and with colleagues both in and out of teaching" (Little 1993, p. 138). In order to understand teachers' vulnerability and its impact on their lives and careers, it is necessary to "listen" carefully "beyond" the descriptive account of events and to move to the moral and political layers of meaning. In this way too the "author" of the story can come to deeper or even new understandings of his/her career experiences in general and of vulnerability in particular. One could say that it allows them to "read" their story of vulnerability as a chapter or a sub-story in the "book" of their career, encompassing a whole web of stories. Sharing one's way of "reading" (interpreting) with others and listening to their stories of experiencing and coping with vulnerability opens up perspectives for alternative "readings" of one's own experiences. For example, it may help the individual to understand the particularities of person and context, instead of falling back upon more deterministic readings of the experience (e.g. "It's is my character," "It results from my education as a girl"). However, in order to reach the perspectives that facilitate empowering action, those who share their stories should push their reflection beyond technical matters of knowledge and skills to the moral and political roots of the stories. Only then will the basic moral choices and commitments which underlie and drive the individual's teaching and professional identity be revealed. These moral choices and commitments are also political in that they lead to strategies and actions to influence teachers' job situations. This influence can be conservative, directed towards maintaining the status quo, or innovative, directed towards changing the situation.

Teachers' awareness of the moral and political base of their professional behaviour can help them to defend their decisions as thoughtful and responsible, thus providing a more solid basis for their accountability. It can further contribute to teachers' understanding and delineating of their professional responsibilities, e.g. helping them to balance commitment and expected impact on the pupils in order to reduce the vulnerability stemming from inefficacy and from unclear goals (Nias 1989, p. 193). It provides a perspective from which to move beyond the stressful threat of vulnerability and make teaching individually and collegially a personally meaningful, experientially rich and enjoyable job.

This awareness seems especially important in the actual turbulent educational policy contexts of performativity, with its increasing pressure of accountability, together with more and more different demands on teachers' jobs (see Kelchtermans 2007b; Ballet et al. 2006), which result in increasing and often contradictory demands on schools and teachers (Kelchtermans 2007b). In times where, as postmodernism teaches, the big, encompassing "stories" lose their power as sources of existential meaning, people are thrown back on their individual stories, personal reflections and judgements. Even though such individuality may give a sense of personal autonomy and freedom, it also implies high vulnerability to feelings of loneliness, uncertainty and doubts. Acknowledging and understanding one's own career story, especially in the company of others, is one step towards effective coping with these uncertainties.

Post-script: Beyond Emotion, Vulnerability as an Intrinsic Job Characteristic

The text of this chapter was originally published in 1996 in a special issue on "Emotions in teaching" of the *Cambridge Journal of Education*, with Jennifer Nias as guest editor (Nias 1996; Kelchtermans 1996). Since this was the first text in which I presented the issue of teacher vulnerability, I have chosen to stay as close as possible to the original in this chapter. The original manuscript was only slightly edited, with some minor rephrasing for the sake of clarity and the literature was somewhat updated with more recent publications.

Because of the special issue's focus, the article from 1996 emphasised the experiential aspect of vulnerability. Yet, later on I came to realise that vulnerability is not just an experiential dimension in teaching, but indeed a *constitutive characteristic of teaching as such* and thus *a structural condition* teachers (or educators in general) find themselves in (Kelchtermans 2005). Teaching implies an ethical relationship of responsibility and care in which one engages oneself as a person (Fenstermacher 1990, p. 132). This commitment cannot be properly conceptualised as just an instrumental, intentional or technical relationship (see a.o. Ball 2003; Jeffrey 2002). The ethical, interpersonal relationship implies that the teacher never has full control over the situation, nor over the outcomes of his/her actions. As such the educational relationship implies a dimension that radically escapes control and intervention. And as such it contradicts the fundamental activist bias in theory and intentional actions of teaching, with its taken for granted association of doing something, bringing something about. This "entrepreneurial" (Masschelein and Simons 2002), interventionist root metaphor is so strong that it makes it almost impossible to see and acknowledge the aspects of "passivity", of "being exposed" to the other, of "finding oneself in a situation" in which things "can happen, can take place" (instead of "being done"). These aspects are intrinsically also present in the educational relationship. In other words, in order to understand vulnerability in teaching, it should not be conceived primarily as an experiential category, but as a structural condition that constitutes the specific character of the educational relationship and therefore also constitutes the self-understanding of teachers. The condition of vulnerability can bring about both positive and negative emotions, but it is not an emotion in itself, nor an attitude, an agenda or a strategy. Taking this conceptual stance helps us to position the concept towards felt emotions, as well as towards actions and action agendas or coping strategies.

Conceiving vulnerability this way as a structural condition of being a teacher, helps us to understand the wide range of different emotions that go with it, in particular when dealing with calls for change or even more in an international policy environment, where performativity, output measurement and accountability dominate the discourse and the imposed reforms. Since a teacher or educator, because of the fundamental ethical character of the relationship, can never fully prove the effectiveness of his/her actions; since there is no uncontested moral stronghold to justify one's specific actions, etc., being a teacher implies that one's actions and decisions can always be questioned. And thus, teachers will often experience uncertainty, guilt and shame (for failing the students).

The fundamental lack of control or limited efficacy (passivity), the fact that accountability procedures either neglect or instrumentalise (and thus reduce) the interpersonal dimension in teaching, the absence of an ultimate ground for justifying one's actions as a teacher—I would argue—, is a reality teachers have to *endure:* there is no escape from it. This also explains why there are so many teachers—apart from the widespread criticisms that are mostly heard—who tend to be rather positive in their evaluation of standards and standardised testing. Standards and tests promise certainty or a final proof of one's "quality" as a teacher—even if it is a delusive certainty, that demands a very reductionist understanding (and experiencing) of the educational relationship.

Yet, on the other hand, the condition of vulnerability is at the same time that which constitutes the very possibility for the "pedagogical" to happen in the interpersonal relationship between teachers and pupils. The relationship of an ethical and thus vulnerable commitment opens up the chance that education (literally) "takes place". Such encounter makes the teacher feel that he or she is really "making a difference as a person" in the student's life. Joy, pride, existential personal fulfillment are the emotions that go with it. So vulnerability is not only a condition to be endured, but also to be acknowledged, cherished and *embraced.*

References

Ball, S. (1987). *The Micropolitics of the school: Towards a theory of school organization.* London: Methuen.

Ball, S. (1994). Micropolitics of schools. In T. Husen, T. Postlethwaite (Eds.), *The international encyclopedia of education* (2nd ed., Vol. 7, pp. 3824–3826). Oxford: Pergamon.

Ball, S. J. (2003). The teacher's soul and the terrors of performativity. *Journal of Education Policy, 18*(2), 215–228.

Ballet, K., Kelchtermans, G., & Loughran, J. (2006). Beyond intensification towards a scholarship of practice: Analysing changes in teachers' work lives. *Teachers and Teaching: Theory and Practice, 12,* 209–229.

Blase, J. (1988). The everyday political perspectives of teachers: Vulnerability and conservatism. *Qualitative Studies in Education, 1,* 125–142.

Blase, J. (Ed.). (1991). *The politics of life in schools: Power, conflict, and cooperation.* Newbury Park: Sage.

Blase, J., & Anderson, G. (1995). *The micropolitics of educational leadership.* London: Cassell.

Calhoun, C. (Ed.). (1994). *Social theory and the politics of identity.* Oxford: Blackwell.

Doyle, W., & Ponder, G. (1977–1978). The practicality ethic in teacher decision-making. *Interchange, 8,* 1–12.

Fenstermacher, G. (1990). Some moral considerations on teaching as a profession. In J. Goodlad, R. Soder, & K. Sirotnik (Eds.), *The moral dimensions of teaching* (pp. 130–151). San Francisco: Jossey Bass.

Filipp, S.-H. (Ed.). (1990). *Kritische Lebensereignisse.* München: Psychologie Verlags Union.

Goodson, I. (Ed.). (1992). *Studying teachers' lives.* London: Routledge.

Greenfield, W. D. (1991). The micropolitics of leadership in an urban elementary school. In J. J. Blase (Ed.), *The politics of life in schools* (pp. 161–184). Newbury Park: Sage.

Hargreaves, A. (1994). *Changing teachers, changing times: Teachers' work and culture in the postmodern age*. London: Cassell.

Hargreaves, A. (1995). Development and desire. A postmodern perspective. In T. R. Guskey, M. Huberman (Eds.), *Professional development in education: New paradigms and perspectives* (pp. 9–34). New York: Teachers College Press.

Hoyle, E. (1982). Micropolitics of educational organizations. *Educational Management and Administration, 10,* 87–98.

Hoyle, E., & John, P. D. (1995). *Professional knowledge and professional practice*. London: Cassell.

Jeffrey, B. (2002). Performativity and primary teacher relations. *Journal of Education Policy, 17*(5), 531–546.

Kelchtermans, G. (1993). Getting the story, understanding the lives: From career stories to teachers' professional development. *Teaching and Teacher Education, 9,* 443–456.

Kelchtermans, G. (1994). Biographical methods in the study of teachers' professional development. In I. Carlgren, G. Handal, & S. Vaage (Eds.), *Teacher thinking and action in varied contexts: Research on teachers' thinking and practice* (pp. 93–108). London: Falmer.

Kelchtermans, G. (1996). Teacher vulnerability. Understanding its moral and political roots. *Cambridge Journal of Education, 26,* 307–323.

Kelchtermans, G. (1999). The teaching career: Between burnout and fading away? Reflections from a narrative and biographical perspective. In R. Vandenberghe, M. Huberman (Eds.), *Understanding and preventing teacher burnout: A sourcebook of international research and practice* (pp. 176–191). Cambridge: Cambridge University Press.

Kelchtermans, G. (2005). Teachers' emotions in educational reforms: Self-understanding, vulnerable commitment and micropolitical literacy. *Teaching and Teacher Education, 21,* 995–1006.

Kelchtermans, G. (2007a). Macropolitics caught up in micropolitics. The case of the policy on quality control in Flanders. *Journal of Education Policy, 22,* 471–491.

Kelchtermans, G. (2007b). Teachers' self-understanding in times of performativity. In L. F. Deretchin & C. J. Craig (Eds.), *International research on the impact of accountability systems. Teacher education yearbook XV* (pp. 13–30). Lanham: Rowman & Littlefield Education.

Kelchtermans, G. (2009). Who I am in how I teach is the message. Self-understanding, vulnerability and reflection. *Teachers and Teaching: Theory and Practice, 15,* 257–272.

Kelchtermans, G. (2010). Narratives and biography in teacher education. In E. Baker, B. McGaw, & P. Peterson (Eds.), *International Encyclopedia of Education* (Vol. 7, pp. 610–614). Amsterdam: Elsevier.

Kelchtermans, G., & Ballet, K. (2002a). The micropolitics of teacher induction. A narrative-biographical study on teacher socialisation. *Teaching and Teacher Education, 18,* 105–120.

Kelchtermans, G., & Ballet, K. (2002b). Micropolitical literacy: Reconstructing a neglected dimension in teacher development. *International Journal of Educational Research, 37,* 755–767.

Little, J. W. (1993). Teachers' professional development in a climate of educational reform. *Educational Evaluation and Policy Analysis, 15,* 129–152.

Loewenberg-Ball, D., & Wilson, S. M. (1996). Integrity in teaching: Recognizing the fusion of the moral and the intellectual. *American Educational Research Journal, 33,* 155–192.

Masschelein, J., & Simons, M. (2002). An adequate education for the globalized world? A note on the immunization of being-together. *Journal of Philosophy of Education, 36*(4), 565–584.

Measor, L. (1985). Critical incidents in the classroom: Identities, choices and careers. In S. Ball, I. Goodson (Eds.), *Teachers' lives and careers* (pp. 61–78). London: Falmer.

Nias, J. (1989). *Primary teachers talking. A study of teaching as work*. London: Routledge.

Nias, J. (1996). Thinking about feeling: the emotions in teaching. *Cambridge Journal of Education, 26*(3), 293–306.

Schein, E. (1985). *Organizational culture and leadership: A dynamic view*. San Francisco: Jossey Bass.

Staessens, K. (1993). Identification and description of professional culture in innovating schools. *International Journal for Qualitative Studies in Education, 6,* 111–128.

Strike, K. A. (1990). The legal and moral responsibility of teachers. In J. I. Goodlad, R. Soder, & K. A. Sirotnik (Eds.), *The moral dimensions of teaching* (pp. 188–223). San Francisco: Jossey Bass.

Part II
Educational Change

Chapter 6
Teachers' Emotions in a Mandated Curriculum Reform: A Chinese Perspective

John Chi-Kin Lee and Hong-Biao Yin

Emotion has been one of the issues that had experienced dramatic increase in teaching and educational research since mid-1990s. In 1996 and 2005, two reputable academic journals in education field, i.e. *Cambridge Journal of Education* and *Teaching and Teacher Education*, published a special issue on teacher emotion in teaching and educational change, respectively. Recently, some authors conducted more thorough explorations on the roles of teacher emotion plays in teaching (Zembylas 2005), educational leadership (Leithwood and Beatty 2008), and education in general (Schutz and Pekrun 2007). In these studies, teacher emotion was usually viewed as a social-cultural construct rather than merely a psychological process as it is in popular conception (Hargreaves 2001; Jeffrey and Woods 1996; Zembylas 2002, 2005), which enriched our understanding about the nature and operation of teacher emotion in professional situations.

The Emotional Side of Educational Change

Emotion has been one of the most neglected dimensions of research in and practice of educational change for a long time (Hargreaves 1998a, b; Marshak 1996). However, the silence of emotion in educational change was broken in the mid-1990s. More and more researchers found that the educational change, especially the mandated large-scale one imposed from the outside, can bring both cognitive and emotional impacts on teachers, leaders, and other people charged with accomplishing it. Various aspects of teachers, including their life experiences, aims and purposes, working conditions, and work culture, can be significantly influenced by the imposed change (Sikes 1992). Nonetheless, under the assumption that teachers lack knowledge and skills, teachers' voices, perspectives, and feelings are frequently marginalized in implementing the mandated educational change (Bailey 2000). Because educational change contains so many human elements such as the

J. C.-K. Lee (✉)
Hong Kong Institute of Education, Tai Po, New Territories, Hong Kong SAR
e-mail: jcklee@ied.edu.hk

C. Day, J. C.-K. Lee (eds.), *New Understandings of Teacher's Work*, Professional Learning and Development in Schools and Higher Education 6,
DOI 10.1007/978-94-007-0545-6_6, © Springer Science+Business Media B.V. 2011

relationships, the interactions and the dynamics of people (Norman 2001), loss as well as gains (Marshak 1996), emotion is inevitably one part of the commitment that teachers offer to the change process. Jeffrey and Woods (1996) found that teachers felt a lot of negative emotions, e.g. confusion, anxiety, dehumanization, and mortification when they implemented the deprofessionalized change imposed by the government. Emotions reflect the beliefs that teachers deeply hold about good education in their self-understanding, but reform agendas are inclined to impose different normative beliefs and change the definitions of good professional performance (Kelchtermans 2005). Therefore, if teachers experience congruence between their own professional orientations and the mandated reform agendas, they will react to the change more positively, but those teachers who experience incongruence will react more negatively or in ways of seeking self-preservation (van Veen and Sleegers 2006).

In fact, the relationship between educational change and teacher emotion is not one-way but reciprocal. As Hargreaves (2004, p. 287) suggested, both change and emotion imply "movement". They always go side by side, and each implicates the other. Research on whole school renewal or comprehensive school reform reckoned that teachers need emotionally safe space for learning and growing with school leaders (Beatty 2007), and they also need the emotional support to take reasonable risks without concerning about the possible bad consequences (Schmidt and Datnow 2005). In a study on teachers' life stories, Oplatka (2005) found that although teachers might experience some negative emotions; externally mandated change can stimulate their self-renewal which is largely facilitated by teachers' emotional commitment characterized by strong emotional bonds with their students. In Hargreaves' (1998a) study, the emotional bonds between teachers and their students were also found to be an emotional filter which influenced on teachers' response to change.

The Characteristics of Emotion in Chinese Culture

In the area of cross-cultural studies, Hofstede (1980) defined culture as a kind of collective programming of the mind, which distinguishes the members of one category of people from another. He and his associates identified five dimensions to define and differentiate various cultures after comparing the data from 53 countries (Hofstede 1980, 1991): (1) power distance, which means the extent to which the less powerful members of organizations accept that the power is distributed unequally; (2) uncertainty avoidance, which refers to the extent to which people feel threatened by unstructured situations that are perceived as unknown or different from usual; (3) individualism versus collectivism, which describes the degree to which individuals are integrated into groups; (4) masculinity versus femininity, which reflects a situation in which the dominant values in society are either assertive such as success, money, or things, or nurturing such as caring for others and the quality of life; (5) Confucian dynamics, later labelled as long-term orientation versus short-term orientation (Hofstede 1991), which reflects the degree to which the culture put emphasis on a more dynamic, future-oriented mentality, or on a more static, tradition-oriented mentality. Through this lens, it can be found that the "Chineseness" of Chinese culture lay in its relatively high power distance, high collectivism, risk-avoiding, medium femininity, and high Confucian dynamics (Hofstede 1991; Hofstede and Bond 1988).

As Qu and Zhang (2005) observed, the Chinese, who live in collectivist cultures emphasizing interdependence of self and social harmony, may experience and express more other-focused emotions (e.g. sympathy, shame) and underline meeting social obligations and responsibilities. Therefore, in Stipek et al. (1989) study, they found the Chinese tend to de-emphasize the importance of personal achievement and stress group goals and accomplishments, and "may only report experiencing pride for achievements that benefit others" (p. 110). Anolli et al. (2008) found the vocal expression of emotions by the Chinese is characterized by a more restrained style than that of their Italian counterparts, which is because in Chinese culture emphasizing relational harmony and concern about the impact that emotional practices may have on others, expansive vocal expression may be considered a signal that the individual is taking more than their proper place, so Chinese people are induced to dampen their vocal expression of emotion. These studies on emotion in Chinese culture, although not in the educational field, provide some empirical and theoretical clues for this investigation of Chinese teachers' emotions in a mandated national curriculum reform.

In short, just as Hargreaves (1998b) mentioned, if we ignore the emotional side of educational change, we not only miss the chance of improvement from teachers' voices and feelings, but also let teachers' emotions enter the change process by the back door, in damaging ways. While there are a lot of studies of teacher emotion in educational change in the West, there is a remarkable dearth of studies in East Asia, especially in the vast country of China. If the claim that emotion is a social-cultural construct is true, it can be inferred that Chinese teachers' emotions should have some distinct and indigenous specificities compared with their Western counterparts. However, we know little about that until systemic investigations are conducted. This study attempts to address this question by examining teachers' emotional experiences in the context of a mandated national curriculum reform, i.e. the senior secondary school (SSS) curriculum reform, in mainland China. To be specific, this study aims at exploring the following key question: What are the emotional responses and experiences of Chinese teachers toward the nation-wide curriculum reform?

Context of This Study

At present, curriculum reform is the central agenda of basic education in mainland China. The Chinese Ministry of Education (MoE) initiated the eighth round of national curriculum reform since June, 2001. On the stage of senior secondary school

(SSS), MOE issued the new curriculum project (experimental draft) and curriculum standards for 15 subjects (experimental draft) in 2003. Then, the nation-wide SSS curriculum reform has first been put into practice since September 2004 in four selected provinces including Guangdong, Shandong, Hainan, and Ningxia, and then gradually extended to other provinces such as Jiangsu, Fujian, Liaoning, Zhejiang, etc. By September 2008, there were 19 provinces (autonomous regions and municipalities) and more than 60% students participating in the reform. In June 2007, the first group of students using the new SSS curriculum graduated from the four early-bird provinces.

In short, the ambitious innovative efforts attempted to bring a systemic change to the Chinese SSS curriculum, especially in the following aspects (Ministry of Education, PRC 2003):

- Replacing the existing subject-based SSS curriculum structure with a three-level structure consisting of learning fields, subjects, and modules
- Adopting an elective course and credit system
- Granting the opportunity of choosing courses to students
- Improving students' generic skills of independent inquiry, co-operation, communication, and problem-solving
- Establishing a formative evaluation system and connecting students' academic performance with their growth portfolio
- Decentralizing the existing educational system and encouraging school-based curriculum development

Obviously, the SSS curriculum reform is a large-scale educational change. In some sense, it can also be considered as the response of mainland China to the global tendency of "the return of large-scale reform" since late 1990s (Fullan 2000). In this national curriculum reform, teachers, again, shoulder the high expectations of various groups including policy-makers, educational administrators, parents, etc. to implement the reform successfully.

However, implementing such a large-scale educational change is really a tough job for senior secondary teachers. Just like their counterparts in other countries, teachers have to work under the pressure of heavy workloads and stress, and the SSS curriculum reform makes teachers' work more intensified. At the beginning of the reform, a survey on SSS teachers' readiness in Shandong province found that teachers were full of the feelings of uncertainty, worry and hesitation, and they were wondering how to change their teaching practices to adapt to such a complex change, although they looked forward to the coming of the SSS curriculum reform (Jiang 2004). A case study on the implementation of SSS curriculum reform in Guangdong province found teachers' emotions were significantly influenced by four kinds of dilemmas, i.e. cultural dilemma, professional dilemma, institutional dilemma and resource dilemma, which were caused by the tensions between the reform efforts per se and the situation in which the reform happened (Yin 2006; Yin and Lee 2008a).

Methodology

The present study is a part of a three-year qualitative research project on teacher emotion in curriculum reform in mainland China. In this project, researchers seek to explore teachers' emotional experiences during the implementation of SSS curriculum reform in Guangzhou, Guangdong Province. This paper only reports the results of analyzing data collected from two schools in which a total of 17 teachers involved in the present study. Both schools were the so-called "sample schools" which were selected by the Guangdong education department, and were expected to play the roles of model and provider of experiences or lessons during the implementation of the reform. However, one of them (S1) was a key secondary school in Guangzhou, while the other one (S2) was an ordinary school.

Three rounds of fieldwork were conducted in the present study. The first round of fieldwork was conducted in late 2005 (from October to December). In each school, one director taking charge of teaching affairs and several subject teachers were investigated. The second and the third round of fieldwork were conducted in December 2006 and December 2007, respectively. Based on the findings of the first round of fieldwork, two teachers in each school who knew more about the arrangement of curriculum reform and provided more information than other teachers were deliberately invited to attend the further research. Table 6.1 summarizes the background information of the schools and teachers participating in this study.

Semi-structured interview and document collection were employed to collect the data about teacher emotion. Each interview lasted about one hour and concentrated on eliciting teachers' conversation about the feelings or emotional episodes they experienced during the implementation of SSS curriculum reform, the coping strategies they used, and their opinions on the roles of emotion in teaching and curriculum reform. Following Hargreaves' (2001) and Kelchtermans' (2005) suggestions, teachers were asked to describe the particular incidents that involved their positive or negative emotions. The major interview questions were listed as follows:

- What were the impacts of the SSS curriculum reform on your emotion?
- Facing the challenges brought by the SSS curriculum reform, what did you feel and what did you do?
- Were there any incidents which made you feel joyful (or happy, excited…)/sad (or anxious, worried…) in the implementation of the SSS curriculum reform?

Table 6.1 Background information of the informants

School	School background		Informants involved	
	Sample school	Key school	School administrator	Subject teachers
S1	Yes	Yes	One teaching affair director	9
S2	Yes	No	One teaching affair director	6

- Were there any incidents happening during your interactions with the students, colleagues and administrators in the implementation of the SSS curriculum reform? What were your emotional experiences in these incidents?
- How did you express your feelings about the SSS curriculum reform when you were facing your students, colleagues, and administrators?
- Was there any change of your feelings about the SSS curriculum reform during the implementation of the reform? If there was, why?

In the collection of documents, besides teachers' self reflection journal they wrote about the curriculum reform, some teachers' personal blog and the discussion record of online forum were also used as a source of data. The data from the virtual world, under the cover of anonymity, suggested by some researchers (Beatty 2002; Gronn and Lacey 2004), was more appropriate to deal with these sensitive research topics like teacher emotion.

All interviews were transcribed and analyzed inductively. The overall analytic process was an ongoing cyclical process in which categories and patterns emerged from the data and were later cross-checked (Miles and Huberman 1994). Specifically, the approach of grounded theory was used. The essence of grounded theory is that the researchers do not impose preconceived frameworks or theories on the data; rather, theory emerges from the data, and so is grounded in it. This approach can produce the theoretical perspectives which are more relevant to the situation and enrich our understanding about the problems (Strauss and Corbin 1998). During the data analysis process, NVivo software was used to classify and cluster the data. NVivo is excellent for analyzing qualitative data as a voluminous body of text can be handled in which similar concepts or themes can be encoded and structured. Coding the transcriptions with NVivo enabled researchers to more effectively draw the codes, concepts, and categories step by step, and finally to discover the patterns in the data. Table 6.2 shows the themes, categories, and subcategories in the refined coding system finalized in the present study.

Table 6.2 The refined coding system

Theme	Category	Subcategory
Emotional responses to the coming of curriculum reform	Positive emotions	Being excited, joyful, and passionate Hopeful and expectant
	Negative emotions	Loss of confidence Being tired of the reform waves
	Complex emotions	The contradictory emotion of being happy but scared
		Emotional metaphors for the complex emotional experiences
Issues disturbing teachers' emotions in reform	The new textbooks	Strong emotional impacts brought by the new subject knowledge
		Worried or disappointed about the design and compiling of the new textbooks

Table 6.2 (continued)

Theme	Category	Subcategory
	The new teaching approaches	At a loss about how to organize teaching Being hurried for the prescribed reform schedule
	The new college entrance examination	Being anxious, uncertain and concerned The weather vane of teachers' practice in the curriculum reform
Emotions expressed in public	Facing the students	Encouraging or inspiring students Avoiding the negative influences on students
	Facing the educational administrators outside the school	Being careful of one's own emotions and behaviours Being obedient to the reform policy
	Facing the colleagues	Collaboration in risky times Emotional support from colleagues

Findings

Teachers' Internal Emotional Experiences About the Coming of SSS Curriculum Reform

In September 2004, the SSS curriculum reform was put into school practice in Guangzhou. As proclaimed by the designers of the SSS curriculum reform, this reform intended to correct the long-standing malpractices in senior secondary education in China as follows (Zhong et al. 2003): (1) the curriculum objectives which pursue the master of academic subject knowledge; (2) the curriculum contents which are outdated and academically difficult, and have little to do with students' life experiences; (3) the subject-based curriculum which leaves no space for students' choice; (4) the teaching approaches emphasizing lecturing and rote learning; (5) the values of "all for the college entrance examination" which stress the selecting function of assessment; (6) the highly centralized system of curriculum management. It can be inferred that implementing such a systemic change like the SSS curriculum reform puts forward huge demands on teacher change, including the significant transformations in their materials of learning, approaches of teaching, methods of evaluation and values of education, etc. So, what were teachers' emotional responses to this reform?

Positive Emotions: Excitement

For the teachers who understood these shortcomings of senior secondary education and tried to make a difference, it was just the time for the SSS curriculum reform.

The splendid blueprint of the reform ignited teachers' passion, and made them full of hope about the future. Both teachers and school administrators described most teachers' emotional status when they knew the coming of the reform:

> At the beginning, teachers are excited. Because there are opportunities to take part in training and be in touch with new ideas. Also, these new ideas are felt to be scientific because they match with the needs of our talent development in China. It makes people feel excited and want to get a try. (S1-AM)

> I feel very excited. It is because China's education is too "lengthy" and precipitates too much Chinese traditions such as "the college entrance exam as the baton of teaching". This education is too smothery and very boring. Nonetheless, this reform has brought about some hope like opening a small window. To be personally, I am more excited. (S2-TF-3)

Negative Emotions: Frustrations

However, not all teachers' thought the coming of the reform was a good news because of the huge demands on teacher development. Teachers had to spend lots of time and energy on learning the new ideas, materials and methods, and adapting themselves to these new requirements, which made some teachers tired of the continuous waves of educational change. For some experienced teachers, the unfamiliar curriculum system caused them to lose the confidence about the effectiveness of their teaching.

> At the beginning of this new curriculum reform, it causes a lot of trouble. You should know that it means I have to start learning again. This is quite troublesome. (S2-TM-1)

> At the start it is blank. I feel that "Ah, this thing is so new. Can I accept it?" Also, I think, "Is it easy for new teachers to master? Black paper makes drawing easy! Is it more difficult for teachers with more than ten years' teaching experiences to change?" (S1-TF-3)

Complex, Mixed Emotions

Facing the huge challenges and uncertainties brought by the reform, teachers' internal worlds could be anything but tranquil. In fact, it was difficult to evaluate teachers' emotional experiences using just "positive" or "negative" because they were very complex in many cases. Many interesting metaphors were used by teachers to describe their inner feelings, such as "holding a hot potato", "ant in a hot pan", and "mouse falling onto the scale". A teacher detailed described this kind of complicated feeling:

> As to the emotional responses to the curriculum reform, we are happy with scared...we know the old teaching approaches should not continue any more because they would impair the national quality. So we are very excited about the coming of the new curriculum reform. Nonetheless, teaching is not our hobby but vocation where we settle down and get along with our pursuit, and it directly links with our salary. The new evaluation system is an

> integral part of the reform.... Can we still keep the previous achievements according to the new standards of evaluation? Can we keep our "rice bowl" any more? Therefore, we are also very anxious and afraid of the coming the reform. It is a kind of extremely complex emotional status. (S1-TF-4)

As described by this teacher, teachers had deep understanding of the defects of the previous educational traditions and of the necessity of the SSS curriculum reform. So, they were very excited about the coming of the reform but also they were extremely anxious about whether they could survive in the new curriculum system. The strange emotional status of being rapture but scared became a major feature of teachers' internal worlds.

The Issues Disturbing Teachers' Emotions During the Implementation of Curriculum Reform

Use of New Textbooks and Teaching Materials

Teachers' emotional experiences were the most intensified when the changes brought by the reform directly disturbed teachers' everyday practice in schools. Among all the changes happening in the reform, the change of textbook was the primary one for teachers. Many teachers felt surprised when they got the new textbooks because of the exciting innovations.

> When I see the textbook, I am surprisingly happy. I feel that "Ah, many things have changed." (S2-AM)

> The most affirmative thing for new curriculum is going respect to "endless learning/lifelong learning", and encourage teachers search for this thing. It strongly bombed teachers' old paradigm. So I like the new curriculum very much. (S1-TF-4)

However, using the new materials to teach was a tough task, especially for the experienced teachers who were accustomed to use the old textbooks. So, the feelings of worry and loss of control on teaching were also prevalent among teachers. Interestingly, in face of the high demands on interdisciplinary and integrated knowledge, a female teacher (S2-TF4) used the term of "positive professional anxiety" to describe her own emotional experiences. In her opinion, teachers would do nothing in this reform if they did not have this kind of paradoxical feeling.

> Like the old teaching materials we had been using, we have mastered them efficiently. Now to cope the new materials, I feel a little at a loss. (S1-TM-2)

> New curriculum requires a strong cultural accumulation, and requires teachers to have an integrated knowledge structure, like requiring teachers to be an expert in literature, history, and philosophy. This is in practice impossible, and will bring about professional anxiety.... If a person want to do the thing (curriculum implementation) well, he/she will definitely know his/her deficiencies and will create such emotions. I feel that this anxious emotion superficially is negative, but it is in practice positive. If there is not such an anxiety, he/she may not have any change. (S2-TF-3)

Adoption of New Teaching Approaches

The SSS curriculum reform advocated teachers to employ the new teaching approaches in classroom teaching, such as independent inquiry, teamwork, and self-regulated learning, etc. This meant teachers had to move out of the comfort zone of their professional practice and to embrace the uncertainties of change. In the first year of implementing the reform, teachers almost knew nothing about how to teach at all, and nearly lost all the confidence of their teaching effectiveness. A teacher said she was very confused and depressed in this period of time.

> In the first several months of the first year of curriculum reform, I was very confused and had no idea about how to implement the reform at all, although at that time I was telling students what the new curriculum are! It was so frustrated! I had to make the judgment whether my previous teaching approaches were not consistent with the requirements of the new curriculum.... All of the pressure came upon suddenly. I did not dare to more at all. (S2-TF-1)

For teachers, implementing such a large-scale reform was like to cross an unfamiliar river, and they had to be sure about the stones at the bottom. So, slowing down their pace of teaching in case of acting rashly was a wise choice for teachers in this uncertain situation. Nonetheless, it took teachers more time to adopt these new teaching approaches than to use the traditional lecturing in classroom activities. As expected by the reform, teachers should finish a module in nine weeks and then assess whether students could get the unit of credit. Therefore, teachers were put into a dilemma in which they had to be careful of crossing the river and try their best to make sure the students achieve the standard on one hand, and to move quickly forward and catch up the reform schedule on the other, which caused a lot of emotional burden for teachers.

> For nine weeks, we need to complete a module, like a book! It is unimaginable in that past! Of course the content is less but it is very rushed. Teachers have to teach anxiously and students learn even more rushed.... Because we need to catch up with the teaching schedule, we just rush, rush and rush! (S1-TM-4)

> We are like "crossing the river by touching the stones".... To summarise, it's like teaching four books in one school year. You look, the new things continuously emerge. We just hurried and "forward by running". Such a curriculum reform! (S1-AM)

Influences of the New College Entrance Examination

Besides the new textbooks and teaching approaches, the possible change of college entrance examination was also a critical issue influencing teachers' emotions and practices. In Mainland China, the college entrance examination was usually taken as the baton of teaching. In order to avoid that teachers did too much adjustment according to the new college entrance exam in the reform, the educational administration section in Guangdong province deliberately delayed to enact the change of college entrance examination. Paradoxically, this action made teachers more anxious about the future of reform.

> What is the college entrance examination (CEE) really testing? We feel uncomfortable/unsettled in our hearts. What should you teach your students? CEE, regardless what your think, we think that it is the baton of the teaching. The examination syllabuses are not issued, but the teaching materials have been in print. I feel that it is quite absurd for education.... For anyone, including teachers and students, it is felt as unsettled. (S2-TF-1)

In teachers' eyes, the curriculum reform should go side by side with the change of college entrance examination. If they were separated, teachers could not judge the real direction of the SSS curriculum reform. So, the possible changes of college entrance examination became the weather vane of the implementation of the reform, and all news or gossips about that could affect teachers' emotions and practices significantly.

> How is CEE actually testing? How to cope with it? These matters should be announced earlier. Once these fundamental problems are resolved, we feel relieved.... Now when teachers have heard says, they implement and act immediately. (S1-TM-3)

Teachers' Emotional Expressions in Public

It was obvious that teachers experienced a huge amount of emotion turbulence during this national curriculum reform in Mainland China, no matter whether they were positive, negative, or too complex to name. According to the logic of commonsense, teachers should express them, especially the negative or complex ones, in some manners, which would possibly facilitate or impede the progress of curriculum reform. However, in the opinions of our informants, teachers' emotions seemed too trivial to speak of, and they had little to do with the policy-making or implementation of the SSS curriculum reform.

> I feel that for any frontline teacher, any of his/her emotions and feelings are minute. These [emotions and feelings] will not affect any decisions at the higher level. So the frontline teachers have to learn how to adjust his/her own. It means that one have to change oneself to accommodate the reform, but not let the reform to accommodate you.
> I think that when we express these emotions, it does not bring any meaning of resolving problem or improving the curriculum reform. Yes, it is of no use. We count for nothing! We are just a small potato in this reform. (S2-TM-1)

Then, what did teachers do about their emotions in public if they really experienced so much? Our informants differentiated three kinds of strategies when they faced various stakeholders of the reform, i.e. the students who were inferior to them in status, the outside educational administrators who were superior to them, and the colleagues in schools.

Facing the Students: Expressing Positive Emotions by Encouragement

In short, "do not influence the students badly" was the golden rule for teachers when they were facing the students. In their words, teachers had to pretend to have confidence about and control on the operation of the reform initiatives, and avoid the harmful influences of their own negative feelings on the students.

> If I do not believe, during the process of implementation, we will let students felt that teacher is confused. If it is like that, the consequences will be terrible. So we have to pretend in front of students that we are confident and do not let them feel losing the direction. (S2-TF-3)

> Very few teachers will pass on these emotions to students, and say "Ah, this new curriculum has too many problems." This emotion must not be felt by students. Otherwise, students will definitely feel that "why use us as white mice for experiment?" Right? We definitely can not do that. (S1-TM-4)

In the opinion of our informants, as a teacher, he or she must be careful of his/her words and conduct, including his/her emotions. Encouraging the students rather than complaining before them was a basic requirement on the professional role of teacher.

> In reality, every teacher will affect the life of a student. It is just a matter of large or small [effect].... If you often express grievances and complaining...your image among the students will be affected. If you adopt a positive and optimistic attitude toward life, you teach them how to cope with life without being noticed. (S1-TF-3)

> I will not say such words to students! I will not complain in front of my students. For teachers who serve as a model of other people, some words can not be said. (S2-TM-2)

Facing the Educational Administrators: Being Obedient to the Reform Policy

When teachers were facing the outside educational administrators, e.g. the expert members of textbook designers, the officers in local educational administration section, or the inspectors from Ministry of Education, etc., showing support to the reform policy was very important for them, which required teachers to be an advocate of the reform emotionally and behaviourally. Even if these administrators were coming for collecting teachers' comments on the policies and implementation of the reform, teachers still should keep from expressing the radical or "grey" emotions, such as anger, frustration and worry, and so on (Winograd 2003), because they knew what they were expected to say or to do. If teachers deviated from the expectation too far, they might be stigmatized as the conservative or resistant.

> If experts have a dialogue with thoughtful frontline teachers, it will be a quarrel.... He/She [the experts] will conclude by saying "How the frontline teachers behave like this? They are not actively cooperating with us, not trying hard to promote [new] teaching, but only raising such strange questions?" (S1-TF-4)

A teacher told the expectation of these outside educational administrators on teachers' role in this national curriculum reform. In his eyes, teachers were supposed to be obedient to the reform policy. Expressing proper emotions was also a way of showing teachers' obedience. So, teachers had to suppress their reluctance if they had any and try to enact the reform as expectation.

> They [the reformers] expect us to implement the reform faithfully. They thought we are just a carrier or follower. We have no choice but to follow the ideas advocated by the reformers who are in the superior. You must do according to what the superiors say. (S1-TM-3)

> Despite feeling annoyed, we have to follow his/her instructions. This is certain. You can not say you are against this thing [reform] and do nothing. This can not be permitted. Teachers still have to work hard to follow these syllabuses and implement the teaching objectives. We have to try our best. (S2-TM-2)

Facing the Colleagues in School: Being Collaborative and Providing Support

Compared with facing the students and the outside superiors, teachers had more freedom to express their feelings when they were facing the colleagues in schools, including other subject teachers and the school administrators, because they were the soldiers in the same trench, and they could easily understand each others' situation and the feelings involved, which was defined by Denzin (1984) as emotional understanding. In many cases, just complaining before their colleagues was an emotional relaxation for teachers though maybe no real improvement could be led to.

> Sometimes, we privately have conversations. There are such opportunities. We will use these chances to express our pains. (S1-TM-4)

> Privately we can express grievances to our peers. You cannot resolve the problem at all! (S2-TM-2)

In fact, the function of the colleagues in school was more than an outlet of teachers' negative emotions. The colleagues could also provide emotional support for teachers. In order to reduce the risks of change, teacher collaboration was prevalent in the "sample schools" during the implementation of the SSS curriculum reform. In teachers' words, collectivism and solidarity were more important than ever in the reform. As a result, the relationships among colleagues were improved, which made teachers quite happy.

> Now we are the crew in the same boat, and have a sense of crisis. It means that in facing the new curriculum reform, working together is very important.... We do some research and make modifications. Through these means (of collaboration) inherently reduce teachers' burden, and colleagues' relationships become more harmonious. (S2-AM)

> We are having cross-subject group communications. They are willing to tell me if I ask them some problems. This makes me happy. Our teachers are working in particular happily. (S1-TF-2)

Discussion

The findings from this study reveal that while teachers experienced privately positive, negative, and complex emotions, they tended to display positive emotional behaviors in the public such as encouraging or inspiring students, avoiding the negative influences of the curriculum reform on students, being careful and in control of one's own emotions and behaviors, being obedient to the reform policy as well as offering collaboration to colleagues. This raises the issue whether there could be a Chinese perspective of teachers' emotions in curriculum reform. To address this issue, perhaps we need to answer three or more questions including: Is the context of curriculum reform in China different from the West? Are there differences between the expressions of teacher emotions in China and western countries? Are there any cultural specificities of the reform process and management in China?

Cultural Differences of Reform Context Between China and the West

According to Bascia and Hargreaves' (2000, p. 12) introduction to their co-edited book *The Sharp Edge of Educational Change: Teaching, leading and the realities of reform,* they highlighted the negative impact of contemporary reform efforts on engendering negative emotional labour of teachers ranging from "where teachers' own purposes are overridden or pushed aside by exclusively cognitively driven reform agendas...; where frantic, volatile and capricious change agendas scatter teachers' efforts to the winds as they try to respond to multiple purposes..." to "...guilt-oriented strategies for bringing about ant-racist and ant-sexist education...; political and media-based discourses that shame and blame teachers for educational failure...and willful exclusions of teachers and their expertise from the change and improvement process..." and "conditions prevent, destroy or poison relationships: reform strategies that draw teachers away from their students, divide them from administration, put them under excessive pressure from parents, and isolate them from each other". Compared with their counterparts in the West, teachers in China may also encounter negative impacts of contemporary reform efforts such as curriculum reform (Yin and Lee 2008b) as well as pressure from external inspection and quality assurance measures (Lee et al. 2008) but the context is different in China in the following manners:

- Despite the cultivation of students having a global outlook and mastering life-long and generic skills in the curriculum reform, moral education, and political education are ideological and socialist in orientation, based on the doctrines of Marxism-Leninism and Mao Zedong Thought in the case of China and changing these values education curricula are still not on the main agenda of the curriculum reform.
- The political and media-based discourses in China do not tend, at least in lip service, to blame the teachers of leading to educational failure. Instead, teachers in China tend to portray an image of "an engineer of spirits".
- The prevalence of "examination culture" (Kennedy and Lee 2008) can considerably constrain the implementation of any reform initiatives which ignore the

influences of this special cultural context. Teachers from this study expressed strong concerns on the new college entrance examination because examination was often seen as a "weather vane" of the implementation of curriculum reform. From another perspective, examinations serve not only as a judgement on teachers' teaching practices but also a platform to demonstrate a school's performance.

Students perhaps remain the most significant stakeholder that affects teachers' emotions and curriculum decisions across culture. In this study, teachers were concerned about how to minimize the negative impact of the curriculum reform on students. As Hargreaves (1998a, p. 566) succinctly remarked, "Teachers' emotional connections to students, and the social and emotional goals they wanted to achieve as they taught those students, shaped and influenced almost everything they did, along with how they responded to changes that affected what they did." Nonetheless, culture may have played a part in shaping the issues of concern associated with student learning. Under the influence of Confucian Heritage Culture (CHC), there was an emphasis on students' preparedness to conform to uniform requirements as well as a prevalence of examination-oriented culture calling for students' quest for "excellence" and "perseverance" (Lee and Dimmock 1998; Kennedy and Lee 2008). In this study, one of the reasons that teachers experienced the emotional dilemma was they were not sure whether their students could achieve the previous standard and achievements in the curriculum reform, which made them think the pace of reform was too fast. A teacher (S1-TM-2) used the metaphor of "a hurried passer-by" to describe the students' learning in this reform. Obviously, "a hurried passer-by" does not need to pay much effort in learning, and can by no means achieve the objective of "excellence".

Teachers' Public and Private Faces in Curriculum Reform

The face is the representation of one's emotions. In China, face (*Mianzi*) is maybe the most salient characteristic of Chinese human interactions. In human interactions, face is "the presentation by means of which a person stages his social existence and communicates its meaningfulness" (Cheng 1986, p. 329), which means a person can manipulate his or her social existence to make it consistent with others' expectation, and the actions may cause a gap between ones' internal feelings and external emotional expressions. The former defines ones' "private face", and the latter reflects ones' "public face".

The gap between teachers' private face and their public face was found in this study. As described by our informants, although teachers experienced a lot of emotional impacts during the curriculum reform and engendered many negative emotions, they tended to be careful and control of their "public face", including their emotional expressions and behaviors as well as being obedient to the reform policy. This is probably a reflection of Hofstede's (1991) high power distance and collectivistic culture in Chinese organizations and schools where teacher participation in school-level decisions and managerial tasks is uncommon and teachers as subordinates are "trained" and expected to be obedient to their superiors including the principals and the government officials and accept instructions, at least at a surface level, without challenge (Walker and Dimmock 2000). Under these cultural influences, there could be a tendency of authoritarian leadership and teacher compliance in the interests of respect for authority and maintenance of a harmonious group environment through showing proper "public face".

Interestingly, teachers were not conscious of their "private face". Although they described their internal feelings about the reform, they tended to degrade the significance of these emotional experiences in their professional practice. In the opinions of our informants, teachers' internal feelings were not "useful" to the improvement and implementation of the SSS curriculum reform, therefore the emotional expression in general was not attached much importance by the Chinese teachers, which can be traced back to the assumptions of Chinese culture on emotion and is different from the emotional expression of the Westerners. As Wang (2003, p. 728) observed, "...not only Chinese children are socialized to control their emotions and impulses; Chinese adults also tend to react less strongly to emotionally provocative events than Westerners, which reflects the Chinese values of social hierarchy, interpersonal harmony, and moderation in all matters.... In comparison, strong emotionality is not suppressed to the same extent in American society especially in contexts where the emotion helps assert the rights and needs of the individual".

Some researchers pointed out the similar phenomena elsewhere. Bond (1993) found what differs in Chinese culture is the lower frequency, intensity, and duration with which emotions are typically experienced, and the expression of emotion is carefully regulated in order to maintain interpersonal harmony and status hierarchies. In an investigation of villagers in mainland China, Potter (1988) found emotions are less relevant in China than they are in the West because they do not achieve social ends and are not needed to legitimate social relationships, which can be explained by the fact that a cultural emphasis on group conformity, like Chinese culture, usually stresses the importance of expressing overt behaviour that develops and maintains harmonic relationships with others rather than expressing inner feelings, because it is seen to be relatively unimportant to self and relational development in China (Markus and Kitayama 1991). Hence, Sun (2008, Chap. 9) suggested that in understanding the "inscrutability" or low emotional expressivity of the Chinese, the focus should be shifted from their level of expressivity and toward the importance they attach to emotional expression in social experience, which is echoed by what teachers mentioned in this study.

Cultural Specificities of the Reform Process and Management

In many countries, part of the challenge for curriculum reform and teacher development is "letting go of old conceptions, familiar practices, and comforting practices" (Hargreaves 1998a, p. 571). Such challenge could be more acute in China where there is a strong tradition of expository and textbook-based teaching, exemplified by teachers' concern over the adoption of new textbooks and novel teaching approaches. Nonetheless, one has to be cautious to abandon totally the Chinese pedagogy and its embedded culture, which is seen by some scholars as the oldest and perhaps the most efficient pedagogy and is characterized "by a strongly felt responsibility for moulding the object of learning, for taking learners' point of view into consideration, for finding the balance among repetition, variation and reflection" (Marton 2000, p. 288). In future, one could explore how the progressive practices advocated by the curriculum reform could be organically integrated with the traditional and effective Chinese pedagogy (Lee et al. 2003).

The quest for interpersonal and social harmony in Chinese society and organizations such as schools may have drawbacks on the implementation of school-based decision-making mechanisms and teacher participation in reform initiatives. In the Chinese context that highlights respect for authority and legitimized hierarchy, conversations between principal and senior colleagues/government officials and teachers/frontline practitioners tend to be polite and one-way (i.e. top-down). Open discussion and critical reflection of pros and cons of the curriculum reform as well as honest feedback on school's responses to the reform and teachers' developmental needs especially confronting supervisors' plans is rather unlikely and could be problematic. This could be quite a contrast with the western organizations where western managers tend to have positive management of conflict and confrontations through aggressive conflict handling styles, "help to get to the roots of the issue and to identify the underlying concerns of the two parties and thus to develop integrative solutions which meet the concerns of both parties" and lead to "better understanding, mutual trust, constructive competition and creativity" (Tang and Kirkbride 1986, p. 294). In addition, the potential dominance of authoritarian leadership in China may be at odds with the encouragement of emotional management and leadership in the Western world where leaders are expected to acquire such attributes as communicating effectively, empathizing with others, and valuing and working through teams (cited in Hartley 1999, p. 317 and Humes 2000, p. 44).

To eradicate such drawback, it would be desirable to promote more collaboration and discussion in groups where members are either similar in status or feel comfortable in working with each other as findings from this study showed that teachers tended to voice their grievances among their colleagues. In addition, the role of middle managers as senior teachers needs to be strengthened as they could act on the one hand as a bridge to communicate junior colleagues' views to the senior management and on the other hand as a mentor to advise and develop the younger colleagues based on their needs (Walker and Dimmock 2000). To move further and encourage the positive value of conflict, management experts have proposed the use of cooperative conflict theory in China, which emphasizes that: "the proclivity to show face, use persuasive influence attempts, and communicate interpersonal warmth in Chinese culture…to facilitate a cooperative, open-minded, productive discussion of opposing views" (Tjosvold and Ding 2001, p. 62). Alternatively, from a critical perspective, Zembylas (2005, p. 173) has advocated a critical emotional literacy approach having a pedagogy of discomfort which could be applied to teacher education or in-service staff development course that "pushes the individual and the collective to think beyond the personal and the local and understand how an individual or a community is situated in a social, cultural, and historical context". Such a radical approach to teacher development, however, could be politically sensitive in China.

Moreover, the findings from teachers' interviews showed that they provided emotional support to their colleagues and encouraged collaboration to help colleagues overcome difficulties. These positive messages, serving for pointers for future work, are in line with research on educational change, which emphasize the notions of "listening with empathy", "creating time and mechanisms for personal and group reflection", "allowing intuition and emotion a respected role", "working on improving relationships", and "realizing that hope, especially in the face of frustrations…[as] the last healthy virtue" (Fullan 1997, p. 227).

References

Anolli, L., Wang, L., Mantovani, F., & De Toni, A. (2008). The voice of emotion in Chinese and Italian young adults. *Journal of Cross-Cultural Psychology, 39*(5), 565–598.

Bailey, B. (2000). The impact of mandated change on teachers. In N. Bascia & A. Hargreaves (Eds.), *The sharp edge of educational change: Teaching, leading and the realities of reform* (pp. 112–128). London: RoutledgeFalmer.

Bascia, N., & Hargreaves, A. (2000). Teaching and leading on the sharp edge of change. In N. Bascia & A. Hargreaves (Eds.), *The sharp edge of educational change: Teaching, leading and the realities of reform* (pp. 3–26). London: RoutledgeFalmer.

Beatty, B. (2002). *Emotion matters in educational leadership: Examining the unexamined.* Unpublished EdD dissertation, OISE. University of Toronto, Toronto.

Beatty, B. (2007). Going through the emotions: Leadership that gets to the heart of school renewal. *Australian Journal of Education, 51*(3), 328–340.

Bond, M. H. (1993). Emotions and their expression in Chinese culture. *Journal of Nonverbal Behavior, 17*(4), 245–262.

Cheng, C.-Y. (1986). The concept of face and its Confucian roots. *Journal of Chinese Philosophy, 13*(3), 329–348.

Denzin, N. K. (1984). *On understanding emotion.* San Francisco: Jossey-Bass.

Fullan, M. (1997). Emotion and hope: Constructive concepts for complex times. In A. Hargreaves (Ed.), *Rethinking educational change with heart and mind* (pp. 216–233). Alexandria: Association for Supervision and Curriculum Development.

Fullan, M. (2000). The return of large-scale reform. *Journal of Educational Change, 1*(1), 5–28.

Gronn, P., & Lacey, K. (2004). Positioning oneself for leadership: Feelings of vulnerability among aspirant school principals. *School Leadership and Management, 24*(4), 405–424.

Hargreaves, A. (1998a). The emotion of teaching and educational change. In A. Hargreaves, A. Lieberman, M. Fullan, & D. Hopkins (Eds.), *International handbook of educational change* (pp. 558–575). Dordrecht: Kluwer.

Hargreaves, A. (1998b). The emotional politics of teaching and teacher development: With implications for educational leadership. *International Journal of Leadership in Education, 1*(4), 315–336.

Hargreaves, A. (2001). Emotional geographies of teaching. *Teachers College Record, 103*(6), 1056–1080.

Hargreaves, A. (2004). Inclusive and exclusive educational change: Emotional response of teachers and implications for leadership. *School Leadership and Management, 24*(2), 287–309.

Hartley, D. (1999). Marketing and the re-enchantment of school management. *British Journal of Educational Sociology, 20*(3), 309–323.
Hofstede, G. (1980). *Culture's consequences: Interactional differences in work-related values.* Beverly Hill: Sage.
Hofstede, G. (1991). *Culture and organizations: Software of the mind.* London: McGraw-Hill.
Hofstede, G., & Bond, M. H. (1988). The Confucian connections: From cultural roots to economic growth. *Organizational Dynamics, 16*(4), 5–21.
Humes, W. (2000). The discourses of management. *Journal of Educational Enquiry, 1*(1), 35–53.
Jeffrey, B., & Woods, P. (1996). Feeling deprofessionalised: The social construction of emotions during an OFSTED inspection. *Cambridge Journal of Education, 26*(3), 325–343.
Jiang, L. (2004). Senior secondary school teachers: Wandering in expectation. [In Chinese.] *Contemporary Educational Science, 20,* 17–20.
Kelchtermans, G. (2005). Teachers' emotions in educational reforms: Self-understanding, vulnerable commitment and micropolitical literacy. *Teaching and Teacher Education, 21*(8), 995–1006.
Kennedy, K., & Lee, J. C. K. (2008). *The changing role of schools in Asian societies: Schools for the knowledge society.* New York: Routledge.
Lee, J. C. K., & Dimmock, C. (1998). Curriculum management in secondary schools during political transition: A Hong Kong perspective. *Curriculum Studies, 6*(1), 5–28.
Lee, J. C. K., Lam, W. P., & Li, Y. Y. (2003). Teacher evaluation and effectiveness in Hong Kong: Issues and challenges. *Journal of Personnel Evaluation in Education, 17*(1), 41–65.
Lee, J. C. K., Ding, D. Y., & Song, H. (2008). School supervision and evaluation in China: The Shanghai perspective. *Quality Assurance in Education, 16*(2), 148–163.
Leithwood, K., & Beatty, B. (2008). *Leading with teacher emotions in mind.* Thousand Oaks: Sage.
Markus, H. R., & Kitayama, S. (1991). Culture and the self: Implications for cognition, emotion, and motivation. *Psychological Review, 98*(2), 224–253.
Marshak, D. (1996). The emotional experience of school change: Resistance, loss, and grief. *NASSP Bulletin, 80*(577), 72–77.
Marton, F. (2000). Afterword—The lived curriculum. In B. Adamson, T. Kwan, & K.-K. Chan (Eds.), *Changing the curriculum: The impact of reform on primary schooling in Hong Kong* (pp. 277–292). Hong Kong: Hong Kong University Press.
Miles, M. B., & Huberman, A. M. (1994). *Qualitative data analysis: An expanded sourcebook* (2nd ed.). Thousand Oaks: Sage.
Ministry of Education, PRC. (2003). Curriculum reform project of senior secondary school (experimental draft). [In Chinese.] http://www.moe.edu.cn/edoas/website18/level3.jsp?tablename=1162&infoid=737. Accessed 31 Aug 2004.
Norman, S. J. (2001). The human face of school reform. *National Forum of Educational Administration and Supervision Journal, 18E*(4). http://www.nationalforum.com/Electronic%20Journal%20Volumes/Norman%20Sharron%20Jenkins%20The%20Human%20Face%20of%20School%20Reform.pdf. Accessed 31 March 2005.
Oplatka, I. (2005). Imposed school change and women teachers' self-renewal: A new insight on successful implementation of changes in schools. *School Leadership and Management, 25*(2), 171–190.
Potter, S. L. (1988). The cultural construction of emotion in rural Chinese social life. *Ethos, 16*(2), 181–208.
Qu, R., & Zhang, Z. (2005). Work group emotions in Chinese culture settings. *Singapore Management Review, 27*(1), 69–86.
Schmidt, M., & Datnow, A. (2005). Teachers' sense-making about comprehensive school reform: The influence of emotions. *Teaching and Teacher Education, 21*(8), 949–965.
Schutz, P. A., & Pekrun, R. (2007). *Emotion in education.* Burlington: Elsevier.
Sikes, P. J. (1992). Imposed change and the experienced teacher. In M. Fullan & A. Hargreaves (Eds.), *Teacher development and educational change* (pp. 36–55). London: Falmer Press
Stipek, D., Weiner, B., & Li, K. (1989). Testing some attribution-emotion relations in the People's Republic of China. *Journal of Personality and Social Psychology, 56*(1), 109–116.

Strauss, A., & Corbin, J. (1998). *Basics of qualitative research: Techniques and procedures for developing grounded theory* (2nd ed.). Thousand Oaks: Sage.

Sun, C. T.-L. (2008). *Themes in Chinese Psychology.* Singapore: Cengage Learning.

Tang, S. F. Y., & Kirkbride, P. S. (1986). Developing conflict management skills in Hong Kong: An analysis of some cross-cultural implications. *Management Education and Development, 17*(3), 287–301.

Tjosvold, D., & Ding, D. (2001). Conflict management training in China: The value of cooperative conflict theory. *Journal of Teaching in International Business, 12*(2), 53–75.

van Veen, K., & Sleegers, P. (2006). How does it feel? Teachers' emotions in a context of change. *Journal of Curriculum Studies, 38*(1), 85–111.

Walker, A., & Dimmock, C. (2000). One size fits all? Teacher appraisal in a Chinese culture. *Journal of Personnel Evaluation in Education, 14*(2), 155–178.

Wang, Q. (2003). Emotion situation knowledge in American and Chinese preschool children and adults. *Cognition and Emotion, 17*(5), 725–746.

Winograd, K. (2003). The functions of teacher emotions: The good, the bad, and the ugly. *Teachers College Record, 105*(9), 1641–1673.

Yin, H. (2006). *Teacher emotion in curriculum reform: A case study on the implementation of the senior secondary school curriculum reform in mainland China.* [In Chinese.] Unpublished PhD thesis, The Chinese University of Hong Kong, Hong Kong.

Yin, H., & Lee, J. C. K. (2008a). Analysing the tensions in curriculum reform: Roots, types, and coping strategies. [In Chinese.] *Exploring Education Development,* (24), 49–54.

Yin, H., & Lee, J. C. K. (2008b). *Curriculum change: Theory and practice.* [In Chinese.] Taipei: Higher Education Publishing.

Zembylas, M. (2002). Constructing genealogies of teachers' emotions in science teaching. *Journal of Research in Science Teaching, 39*(1), 79–103.

Zembylas, M. (2005). *Teaching with emotion: A postmodern enactment.* Greenwich: Information Age Publishing.

Zhong, Q., Cui, Y., & Wu, G. (2003). *Interpreting "The Curriculum Compendium of the Senior Secondary Education".* [In Chinese.] Shanghai: East China Normal University Press.

Chapter 7
Teacher Emotions and Socialization-Related Learning in the Context of Educational Change

Thomas G. Reio Jr.

Educational change is ubiquitous, but little appears to change. In the United States, student learning and test scores continue to languish below international standards, despite large, concerted reform efforts to tackle the problem at national, state, and local levels (Gonzales et al. 2008; Planty et al. 2009). From national change mandates related to No Child Left Behind legislation to state change efforts like the Kentucky Educational Reform Act to specified local- and school-level reforms (e.g., Edison Project, Success for All), an emphasis has been placed on evidence-based practices and tactics that boost student achievement. Reform efforts, through interventions, initiate and promote the methodical "process of collecting data, analyzing data, communicating results, and taking action that serves to improve the understanding of instructional practice *and* [emphasis added] educational outcomes" (Schoen 2007, p. 211). In essence, then, educational reform undergirds systematic efforts to continuously improve teaching practice and optimize student-related academic outcomes, particularly in subject areas like science, mathematics, and reading. There is mounting emphasis on writing ("the neglected R"; National Commission on Writing 2003; Sanders-Reio 2010) and civics education (Torney-Purta and Wilkenfeld 2009) as well.

Teachers are the cornerstone of reform (Gusky 2003; Schoen 2007), but the contributions of teachers to successful implementation of such reforms is misunderstood and at best underappreciated (Hargreaves 2005; Lasky 2005). Reform efforts create amplified societal and professional expectations for student and teacher performance improvement, accountability, and nonteaching duties (e.g., required participation in school planning committees) that tend to lack clear direction as to how teachers are supposed to accomplish such feats without time accommodations. Rare is the occasion that teachers are being asked to do less; indeed, educational reform increases teacher workloads (Lasky 2005; Van Veen et al. 2005). Gusky (2003) reminds us that teachers need reasonable time to increase their knowledge, appropriately evaluate student work, and ultimately improve instruction.

T. G. Reio Jr. (✉)
Department of Leadership and Professional Studies, Florida International University, Miami, USA
e-mail: reiot@fiu.edu

C. Day, J. C.-K. Lee (eds.), *New Understandings of Teacher's Work*, Professional Learning and Development in Schools and Higher Education 6,
DOI 10.1007/978-94-007-0545-6_7,

Lacking sufficient time and direction or feeling overwhelmed in meeting reform demands increases the likelihood that teachers will not learn the information needed to successfully participate in and adapt to the change effort. Ambiguous reform efforts can lead to a wide range of emotional reactions, both positive (e.g., joy, optimism) and negative (e.g., anxiety, sadness) (Reio and Lasky 2007). Particularly if the teacher's professional identity has been challenged, negative teacher emotions may ensue which reduce teaching motivation, learning, and performance (Pekrun et al. 2002). Negative emotions, thus, tend to diminish teacher learning and performance (Hargreaves 2005; Lasky 2005), with concomitant negative influences on student learning and performance (Izard 2009), increasing the probability that the reform effort will fail (Borko et al. 2002; Reio 2005).

The aim of this chapter will be to investigate the association between teacher emotions and a special type of learning, i.e., socialization-related learning, in the context of school reform. I present first the conceptual framework guiding this paper, and then I review the salient background literature, discuss the links between teacher emotions, socialization-related learning, and adaptation, and end with some recommendations for practice and a conclusion.

Conceptual Framework

In this section, I present the combination of emotion and socialization theories that serve as the conceptual framework for understanding the relation among teacher emotion, learning, and adaptation in the context of educational reform.

Emotions

There has been burgeoning academic interest in the nature, causes, and consequences of affect or emotions in the behavioral and social sciences over the past 15 years. Emotions have been linked to learning and adaptation for both children and adults (Rusting 1998). Affect is "a broad generic term that covers both the intense feelings and reactions people have, which are commonly referred to as emotions, and the less intense, but no less important feelings often called moods" (George 1996, p. 145). For the purposes of this chapter, we focus on teachers' specific, discrete emotions.

Historically, emotions have been examined primarily from either a broad dimensional approach or an approach where emotions were thought to consist of a number of distinct units (Izard and Ackerman 2000). The broad dimensional approach emerged from Spencer's (1890) conceptualization that emotions were dimensions of consciousness. Wundt (1897) extended Spencer's work and posited that all emotions could be explained in terms of three dimensions: pleasantness–unpleasantness, relaxation–tension, and calm–excitement. This perspective was dominant in psychology until the 1970s. From the 1970s until the present time, the discrete-emotions theoretical perspective has guided the work of a majority of researchers examining emotion-behavior relations (Izard and Ackerman 2000). This perspective stems from Darwin's (1872/1965) notion of the existence of at least 12 discrete emotions that were derived from adaptive functional systems that served evolution. Although acknowledging that emotion expressions could serve adaptive functions, Darwin did not emphasize their adaptive functions in everyday life. Izard's (1977) Differential-Emotions-Theory is but one example of emotion theorists extending Darwin's work where the communication and regulation of emotional experiences are linked not only to adaptive advantage from an evolutionary perspective, but to learning, development, adaptation, and coping in daily life. In the context of daily life, broad dimensions of emotionality, while useful, tend to lack sufficient specificity to tease out the association between the motivation and organization of behavior best. A discrete emotions perspective thus seems to be the most appropriate lens for studying the link between teacher emotions and learning, and adaptation in the context of mandated reform.

Inasmuch as emotions, learning, and adaptation are clearly linked, I introduce the notion of a specific type of learning, i.e., socialization-related learning, associated with teachers' daily activity as professionals in schools.

Socialization

Socialization across the lifespan entails an individual's proactive learning in relation to meeting the challenges and changes of daily life (Fingerman and Pitzer 2007). Socialization is "an information seeking process that relies heavily on [teachers] taking a proactive role in acquiring the information they need to resolve uncertainties and master the technical and interpersonal skills required for their positions" (Reio and Wiswell 2000, p. 9). In essence, socialization involves "learning the ropes" and therefore adapting to an organization. The socialization process includes proactively learning about the norms, values, and procedures of the school or work group one is entering (Ostroff and Kozlowski 1992; Schein 1988).

The learning associated with the socialization process, socialization-related learning, is motivated by curiosity-driven exploratory behaviors (i.e., observing, consulting, directed thinking; Berlyne 1960, 1978) through which teachers proactively acquire the information and knowledge (both technical and interpersonal) needed to perform expected job tasks and roles (Reio and Wiswell 2000). These socialization-related learning efforts, if positive, promote job, workgroup, and organizational adaptation and ultimately, positive organizational outcomes like better job performance and reduced turnover (Reio and Callahan 2004). The teacher socialization process occurs through both formal (e.g., professional development programs) and informal learning processes (e.g., self-directed learning, coaching, mentoring, experimentation, consultation; Lohman 2000; Reio and Wiswell 2000), although most new job-related information and hence knowledge tends to be acquired through informal means (Lohman 2000; Marsick et al. 1999).

Socialization-related learning is impacted by teachers' emotional reactions to daily environmental contingencies. In the context of ambiguous, but mandated change where teacher's professional identity can be challenged, negative discrete emotions such as anxiety reduce teacher information seeking and socialization-related learning; on the other hand, positive emotions like optimism promote both (Reio and Callahan 2004). In schools, therefore, socialization-related learning is vital for facilitating the continuous learning and adaptation of all teachers faced with increasing demands for change (Reio and Callahan 2004; Schein 1988).

I focus the socialization process on teacher learning in the context of schools undergoing mandated reform. This highly variable context increases the probability of uncertainty for teachers, as the likelihood of ambiguity can be great, and the problems related to meeting challenges generated by information gaps are not few. Teachers' perceptions of themselves as professionals can become less favorable in such an environment because of professional development demands that seem incongruous with present notions of best teaching practice and content knowledge (Lasky 2005). Such ambiguous, challenging conditions engender a wide range of discrete emotional reactions from teachers that can either foster or dampen curiosity and socialization-related learning. Without a satisfactory degree of socialization-related learning, teachers' successful adaptation to reform initiatives is far less likely.

Review of the Background Literature

Reform initiatives increase pressures for teachers to participate in professional development activities, strengthen their content and pedagogical knowledge, collaborate among peers, and align evaluation results with instructional improvement, to name but a few requirements (Gusky 2003; Lasky 2005; Zembylas 2005). Indubitably, teachers cannot rely on past tried-and-true methods to plan and implement their teaching practice when change is mandated; they must change and adapt or risk suffering professionally. Schmidt and Datnow (2005) caution, however, that teachers' understanding of school reform is often imprecise. Unless the time is taken to allow teachers ample opportunity for meaning making related to a change effort, its successful implementation is far less likely.

Teachers' professional development is one key means of implementing reform where teachers are provided time to make sense of a dizzying array of discrepant information from administrators and colleagues for the purpose of learning (Fishman et al. 2003; Garet et al. 2001). Valuable professional development time is often fleeting, nevertheless, if evidence of support from educational leaders is unenthusiastic and equivocal (Lasky 2005; Schmidt and Datnow 2005; Van Driel et al. 2001). One must remember that reform efforts are multidimensional and complex; that is to say, reform initiatives are not merely simple and discrete. Instead, reform is often a three or more year *process* replete with divergent understandings of how best to implement it among legislators, district- and school-level personnel, parents, businesses, and other interested citizens in the community (Lasky 2005).

Professional development workshops tend to be aligned with increasing teacher content and pedagogical knowledge in particular. During reform, however, professional development encompasses a wide array of additional areas associated with understanding the specific reform and planning how to implement it best. Van Driel et al. (2001) stressed that long-term professional development programs are necessary to achieve lasting changes in teachers' practical knowledge, defined as an integration of experiential and formal knowledge, and personal beliefs. Learning in networks, peer coaching, collaborative action research, and the use of case studies were presented as useful strategies for increasing teachers' practical knowledge and thereby increasing the likelihood of successfully implementing reform. Similarly, Fishman et al. (2003) revealed that teacher professional development activities incorporating reflection, observation, and on-going student assessment influence significant teacher learning and student performance.

Teacher emotions are also affected by reform. Reform impacts teachers' sense of who they are as teaching professionals (Johnson 2003), which subsequently influences their emotional reactions to change (Hargreaves 2005). Teachers' emotions subsequently influence their learning and development, and ultimately performance. Unclear, perplexing messages from school leaders concerning the reform's time and duration of implementation, curricula and lesson plan alignment, access to professional development opportunities, and performance expectations create teachers' negative emotional reactions such as anxiety, frustration, sadness, and even anger. Negative emotions can arise because the state of uncertainty associated with change efforts challenges teachers' identity as successful teachers (Lasky 2005; Zembylas 2005). This state of affairs is especially so with regard to their subject matter expertise, teaching methods, classroom management skills, administrator and parent relationships, and student academic performance. Systematic reform requires ample learning and development opportunities for teachers to meet the increasing demands for greater teaching expertise; yet, the negative emotions often associated with mandated reform can deter the learning required to improving this expertise (Borko et al. 2002).

To be sure, positive emotions can be associated with educational change (Hargreaves 2005; Reio and Lasky 2007). In a study of risk-taking teacher motivation at a middle school in the southwest United States, Reio and Lasky (2007) found positive teacher emotions and learning associated with comprehensive change initiatives. Teachers were provided ample opportunities to travel to conferences and other school districts over a period of three years where they learned the latest information about their respective subject-matter areas, as well as about the curriculum enhancement and teaching practices associated with the change effort. Being allowed to travel left the teachers feeling comfortably supported by both the district and principal in their professional development activities. The school principal's leadership style fostered a school climate which was open and teacher-centered. Because district-level administrators and the principal openly embraced the change over time and were clear about the intervention, teachers reacted quite positively. The teachers felt safe experimenting and taking risks for the sake of enhancing both their own and their students' learning.

In contrast, teachers' emotions varied in Hargreaves' (2005) study of educational change in Toronto, Ontario, Canada. First, the educational reform effort lacked the strong, unambiguous support of policymakers and principals. The younger, early-career teachers in Hargreaves' study were enthusiastic, optimistic, and ready to learn about and adapt to the change initiative. Conversely, the late-career teachers were ambivalent and consequently resistant to the change efforts outside the classroom. They focused instead on teaching and accomplishment inside their classrooms. According to several of the study's mid-career participants, the older teachers' ambivalence was a result of their being set in their ways and unmotivated to learn in general. Consequently, in their eyes, it was not surprising that the late-career teachers resisted learning about and adapting to anything outside their classrooms. Mid-career teachers, while more confident than early-career teachers and still somewhat open to learning and change, were less enthusiastic and more selective about the change initiatives they adopted. The teachers' emotions and desire to learn thus interacted with and varied depending on the teacher's age, career stage, and generational identity.

Despite evidence of positive emotions, Hargreaves warned that educational change could not be sustainable at schools without a mixture of teacher age groups (e.g., schools with mostly early-career teachers struggle when faced with change because these teachers lack sufficient experience to draw upon), mentoring across generations, and organizational memory of collective learning from prior change efforts. He suggested that if policy makers and school leaders are to realistically expect meaningful change, they need to be mindful of how mandated change can challenge teachers' professional identities, evoke a wide range of positive and negative emotional reactions, and motivate learning differentially among age, career, and generational cohorts.

Finding the optimal mixture of teacher age groups at schools for effectively managing educational reform is problematic, especially in urban settings. It is not unusual to see a faculty of primarily early-career teachers serving low-achieving schools. One of the unfortunate outcomes of mounting pressures on teachers in response to reform is an increase in teacher burnout and subsequent turnover. Guin (2004) notes that schools comprised of 50% or more minority students experience twice the rate of teacher turnover than those with lower minority populations. Teachers who transfer between schools are more likely to have taught at schools with a greater proportion of minority, low SES, and low-performing students. Further, the teachers who leave generally have better skills than those that remain behind. The high turnover problem tends to disproportionally affect low-income and minority students by leaving the low-achieving school with the least-qualified and inexperienced teachers.

This state of affairs leaves such schools less able to deal successfully with reform mandates because these schools are less able to coordinate, for example, the short- and long-term curriculum enhancement activities necessary to implement the reform. Because of the almost overwhelming uncertainty inherent in schools suffering high teacher turnover, compounded by reform pressures, negative teacher emotions like anxiety and frustration work against sustaining positive working associations among teachers (Guin 2004). Exacerbating the problem further in low-performing schools, implementing professional development activities for teachers is generally inefficient because the teachers do not remain in the school where they were trained. Guin (2004) called for incentive programs in low-performing schools to recruit and retain high-quality teachers to make teacher and student learning improvements more likely in such contexts.

In sum, educational reform requires sustaining teacher learning for the sake of improving teachers' subject-matter and pedagogical knowledge, which ultimately supports student learning and improves achievement (Fishman et al. 2003; Garet et al. 2001; Reio and Lasky 2007). Uncertainty associated with a reform must be kept to a minimum by legislators and administrators (Van Driel et al. 2001), too, to reduce negative teacher reactions such as anxiety and frustration, which tend to dampen learning motivation (Reio and Lasky 2007). If there has been a lack of quality learning opportunities presented through professional development and other learning-related activities, such as peer consultation and observation (Berlyne 1960, 1978; Lohman 2000; Reio and Wiswell 2000), the likelihood of poorer teacher and student learning and performance outcomes increases (Fishman et al. 2003). Teachers, then, must learn continuously if the transformation required to implement educational change in the classroom is to be successful.

Socialization-Related Learning

As with any professional, teachers must possess a positive, proactive orientation to learning if they are to remain current with the technical and interpersonal knowledge required to perform their jobs. Beyond the vital professional development activity that is a cornerstone of reform (Fishman et al. 2003; Garet et al. 2001), the socialization process (i.e., socialization-related learning; a kind of mostly informal learning) is another principal source of information for teacher learning and development.

Mentoring is an organizational activity that provides a venue for socialization-related learning, where mentees obtain the information necessary to fit into their jobs, schools, and professions (Fisher 1986; Reio and Sutton 2006; Schein 1988). Positive mentoring experiences arouse positive, discrete emotions like passion, enthusiasm, and joy and then, learning. Mentoring supports teacher professional identity development (Johnson 2003) and is mutually beneficial to both the mentor and mentee (Garet et al. 2001; Ragins 2009). However, time constraints associated with reform implementation may limit mentoring activity and be almost nonexistent in low-performing schools, where many teachers are novices (Guin 2004; Hargreaves 2005). Thus, mentoring experiences in such environments may be negative where sadness, frustration, and anger prevail, unnecessarily constraining learning opportunities and subsequent adaptation. Without quality mentoring and its associated socialization-related learning experiences for early-career teachers, the likelihood of turnover from both the school and profession increases, fueling a never-ending cycle of teaching inexperience and student under-performance (Guin 2004).

Self-directed learning where the teacher takes both the responsibility and control over their own learning facilitates socialization-related learning (Marsick et al. 1999). Faced with information gaps and the need for information and knowledge, teachers must take the initiative to be curious to find and develop the knowledge they need to adapt and perform. This type of self-development is essential because professional development activities cannot be expected to fulfill all the learning and development needs of teachers. Notwithstanding, a lack of time, resources, and meaningful rewards for learning or the presence of limited decision-making power in school management dampens positive emotions to the detriment of learning and adaptation, especially for early-career teachers and other teachers new to the school or anyone experiencing a new principal (Lohman 2000).

Socialization-related learning can be fostered too through consultation. Teachers must feel comfortable and safe consulting with their colleagues and supervisors to find the answer to their questions. When questions arise about the subtle nuances of the reform, for instance, teachers cannot hope to reliably find the answers to their questions through checking noninterpersonal sources like the Internet or training manuals (Ostroff and Kozlowski 1992). Tremendous amounts of wasted time can be avoided by proactively asking more experienced peers and supervisors for information related to answering their questions. However, if the school's climate does not facilitate such activity due to fear of failure or frustration, the prevalence of consultation activity suffers and optimal performance becomes less likely.

Positive and Negative Discrete Emotions, Socialization-Related Learning, and Adaptation

As with any learning endeavor, therefore, we must remember that both positive and negative emotional reactions to contextual influences like reform can influence teachers' socialization-related learning and performance. Positive emotions like joy and enthusiasm can influence the degree to which teachers become curious about and attend to tasks related to learning about and implementing a reform (Izard 2009). The positive emotions can be transformed into interest and motivate the teacher to put more effort into socialization-related learning activities, thereby increasing the likelihood of successful adaptation. Thus, principals and other leaders need to find productive means to implement reform unambiguously, provide time for professional development, and seek meaningful teacher input to create a school climate where the arousal of positive emotion is more likely.

Teachers' positive emotions influence children's classroom learning. When teachers exhibited high levels of positive affect in their classrooms, the children were more likely to exert more effort and remain on task longer. Accordingly, creating a classroom climate with high levels of positive affect would seem to be a useful teaching strategy for improving student learning and development (Hargreaves 2000).

Anxiety, a negative emotion, is related to an individual's sense of situational control (Chorpita and Barlow 1998), which often seems ambiguous in the context of reform. Indeed, the level of control and influence a teacher has within his or her immediate environment can be a potent motivator of behavior. When teachers are uncertain about his or her ability to control outcomes, their anxiety becomes aroused, which can impede their curiosity and subsequent socialization-related learning if the anxiety is too high (Reio and Callahan 2004). Tobias (1985) attributes decreased learning when anxious to divided attention and decreased concentration. A teacher's ability to influence and control events and outcomes, then, can determine the extent to which he or she is willing to commit to the task at hand, such as the socialization-related learning necessary to adapt to a reform effort.

Anxiety is an important variable in the context of reform in that the teacher socialization process by its very nature is often anxiety-inducing and taxing (Fisher 1986; Saks and Ashforth 1997). Teachers must proactively engage in socialization-related learning activities like information seeking and knowledge acquisition to reduce these high levels of uncertainty (Miller and Jablin 1991; Morrison 1993; Wanberg and Kammeyer-Mueller 2000). Reichers et al. (1987) suggested that the rapid acquisition of information reduces the anxiety of workers, thereby accelerating their adaptation process. They further recommended that high levels of anxiety be avoided because they impede proactive information seeking and employee learning, that is, socialization-related learning. Therefore, to best facilitate the socialization-related learning required to support reform efforts, administrators must find productive means to provide teachers with the information needed to reduce undue teacher anxiety.

In addition to anxiety, moderate-to-high levels of anger have been shown to impede learning, decision-making, interpersonal relations, and performance, especially in stressful environments (Caffray and Schneider 2000; Fitness 2000). In general, anger is negatively associated with learning, but low levels of anger may allow the teacher to develop and emulate appropriate, intrinsic skills for solving problems effectively (Deffenbacher et al. 1994). There is evidence though that low levels of anger can have a beneficial effect on socialization-related learning (Reio and Callahan 2004). Thus, it is plausible that low levels of anger may be associated positively with socialization-related learning because it might drive an individual to be curious, explore, and consequently learn new ways to achieve seemingly thwarted goals (Reio and Callahan 2004). Still, the implementation of ambiguous, unclear reform efforts is more likely to arouse higher levels of teacher anger that inhibits socialization-related learning, especially if the changes are associated with their performance evaluations and eventual compensation. Again, administrators must find ways to mindfully implement change to avoid arousing negative emotional reactions like anxiety, sadness, frustration, and anger because teacher learning will suffer unnecessarily, and the reform effort will likely be unsuccessful (Borko et al. 2002).

Teachers' negative emotions can be unproductive for children's learning too (Izard 2009). When teachers display negative emotions in classrooms, children are not as motivated to remain attentive and persist on academic tasks. Further, we must remember that boys and girls respond differently to teachers' negative emotions. Klingman and Zeidner (1993) discovered that boys respond to teacher anger with aggressive acts (e.g., acting out in class) and an outward expression of anger. Alternatively, girls tended to respond with internal expressions of emotion like anxiety and sadness. For both boys and girls, teachers' negative emotional modeling was associated with poorer quality teacher–child relationships, worsening as the children progressed into middle and high school. Poor-quality teacher–child relationships developing from teachers' negative emotional responses strongly predict poor social and emotional competence, negative health-related risk-taking, and leaving school prematurely (Reio et al. 2009). Besides the need for creating a positive emotional work climate for teachers to promote their own socialization-related learning and adaptation to a reform initiative, teachers could benefit too from professional development activities in general where conflict and anger management competencies may be developed with an eye toward improving the emotional climate in their respective classrooms.

Conclusions and Recommendations for Practice

I start by making some recommendations for practice and finish with a brief summary.

Recommendations for Practice

1. Teacher socialization practices that lead to optimal socialization-related learning requires principals to develop collaborative learning relationships in schools that would allow free flow of information, particularly between new teachers and their supervisors (Reio and Wiswell 2000). Open communication between all key stakeholders is indeed key to managing reform efforts. Teachers must feel safe being curious and seeking answers, modeling their curiosity to peers and students, and taking risks for the sake of learning (Reio 2010).
2. Negative emotional reactions to reform initiatives can be reduced appreciably by reducing the uncertainty inherent in reform through increased communication and the free flow of information not only between district personnel, principals, and teachers, but between teachers and peers as well. Creating reasonable time allowances for teacher learning and development are critical for bringing about more positive perceptions of control, thereby reducing the possibility of negative emotional reactions related to a mandated change (Hargreaves 2005).
3. Principals can play a critical role in supporting their teachers' socialization-related learning by helping them to learn how to fit in at the school, even in the face of constant reform, making available important information to navigate the many nuances of the reform's planning and implementation, and providing regular feedback on their performance (Reio and Callahan 2004).

4. Professional development activities can assist teachers in developing their emotional competencies with an emphasis on how to appropriately display their emotions to both males and females. Professional workshops also need to alert teachers and principals about how vital is to develop positive relations with their students and how to do so, starting with managing the emotional climate in the classroom.
5. Encourage coaching and mentoring, self-directed learning, and consultation activities to promote socialization-related learning, adaptation, and performance. A mixture of early-, mid-, and late-career teachers must be present for optimal results. In poorly performing schools, ways should be found to encourage experienced teachers to remain for the sake of both teacher and student learning.
6. Teachers must be provided ample opportunity to learn. Teachers must have access to learning opportunities (e.g., being able to visit colleagues in neighboring schools, attending conferences) and adequate technology to promote their learning, as well as be rewarded for their proactive learning.

Summary

To summarize, teacher learning and development are central to the mission of reform. Professional development activities that enhance teachers' content and pedagogical knowledge have been linked to student achievement gains (Gusky 2003; Van Driel et al. 2001). Reform efforts, however, can arouse teachers' positive and negative discrete emotions, especially when a teacher's professional identity has been challenged. Further, teachers' emotional reactions can either foster or dampen their own learning and subsequent adaptation to change. Socialization-related learning is presented as an important kind of primarily informal learning that unleashes teachers' expertise and develops job-related competencies, thereby promoting optimal teacher performance (Reio and Sutton 2006) and ultimately student learning (Izard 2009).

References

Berlyne, D. E. (1960). *Conflict, arousal, and curiosity.* New York: McGraw-Hill.

Berlyne, D. E. (1978). Curiosity and learning. *Motivation and Emotion, 2,* 97–175.

Borko, H., Elliott, R., & Uchiyama, K. (2002). Professional development: A key to Kentucky's educational reform effort. *Teaching and Teacher Education, 18,* 969–987.

Caffray, C. M., & Schneider, S. L. (2000). Why do they do it? Affective motivators in adolescents' decisions to participate in risk behaviours. *Cognition and Emotion, 14,* 543–576.

Chorpita, B. F., & Barlow, D. H. (1998). The development of anxiety: The role of control in the early environment. *Psychological Bulletin, 24,* 3–21.

Darwin, C. E. (1965). *The expression of the emotions in man and animals.* Chicago: University of Chicago Press. (Original work published in 1872)

Deffenbacher, J. L., Thwaites, G. A., Wallace, T. L., & Oetting, E. R. (1994). Social skills and cognitive-relaxation approaches to general anger reduction. *Journal of Counseling Psychology, 41,* 386–396.

Fingerman, K. L., & Pitzer, L. (2007). Socialization in old age. In J. E. Grusec & P. D. Hastings (Eds.), *Handbook of socialization: Theory and practice* (pp. 232–256). New York: Guilford.

Fisher, C. D. (1986). Organizational socialization: An integrative review. In G. F. Ferris & K. M. Rowland (Eds.), *Research in personnel and human resources management* (Vol. 4, pp. 101–145). Greenwich: JAI.

Fishman, B. J., Marx, R. W., Best, S., & Revital, T. T. (2003). Linking teacher and student learning to improve professional development in systemic reform. *Teaching and Teacher Education, 19,* 643–658.

Fitness, J. (2000). Anger in the workplace: An emotion script approach to anger episodes between workers and their superiors, co-workers and subordinates. *Journal of Organizational Behavior, 21,* 147–162.

Garet, M. S., Porter, A. C., Desimone, L., Birman, B. F., & Yoon, K. S. (2001). What makes professional development effective? Results from a national sample of teachers. *American Educational Research Journal, 38,* 915–945.

George, J. M. (1996). Trait and state affect. In K. R. Murphy (Ed.), *Individual differences and behavior in organizations* (pp. 145–171). San Francisco: Jossey-Bass.

Gonzales, P., Williams, T., Jocelyn, L., Roey, S., Kastberg, D., & Brenwald, S. (2008). *Highlights from TIMSS 2007: Mathematics and science achievement of U.S. fourth- and eighth-grade students in an international context* (NCES 2009–001 Revised). Washington: National Center for Education Statistics, Institute of Education Sciences, U.S. Department of Education.

Guin, K. (2004). Chronic teacher turnover in urban elementary schools. *Educational Policy Analysis Archives, 12*(42), 1–30.

Gusky, T. R. (2003). Professional development that works: What makes professional development effective? *Phi Delta Kappan, 84,* 748–750.

Hargreaves, A. (2000). Mixed emotions: Teachers' perceptions of their interactions with students. *Teaching and Teacher Education, 16,* 335–353.

Hargreaves, A. (2005). Educational change takes ages: Life, career and generational factors in teachers' emotional responses to educational change. *Teaching and Teacher Education, 21,* 966–987.

Izard, C. E. (1977). *Human emotions.* New York: Plenum.

Izard, C. E. (2009). Emotion theory and research: Highlights, unanswered questions, and emerging issues. *Annual Review of Psychology, 60,* 1–25.

Izard, C. E., & Ackerman, B. P. (2000). Motivational, organizational, and regulatory functions of discrete emotions. In M. Lewis & J. M. Haviland-Jones (Eds.), *Handbook of emotions* (2nd ed., pp. 253–264). New York: Guilford.

Johnson, K. A. (2003). "Every experience is a moving force": Identity and growth through mentoring. *Teaching and Teaching Education, 19,* 787–800.

Klingman, A., & Zeidner, M. (1993). School-related anger in Israeli adolescent students. *School Psychology International, 14,* 339–353.

Lasky, S. (2005). A sociocultural approach to understanding teacher identity, agency and professional vulnerability in a context of secondary school reform. *Teaching and Teacher Education, 21,* 899–916.

Lohman, M. C. (2000). Environmental inhibitors to informal learning in the workplace: A case study of public school teachers. *Adult Education Quarterly, 50,* 83–101.

Marsick, V. J., Volpe, M., & Watkins, K. E. (1999). Theory and practice of informal learning in the knowledge era. In V. J. Marsick & M. Volpe (Eds.), *Informal learning on the job* (pp. 80–95). San Francisco: Berrett-Koehler.

Miller, V. D., & Jablin, F. M. (1991). Information seeking during organizational entry: Influences, tactics, and a model of the process. *Academy of Management Review, 16,* 92–120.

Morrison, E. W. (1993). Newcomer information seeking: Exploring types, modes, sources, and outcomes. *Academy of Management Journal, 36,* 557–589.

National Commission on Writing. (2003, April). The neglected "R": The need for a writing revolution. http://www.writingcommission.org/report.html. Accessed 16 Jan 2009.
Ostroff, C., & Kozlowski, S. W. (1992). Organizational socialization as a learning process: The role of information acquisition. *Personnel Psychology, 45,* 849–874.
Pekrun, R., Goetz, T., Titz, W., & Perry, R. (2002). Academic emotions in students' self-regulated learning and achievement: A program of qualitative and quantitative research. *Educational Psychologist, 37,* 67–78.
Planty, M., Hussar, W., Snyder, T., Kena, G., KewalRamani, A., Kemp, J., Bianco, K. & Dinkes, R. (2009). *The condition of education 2009* (NCES 2009–081). Washington: National Center for Education Statistics, Institute of Education Sciences, U.S. Department of Education.
Ragins, B. R. (2009). Positive identities in action: A model of mentoring self-structures and the motivation to mentor. In L. M. Roberts & J. E. Dutton (Eds.), *Exploring positive identities and organizations: Building a theoretical and research foundation* (pp. 237–263). New York: Routledge.
Reichers, A. E., Wanous, J. P., & Steele, K. (1987). Design and implementation issues in socializing (and resocializing) employees. *Human Resource Planning, 17,* 17–25.
Reio, T. G., Jr. (2005). Emotions as a lens to explore teacher identity and change: A commentary. *Teaching and Teacher Education, 21,* 985–993.
Reio, T. G., Jr. (2010). What about adolescent curiosity and risk taking? [invited]. In J. L. DeVitis & L. Irwin-DeVitis (Eds.), *Adolescent education: A reader* (pp. 99–109). New York: Peter Lang.
Reio, T. G., Jr., & Callahan, J. (2004). Affect, curiosity, and socialization-related learning: A path analysis of antecedents to job performance. *Journal of Business and Psychology, 18,* 35–50.
Reio, T. G., Jr., & Lasky, S. L. (2007). Teacher risk taking changes in the context of school reform: A sociocultural and cognitive motivational perspective. In D. M. McInerney & S. Van Etton (Eds.), *Standards in education: Vol. 7. Research on sociocultural influences on motivation and learning* (pp. 13–32). Charlotte: Information Age.
Reio, T. G., Jr., & Sutton, F. C. (2006). Employer assessment of work-related competencies and workplace adaptation. *Human Resource Development Quarterly, 17,* 305–324.
Reio, T. G., Jr., & Wiswell, A. (2000). Field investigation of the relationship among adult curiosity, workplace learning, and job performance. *Human Resource Development Quarterly, 11,* 5–30.
Reio, T. G., Jr., Marcus, R. F., & Sanders-Reio, J. (2009). The contribution of student and instructor relationships and attachment style to school completion. *The Journal of Genetic Psychology, 170,* 53–72.
Rusting, C. L. (1998). Personality, mood, and cognitive processing of emotional information: Three conceptual frameworks. *Psychological Bulletin, 124,* 165–196.
Saks, A. M., & Ashforth, B. E. (1997). Organizational socialization: Making sense of the past and present as a prologue for the future. *Journal of Vocational Behavior, 51,* 234–279.
Sanders-Reio, J. (2010). *Investigation of the relations between domain-specific beliefs about writing, writing self-efficacy, writing apprehension, and writing performance in undergraduates.* Unpublished doctoral dissertation, University of Maryland, College Park, MD.
Schein, E. H. (1988). Organizational socialization and the profession of management. *Sloan Management Review, 30,* 53–65.
Schmidt, M., & Datnow, A. (2005). Teachers' sense-making about comprehensive school reform: The influence of emotions. *Teaching and Teacher Education, 21,* 949–965.
Schoen, S. (2007). Action research: A developmental model of professional socialization. *The Clearing House, 80,* 211–216.
Spencer, H. (1890). *The principals of psychology* (Vol. 1). New York: Appleton.
Tobias, S. (1985). Test anxiety: Interference, defective skills, and cognitive capacity. *Educational Psychologist, 20,* 135–142.
Torney-Purta, J., & Wilkenfeld, B. S. (2009). *Paths to 21st century competencies through civic education classrooms: An analysis of survey results from ninth-graders.* (*A technical assistance bulletin*) Chicago: American Bar Association Division for Public Education.
Van Driel, J. H., Beijaard, D., & Verloop, N. (2001). Professional development and reform in science education: The role of teachers' practical knowledge. *Journal of Research in Science Teaching, 38,* 137–158.

Van Veen, K., Sleegers, P., & van de Ven, P. (2005). One teacher's identity, emotions, and commitment to change: A case study into the cognitive–affective processes of a secondary school teacher in the context of reforms. *Teaching and Teacher Education, 21,* 917–934.

Wanberg, C. R., & Kammeyer-Mueller, J. D. (2000). Predictors and outcomes of proactivity in the socialization process. *Journal of Applied Psychology, 85,* 373–385.

Wundt, W. (1897). *Outlines of psychology* (trans: Judd, C.H.). New York: C. E. Stechert.

Zembylas, M. (2005). Discursive practices, genealogies, and emotional rules: A poststructuralist view on emotion and identity in teaching. *Teaching and Teacher Education, 21,* 935–948.

Chapter 8
The Importance of Affective Containment for Teacher Effectiveness and Successful Educational Change

Chris James

Introduction

For teachers, lecturers and those with leadership and management responsibility in schools and colleges, controlling the experience of feelings—especially difficult feelings—and the feelings experienced by others can be extremely hard. Furthermore, attempts by individuals and organisations to protect themselves against unwelcome feelings by engaging in defensive behaviours may not be helpful. Such efforts can create distance, defensiveness and "affective anorexia", where the affective experience of teaching and managing is minimised, and can reduce both individual and collective effectiveness and change capability. Another and arguably more productive way of working with feelings is affective containment where feelings can be "held" individually and collectively (placed and secured in a "container" in a metaphorical sense), reflected upon, learned from and used to good effect. This transformation process, which is known as affective containment, can enhance individual and collective effectiveness and capacity to change. The intention of this chapter is to develop the notion of affective containment and to consider its potential role in securing and augmenting teacher effectiveness and helping to bring about successful educational change.

Following this introduction, there is a discussion on the nature of affects—feelings, moods and emotions. The sections that follow consider the notions of affective control and defences against unacceptable feelings, and develop the notion of affective containment. The final section then considers how affective containment may be established and the role it can play in improving the effectiveness of teaching and the successful organisation of educational change.

C. James (✉)
Department of Education, University of Bath, Bath, UK
e-mail: cj234@bath.ac.uk

C. Day, J. C.-K. Lee (eds.), *New Understandings of Teacher's Work*, Professional Learning and Development in Schools and Higher Education 6,
DOI 10.1007/978-94-007-0545-6_8,

The Nature of Affective Experience: Feelings, Moods and Emotions

Affects are the particular mental conditions we experience and three kinds can be distinguished: feelings, moods and emotions (Forgas 2000). The central concern of this chapter is with the containment of social affects that arise through experience of the social world. These social affects contrast with sensations such as smell and sound that are discerned by the senses. Social affects are important and they appear early in human development. The experience of affects is important in organisations as a source of creativity, dynamism and passion in individuals and groups (James 2004; Day 2004; James et al. 2006).

Distinguishing between feelings and moods is difficult but the generally accepted differences are shown in Table 8.1.

For many theorists from different fields and standpoints, such as Oatley and Jenkins (1996), Niedenthal et al. (2006), Hochschild (1983), and Goleman (1995), the terms "feeling/moods" and "emotion" are synonyms. Others, such as Forgas (2000), Fineman (2003), James et al. (2006), James (2008) and James (2010), make a distinction: feelings/moods are affects that are experienced whereas emotions are feelings/moods affects that are displayed. This distinction is useful for analytical purposes and because it establishes emotions as particular kinds of actions that have an affective rationale.

The display of feelings as emotions may be engaged in collectively, for example, when the pupils in a class smile as the teacher tells a "funny" story. Other displays of feelings, such as crying or laughing (some of the pupils may even have laughed during the teacher's funny story!), are also emotions. This display of feelings may be controllable by will-power but of course such control is not always possible especially when the feelings or indeed the desire to show them are strong.

Importantly, feelings can be made apparent to others in a variety of ways as actions of a range of kinds, some of which would not normally be considered to be emotions. For example, a teacher who remains calm, quiet and apparently accepting during a reprimand from the headteacher that she considers unwarranted but who slams the door to his office as she leaves, is displaying her feelings as emotion. The pupil who makes a rude sign behind a teacher's back when he has been given an unexpected (and he would say an unjustified) low mark for a piece of coursework, is displaying his feelings as emotion—albeit not to the teacher. The

Table 8.1 Generally accepted differences between feelings and moods

Characteristics	Feelings	Moods
Timescale	Temporary	Persistent
Intensity	High	Low
Reason	Usually have a clear explanation	May not be easily explained
Definition and description	Can usually be clearly defined and described	May be difficult to define beyond the use of general descriptors such as "good" or "bad"

key point here is that emotions are mobilisations of power. The "emotional" is thus the "political".

Anxiety is a particularly significant social feeling for a variety of reasons:

1. Anxiety is inter-linked with powerful physiological responses through complex pathways that involve reflexes and the activity of physiological systems, which cannot be easily controlled by will-power.
2. It has an important arousal function driving alertness, responsiveness and performance. It is always present, although we may not realise it, and indeed, it is essential to human activity.
3. There is a link between anxiety and other feelings and/or the anticipation of those other feelings. This link may be with unpleasant feelings. For example, a headteacher may feel anxious about how he will be viewed as a headteacher if an important event at the school does not go well. But anxiety may also be connected to pleasurable feelings, for example, through the potential ending of a pleasing feeling. So, a teacher may feel anxious about how she is going to feel when her favourite teaching group leaves the school.
4. Anxiety is a deeply seated and primitive response to perceived danger and has a distant origin in human and probably pre-human evolution.

Importantly, anxiety is not the same as fear although they are both responses to danger. From a Freudian psychoanalytic perspective, "fear is a response to a known and external danger, anxiety to an internal and unknown one" (Brown 1972, p. 32). With anxiety, a source of danger is the threat that the id and the powerful and forbidden desires that are repressed in the unconscious may overwhelm the ego and endanger and destroy the individual's relations with others. There is also the danger that the ego will not match the standard set by the super-ego, the so-called "ego ideal", which is the part of the psyche that is responsible for self-criticism and self-monitoring. The ego thus has the very difficult task of arbitrating between these two powerful inner forces—the id and the super-ego (Gabriel 1999, p. 308)—and mediating between the individual's internal world and the environment. The task is a difficult balancing act that involves keeping the boundary between the internal and the external spheres, self-preservation, and maintaining the mental integrity between the psyche's different components. Very importantly, when there is a change in the "external sphere"—something new in our external world—the ego needs to adjust its balancing act and the potential for failure in its task arises and the experience of anxiety occurs. Organisational change including educational change is something new in our world in a sense which is why it is always associated with anxiety.

Arguably, the ego's failure in its task is interpreted as a loss which is arguably the generator of anxiety at all stages from early infanthood, where the danger from the possible loss of the other to which the infant is attached, to old age, where the danger of the potential loss of life itself may provoke powerful though perhaps repressed anxiety. It is at the heart of primitive anxiety, which is one of the three interlinked forms that can be experienced in work settings (Obholzer 1994). Primitive anxiety is the ever-present, all pervading anxiety that we all experience to varying degrees. It is a foundational and essential aspect of the human condition.

The second kind is work-related anxiety which arises from the nature of work and our feelings about it: failure to do it well enough and the resultant anxiety generated by losing the respect of valued others in our lives; the burden of responsibility for doing it and not being able to bear that responsibility and the anxiety that generates; concern about what working denies us and the anxiety about what we lose as a result, and so on. The loss resulting from unwelcome change can also be significant—especially during educational change (James et al. 2006; James 2010). The third form, personal anxiety, is triggered by elements of past conscious—and even unconscious—experience. So, for example, a pupil bursting into tears when she has receives a low mark for a piece of work may call up the teacher's own experience of failure at school and what it meant to him—the loss of esteem, hope and potential.

In a range of ways we seek to protect ourselves from these forms of anxiety and the feelings associated with them. The ego has a set of defensive processes that are the basis of social defences, which can be brought onto play in social settings and have the purpose of protecting from difficult feelings including anxiety.

Social Defences

Social defences are patterns of behaviour that reduce the prospect of unacceptable feelings, typically anxiety, or eliminating influences threatening mental survival (James et al. 2006; James 2010). These patterns are often taken for granted aspects of current individual and organisational practice but they may also be called up in response to unacceptable feelings such as those resulting from unwelcome educational change. These defensive behaviours may not be deliberate since they are largely the result of unconscious processes. Social defences are likely to be present in organisations that experience high levels of affective intensity such as schools and they can become such an implicit part of working and organising that their defensive purpose may not be immediately apparent or understood. Indeed, for a variety of reasons individuals and groups are likely to cover over the affective rationale with an apparently valid and sensible cognitive explanation of their behaviour.

There are different forms of defence (James et al. 2006; James 2010): routines, which may become ritualised, projection and the related process of introjection, regressions, repressions, resistance, splitting and task-related defences. They are often linked, which is perhaps unsurprising as they are all the outcome of mental forces between parts of the psyche and between the inner and outer worlds, the purpose of which is to maintain mental stability.

Three particular social defences—routines, resistance, task-related defences and splitting and projection are of especial interest because they are so familiar and because they are particularly significant in teaching practices and the management of educational change. These four defences are dealt with here.

Routines

Organisational routines are the practices that are repeatedly engaged in that then become the taken-for-granted ways of working. Such behaviours may have little apparent connection to any rational understanding of experience or may have a cognitive rationale that overlays and belies their deeper affective purpose. They can be engaged in both individually or collectively (Menzies 1960). Importantly, routines satisfy both the conservative impulse (they provide a consistent secure pattern) and the protective purpose (they afford a defence against difficult feelings). Examples of routines in schools that are likely to have a defensive function include: school uniforms (for both pupils and staff, in terms of what is acceptable and expected, which reduces the anxiety arising from the threat associated with competition); teachers being referred to as "Sir" or "Miss" (provides affective distance and respects status and the anxiety that threats to status bring); always teaching a topic a particular way (the teacher knows it will work and the risk of failure and the anxiety it calls up is minimised); and never releasing a class before the end of lesson bell goes (minimises the likelihood of unacceptable and perhaps threatening pupil behaviour and the associated difficult feelings such as envy for those still in classes knowing that other pupils and teachers are no longer working).

Educational change may well alter defensive routines and the order they give and may also involve the loss of an attachment (Fonagy 2001) to a "much loved" way of working. This consequence of change can be particularly important when routines have become rituals (ways of working that have particular symbolic significance) which then have cultural importance (Schein 1992). So, deciding to: do away with the school sports day or the annual grand prize-giving ceremony; not have school prefects; or disband the special needs department will have particularly difficult because they are changes to significant ways of working that have symbolic significance. The importance of the defensive function of routines and rituals can help to explain why it can be very difficult to bring about culture change in schools. The key point here is not that routines should not have a role in working with the feelings of teaching and organising in schools. Routines can be very helpful. Rather it is saying that, as with all social defences, routinised ways of working need to be engaged with, reflected on and learned from.

Resistance

Resistance is a direct refusal to accept information or to defy or oppose a proposal, request or order of some kind (Gabriel 1999; Fineman 2003; James et al. 2006). Arguably, it is different in kind from the other social defences in that it is a response to change—it is change that is resisted. In psychoanalysis, resistance comes into play when defences are threatened. Much the same happens in individuals and groups in work organisations when defences are threatened. Understanding the nature of resistance can help to explain why educational change can be particularly difficult especially if teaching or organisational practices have become routinised in an unreflective way or have become very defensive in other ways. As argued above, any educational change brings anxiety with it. So, educational change, which brings anxiety, may involve changing social defences which have been put in place to prevent unpleasant feelings and anxiety. So the potential threat is doubled, an experience which has been referred to as the "double whammy of educational change" (James and Connolly 2000) because it brings the "double dose of dreadful dreads" (James et al. 2006). Imposed educational change may disrupt social defences, which is why resistance to it can be so strong. Powerful displays of feelings as emotions may therefore accompany imposed and unwelcome change.

Task-Related Defences

The notion of the organisational task, how it is defined and interpreted is important in understanding the nature of work organisations—including schools and colleges. The primary task concept, which is derived from group relations theory, can be very useful in gaining an understanding of the work task and individual and group relationships with it. Miller and Rice (1967) define the task as "what an organisation must do to survive". The term "survive" is deliberately used; it means to last, to endure and to continue. In a deeper sense, it also means to stay alive, to live on and to continue to exist.

Many work organisations have a given or defined primary task which is known as the normative primary task. So, this normative primary task for the teaching staff of a school may be defined as "to teach the pupils". Thus if the teaching staff in a school do not teach the pupils, they will not survive as a teaching staff—well probably not for long. If the teachers in the science department in a secondary school decide to teach religious education instead of science they will not survive as a science department for long.

Even when the task is defined in a normative sense, the members of a work organisation have to interpret it and then engage in work on it. This interpretation of the primary task is the existential primary task and it is what organisation members understand or believe the primary task to be (Lawrence 1977; James et al. 2006). So a teacher may interpret the task "to teach the pupils" as "to get the best examination results I can" which will have implications for the way she teaches. Under a range of influences all of which will have an affective component, she has arrived at this particular interpretation of the primary task. It is what she believes she must do to survive. A headteacher may interpret the primary task of the school as "to get a good Ofsted inspection report" which will have implications for the way teaching is organised in the school. It is what she believes the school must do to survive. The primary task can also be inferred from teaching and organising processes in the school, which is linked to the organisation members' interpretation of the primary task. This inferred task is the phenomenal primary task (Lawrence 1977; James et al. 2006). So, the primary task of a school characterised by harsh discipline, a high level of punishment and an eerie calm may be understood as "to quell the pupils". It is the teaching staff's interpretation of the primary task. Teaching the pupils for them is quelling the pupils and it is what they must do to survive. Organisation members re-defining of the normative primary task may be a defence against the anxiety of engaging with it.

Arguably the normative task still has to be understood by the organisation members—"defined in the mind"—if collective work on it is to be successful. And to be clear, perhaps teaching to the test, getting through an Ofsted inspection and keeping the pupils calm, should be the primary task on a temporary basis if it enables the school teachers, the headteacher and the school to survive in the short term. In the longer term, however, the group must return to the normative primary task and engage in work on that task it is to survive. But failing to develop a shared definition of the primary task that is understood by all the organisation members may in itself be a defensive behaviour. The defensive value of not clarifying a definition of the primary task allows scope for re-interpretation which may afford protection against difficult feelings and anxiety.

Work organisations—especially schools—may use a range of strategies to avoid interpreting and defining the normative primary task for themselves and then accepting it. Many of the strategies are familiar in schools and, although they may address substantive issues, they do have a defensive purpose. They enable an escape from the anxieties associated with having a clearly defined primary task. Here are some examples.

Deciding that Defining the Primary Task Is Too Difficult "Yes, but the work teachers do is so complicated, defining our task is simply too hard…."

Having More than One Primary Task The problem here is that with more than one task there always comes the additional task of managing the balance of resources between the different tasks. Thus, as tasks are added, the total number of tasks actually increases exponentially.

Over-Complicating the Primary Task "Yes, but if my task is to teach the pupils and I get the class to read for half an hour and they learn something, have I taught them?"

Focusing on Considering Ways of Doing the Task as Opposed to Defining the Task Itself "Yes but surely it's how we engage the pupils in learning that's important."

Concentrating on Related Aspects of the Task Rather than the Task Itself "Yes but first and foremost our work is caring for the pupils and forming relationships with them."

Lack of task definition also facilitates withdrawal from the task. Again this defence is a familiar one in schools. It takes a number of forms and arguably they all result from the anxiety-laden nature of the task and the need to gain protection from that anxiety. Many of them are complicities with the students' lack of desire or ability to learn. Interestingly, many of these defences do end up being counter-productive—they can actually make more work for the teacher or manager and make the normative primary task ultimately more difficult. Here are some everyday examples.

Collusion On a Friday afternoon, or in the afternoon before the end of term, a teacher may decide not to teach the class or may even suggest they bring in games to while away the last few hours. "It's really not worth bothering, they're in no mood to do any learning…." Here the teacher conspires with the students and their anticipated lack of desire to learn. However, the problem is that managing the class as they pass time is much more difficult than teaching a normal lesson and changing this usual practice may be more demanding in the end.

Low Expectations This defence can be familiar one especially when teaching pupils from disadvantaged settings or when teaching pupils with learning difficulties (James et al. 2006). It amounts to scaling down the task, so lessons may not be fully prepared ("Why bother?"), effort by the teacher during the lesson will be minimised ("Why bother?") or homework may not be set ("Why bother?" It's not worth the hassle, you know they're not going to so it….). This low expectation defence makes raising expectations in the future more difficult.

Off-Task Working In this defence, the teacher expends energy working on tasks other than the primary task. Some of these activities may be valuable, but they may also be defensive. So a headteacher may say of a teacher: "Yes, Jeff does some fantastic display work in his classroom…it's pity that his pupils aren't really enthused by his teaching, they seem to learn so little…." or "Yes, Suzie is a wizard with the interactive whiteboard, it's a shame her class's SATs result were so poor this year, the pupils didn't seem to learn much…."

Splitting and Projection

The social defence of splitting is when difficult feelings about objects and experiences that generate painful or threatening internal conflicts are separated from other more acceptable feelings (Halton 1994). It is often associated with projection in which case the difficult split feelings are "launched", that is, displayed either unconsciously or consciously. They are either projected directly onto another person who then becomes the embodiment of those feelings or simply projected into the outer world, where they may be introjected—taken in—by another person or group. Because feelings are important rationales for actions, emotions and actions are usually inter-linked. When both the feeling and the action are experienced by others the projection may well be strong.

Projection can happen at a number of levels. Consider the example of a teacher in a staff meeting arguing vehemently against a change in the school and at the end of his speech getting up and striding out of the room. Other colleagues may follow because they feel the same; others may follow because they have introjected his feelings and are acting on the basis of them. The actions of the latter group are an example of projective identification, which is to control the other by means of projections. The latter group have been controlled by the teacher's display of feelings. The defensive value of projection at this level is that difficult feelings are got rid of, disowned and located in others.

At a deeper level, the projection will relate to significant previous experiences and may powerfully condition a person's or a group's view of the world. So a teacher who has experienced disdain, lack of consideration, and condescension by figures of authority in the past may well view all authority figures in the same way. He may thus view the headteacher in the same way having projected those feelings onto his current headteacher for no reason grounded in reality. So, when a change in the way the school is organised is being planned, regardless of what the headteacher does, the teacher will be expected to be treated in that (expected) way. The headteacher may feel as though he wants to treat him in a disparaging way, through a process known as transference, where the projections are strongly experienced. Indeed, the headteacher may actually treat the teacher in that way if he has introjected the projected feelings, a process which is known as countertransference. The defensive value of the projection at this level is that it satisfies both the conservative impulse, providing a consistent secure pattern, and the protective purpose, allowing difficult feelings to be projected elsewhere and renounced.

The outcomes of this kind of projection are often lived out in relationship patterns in schools, where, for example, a young teacher may project "fatherly feelings" onto the much older male headteacher, who then through introjection, transference and countertransference then takes up that role. His behaviour in turn reinforces the projective behaviour of the young teacher. These familiar patterns are known as covert coalitions (Hirshhorn 1988) which can be very productive but can also be quite limiting and restricting and can exacerbate the difficulties of organisational change.

For individuals and organisations, the consequences of splitting and projection can be very damaging (Dunning et al. 2005) and can undermine the development of securely grounded personal and collective authority (James et al. 2006). By getting rid of difficult feelings, individuals and groups may feel better temporarily and indeed it may enable some partial status to be gained. For example, the "leader" of the group of teachers who sit in the corner of the staff room who are always whingeing about some aspect of the school will have some status with that group. But the real status and authority comes being able to hold both positive and negative feelings. It provides the strongest basis for authentic action that is grounded in a realistic sense of the social world. This alternative to splitting and projection is what Melanie Klein termed the depressive position (Segal 1979) where the full range of difficult and often contradictory feelings is held together in an integrated mental state.

The key point here is that in a whole range of ways we seek to defend ourselves from difficult feelings and anxiety associated with being in a complex organisation like a school and taking the responsibility for the very affectively challenging activities of teaching and organising. The problem is that these defences when engaged in extensively both individually and in groups can result in organisations that are ineffective and difficult to change. One way of overcoming this problem is to transform these difficult feelings through affective containment rather than attempting to control them or defend against them.

Schools Are Locales of High Affective Intensity

It is a truism that schools and colleges are places with high levels of affective intensity and anxiety (James 1999, 2008; James and Connolly 2000; James et al. 2006). At the heart of this affective intensity, is the role of schools and colleges as institutions with important and significant social purposes. In this role, schools and those who work in them are in effect assigned the responsibility for the education of young people. It is a significant responsibility—what these young people learn will in affect secure society's future. The work schools undertake in educating young people will help to enable society to survive and to live on. The very significant feelings including anxiety that accompany this responsibility have to be dealt with. They are held by schools, progressively transformed and returned, until, as the young people reach adulthood, the anxiety is discharged. This role as an affective container, a concept which is discussed and developed in the following sections, is the basis of the affective intensity of schools.

Change to institutions can disrupt the containment function. So changes to schools both disrupt their containment function for society and for those who work in them. The problem is that without change, institutions may become out of touch with the needs of the wider environment and the task they are engaged in may no longer be deemed to be appropriate. As a result they are putting their very existence at risk. So, all institutions are in a double bind. They must change to respond to changes in demands from society but they must also stay the same to fulfil the deeper purpose they serve for society.

The Nature of Affective Containment

Affective containment is the process of providing an environment that brings about effective and authentic receptiveness of feelings and reflection on our affective experience and learning from it and then harnesses the feelings and the insights gained for productive use. The idea was developed by Bion (1961) to describe the creation of the conditions during psychoanalysis under which the experience of feelings, especially anxiety can be lodged and held securely, articulated, that is brought to the surface and out into the open, and reflected upon in a respectful, thoughtful and sensitive way. The concept of the container relates to Winnicot's idea of a holding environment (Winnicot 1958, 1965)—an environment provided for the infant by the mother, in which the child is separate from the mother but close enough to feel safe and secure. Affective containment viewed in this way is therefore a natural process.

From infancy, we develop an understanding and an expectation that we can gain relief from difficult feelings by seeking an affective container. As adults, the desire continues as we try, perhaps unconsciously, to get rid of difficult feelings. In adults, just as with children, there is the hope that the receiver of the projected distress will be able to bear what we cannot stand. For adults, there is also the possibility that by articulating the feelings that are so unacceptable, and thereby bringing those thoughts out into the open in a containing environment that our own capacity to contain, reflect upon and learn from our affective experience will develop.

Affective Containment in Educational Institutions

As already discussed, the work of teaching and organising in educational institutions carries a very high level of affective intensity. Work in schools results in the experience of a very wide range of feelings—some acceptable, some unacceptable. Handling the unpleasant feelings—including anxiety—can be very difficult. Affective containment enables the difficult feelings to be accepted by others (as opposed to being introjected by others) and returned in an agreeable form. This reconnection with these feelings in a comfortable form helps to create the depressive position which in turn provides a basis for authentic and authorised practice. During educational change, affective containment can be very important. It facilitates the psychic readjustment that is required during educational change as the ego struggles to maintain the balance between the internal and external worlds and the anxiety that any imbalance engenders. At the individual and organisational levels, there is a need for the ongoing containment of institutional anxieties to safeguard depressive functioning.

In schools, individuals and groups can act as affective containers.

The Individual Level Anyone can have a containment role for their colleagues but arguably those in leadership and management positions should be ready to take on the role. Many senior members of staff may do so naturally. The typical example would be a teacher, fuming with anger, storming into the head teacher's office and sounding off about a particularly difficult pupil while the headteacher simply listens intently and empathetically. At the end of the diatribe, the headteacher says he understands, that it must have been difficult for the teacher but, that it sounds as though as usual she handled the situation well. He then asks if there's anything he should by way of follow-up, to which the teacher replies, "No, nothing, I've I think I'm OK about it, sorry, I just wanted to get it off my chest…."

There is a very good case for arguing that all teachers should have some kind of supervision—in a clinical sense—to allow the difficult feelings that can be part of teaching—especially teaching challenging pupils with troubled backgrounds to be contained. This kind of supervision is an accepted part of the work in other professions, such as social work, that bring close and often difficult encounters with clients. And of course another issue is the question of "Who contains the feelings of those doing the containing?" In the example above, what support is available to the headteacher to enable him to work with his difficult feelings? There is an expectation that the headteacher will be able to cope but that may not always be the case and there are limits to an individual's capacity to take on the containment role and responsibility. Often those in that position make recourse to their families, professional friends or perhaps for the headteacher, the chair of the governing body, who hopefully have the right capabilities for affective containment work.

The Group Level Groups within the institution can also help to contain the difficult feelings associated with the work of teaching and managing and they can play a particularly significant role during times of substantial change. Indeed, "the group" has always offered a protection against primitive anxiety. Since prehistoric times, human beings have gathered together in bands and tribes to give protection from personal and social breakdown, to give us a sense of belonging and save us from feeling alone. Indeed anything that cuts us off from "the tribe"—dismissal, redundancy, retirement, changing jobs, changes in organisational arrangements can submerge us in anxiety. It is no surprise that collaborative practice—joint work that focuses on a primary task in a reflective way—is such a successful way of working and deemed to be at the heart of professional work in education (James 2007; James et al. 2007).

Before feelings can be openly explored in a collaborating group, particularly when the members work together on a day-to-day basis, it is necessary to provide conditions of safety, respect and tolerance so that anxiety and insecurity can be contained and examined properly. Isobel Menzies Lyth was one of the first theorists to study the ways in which work in professional settings is constructed to defend against and contain anxiety in professional settings (Menzies Lyth 1988). In the 1950s and 1960s, she studied nurses at work in settings such as intensive care for children that were particularly challenging from an affective standpoint. The nurses had to deal with situations that were traumatic and rapidly changing—for the children themselves and for their families and of course for the nurses. She identified a number of organisational aspects that facilitated affective containment which included the following.

The Permanence of Staff A continual turnover of staff reduced the capacity of the organisation to act as a container for difficult feelings and anxiety. A stable staff group facilitated affective containment.

The Nature of the Staff Group Affective containment was helped by having a highly integrated group of staff, who have built up mutual trust and cooperation and know each other's strengths and weaknesses and who are deeply concerned for each other's welfare.

Boundary Management Establishing secure boundaries around roles and working practices and managing those boundaries thoughtfully enabled feelings to be contained.

A "Culture of Quiet" Creating a calm, peaceful and tranquil working environment was important in containing the affective aspects of professional practice.

A "Private Space" This practice involved creating opportunities for the staff to withdraw for reflection and thoughtful deliberation—"to have a quiet think or read" as she put it (Menzies Lyth 1988, p. 182).

The Experience of Difficult Feelings Menzies Lyth was at pains to make clear that in places with high levels of affective intensity, it is understandable and acceptable to have difficult feelings.

A Talking Culture In addition to the formal meetings to discuss professional matters, Menzies Lyth argued for continual discussions about professional matters as colleagues met informally. In this "talking culture" as she called it "important issues could be aired, confronted and sometimes, though not always, resolved" (Menzies Lyth 1988, p. 188).

All these organisational features are directly transferable to educational settings and may help to contain difficult feelings especially during periods of educational change.

Obholzer (1994) makes a number of suggestions which can sustain the containing role of the whole organisation—the school or college—and also reduce the turmoil and disarray that can be part of educational change.

Clarity and Ongoing Discussion About the Primary Task in Relation to Changes in the Requirements of the External Environment By continuing this discussion, required changes can be more acceptable—the processes of considering change and what the organisation is there for have been practiced.

Consideration of the Value of Proposed Change It is important to consider the value of any proposed externally mandated organisational change. Will the change support work on the primary task? A consideration of any resistance to organisational change is important. Is the resistance against an attempt to enhance the focus on the primary task and thereby improve practice? Or is the resistance intended to preserve the primary task and work on it because the proposed changes are in fact "anti-task"?

Authority Structures, Systems and Processes Need to Be Clear With the attention being given to flexibility, adaptability and leadership distribution in schools, arguably the usefulness of clear systems, structures and processes in educational organisations has been under-played. Clarity in all these aspects of organisation can be very helpful in containing difficult feelings and anxiety. It is question of knowing how things should be done and who is responsible for what and it is the task of those responsible for the system—managers—to ensure that happens.

Clear and Open Communication Needs to Be Maintained Between All Sectors Good communication ensures that people know what is going on and what is going to happen. The risk of uncertainty and the experience of the associated difficult feelings are reduced; the difficult feelings that can arise from not being "in the loop"—the experience of the so-called narcissistic injury—can be minimised; and the process of communicating shows respect for others' status and integrity. Arguably, part of this communication needs to be a forum for debate, where feelings can be allowed to surface and be worked with in a respectful and understanding way. Meetings with secure boundaries are therefore important. So they should held in a room with a closed door, have fixed and known start and finish times, and follow an agenda. Holding meetings on the same day and at the same time each week can help to increase the sense of containment. Ending meetings on time can be particularly important. It is not a question of being formal and punctual for the sake of it. Group members are highly likely to feel disturbed if they sense that their affective experience determines the structure of the meeting as well as its tone and subject matter. The basic disposition of those chairing meetings is important. For affective containment to work, the chair should not judge or blame, be seen to be too knowledgeable, or provide answers too early in the discussion. It can also be helpful to have the same membership for the meetings too.

Work-Related Staff Support Systems There is a very good case for arguing that formal support systems for teachers and educational leaders and managers would help to contain the anxieties resulting from the work itself and the difficult feelings that arise from the process of educational change.

Concluding Comments

The argument built in this chapter is that educational institutions are places of affective intensity and that many of the feelings experienced by those who work in them are "difficult", and one of the most difficult is anxiety. Feelings are very hard to control and defending against them is not helpful. Both affective control and defence can reduce teacher effectiveness and make educational change more problematic. The alternative is affective containment—by individuals, groups and the whole organisation—where feelings can be brought to the surface, talked about, reflected upon, learned from, accepted and re-owned. This process helps to establish the fully authorised and authentic integrated position where the whole range of feelings is held by individuals and groups as a resource for productive work. This depressive position is in contrast with the defensive state where protection from particular feelings is the aim, or the repressed state where difficult feelings are held down and hopefully controlled. Importantly, in educational change, the containment processes can: prevent the development of defensive responses; enable the meaningful objects that may be lost during the change to be appropriately valued; and can facilitate re-attachment to the new.

An additional benefit of containment as opposed to defence or control is the potential it offers for the development of creativity. Individuals, groups and indeed whole institutions are not trapped by their defensive routines or held in check in a state of controlled affective anorexia but are in touch with their feelings and the well-spring of creativity.

References

Bion, W. R. (1961). *Experiences in groups and other papers.* London: Tavistock.
Brown, J. A. C. (1972). *Freud and the post-Freudians.* Harmondsworth: Penguin.
Day, C. (2004). *A passion for teaching.* London: Falmer.
Dunning, G., James, C. R., & Jones, N. (2005). Splitting and projection at work in schools. *Journal of Educational Administration, 43,* 244–259.
Fineman, S. (2003). *Understanding emotion at work.* London: Sage.
Fonagy, P. (2001). *Attachment theory and psychoanalysis.* London: Other Press.
Forgas, J. P. (2000). Introduction: The role of affect in social cognition. In J. P. Forgas (Ed.), *Thinking and feeling: The role of affect in social cognition* (pp. 1–30). Cambridge: Cambridge University Press.
Gabriel, Y. (1999). *Organizations in depth.* London: Sage.
Goleman, D. (1995). *Emotional intelligence: Why it can matter more than IQ.* New York: Bantam.
Halton, W. (1994). Some unconscious aspects of organisational life. In A. Obholzer & V. Z. Roberts (Eds.), *The unconscious at work* (pp. 11–18). London: Routledge.
Hirshhorn, L. (1988). *The workplace within: Psychodynamics of organisational life.* Cambridge: MIT Press.
Hochschild, A. R. (1983). *The managed heart: Commercialisation of human feeling.* Berkeley: University of California Press.
James, C. R. (1999). Institutional transformation and educational management. In T. Bush, L. Bell, R. Bolam, R. Glatter, & P. Ribbins (Eds.), *Educational management: Redefining theory, policy and practice* (pp. 142–154). London: Chapman/Sage.
James, C. R. (2004). The work of educational leaders in building creative and passionate schools and colleges. In H. Tomlinson (Ed.), *Educational management: Major themes in education.* London: Taylor & Francis.
James, C. R. (2007). Collaborative practice: The basis of good educational work. *Management in Education, 21*(4), 32–37.
James, C. R. (2008). Teaching as affective practice. In H. Daniels, J. Porter, & H. Lauder (Eds.), *Companion in education.* London: Routledge.
James, C. R. (2010). The psychodynamics of educational change. In A. Hargreaves & D. Hopkins (Eds.), *The international handbook of educational change.* London: Sage.
James, C. R., & Connolly, U. (2000). *Effective change in schools.* London: Routledge.
James, C. R., Connolly, M., Dunning, G., & Elliott, T. (2006). *How very effective primary schools work.* London: Sage.
James, C. R., Connolly, M., Dunning, G., & Elliott, T. (2007). Collaborative practice: A model of successful working in schools. *Journal of Educational Administration, 45*(5), 541–555.
Lawrence, W. G. (1977). Management development…some ideals: Images and realities. *Journal of European Industrial Training, 1*(1), 21–25.
Menzies, I. E. P. (1960). A case study in functioning of social systems as a defence against anxiety. *Human Relations, 13,* 95–121.
Menzies Lyth, I. (1988). *Containing anxiety in institutions. Selected essays* (Vol. 1). London: Free Association Books.
Miller, E., & Rice, A. K. (1967). Systems of organisation. In A. D. Coleman & W. H. Bexton (Eds.), *Group relations reader 1* (pp. 43–68). Jupiter: Rice Institute.
Niedenthal, P. M., Krauth-Gruber, S., & Ric, F. (2006). *Psychology of emotion: Interpersonal, experiential and cognitive approaches.* London: Psychology Press.
Oatley, K., & Jenkins, J. M. (1996). *Understanding emotions.* Oxford: Blackwell.
Obholzer, A. (1994). Afterword. In A. Obholzer & V. Z. Roberts (Eds.), *The unconscious at work* (pp. 11–18). London: Routledge.

Schein, E. H. (1992). *Organisational culture and leadership.* San Francisco: Jossey Bass.
Segal, H. (1979). *Klein.* London: Fontana.
Winnicot, D. W. (1958). *Through paediatrics to psychoanalysis.* London: Hogarth.
Winnicot, D. W. (1965). *The maturational process and the facilitating environment.* New York: International Universities Press.

Part III
Teacher Education

Chapter 9
"But That's the Thing; Who Else Is Going to Teach Besides the Idealist?" Learning to Teach in Emotional Contexts

Diane Mayer

> I'm frustrated because nothing can prepare you and it's unfair because the first two years have to be so stressful and so hard. [The program] attracts people like me, that come in with idealism. I've struggled with that; the deflation of all my ideals. But that's the thing, who else is going to teach besides the idealist? (Cathy)

These words from Cathy,[1] a second-year teacher, highlight the importance of understanding the role of vision and teacher identity as new teachers negotiate their early years of teaching. This chapter examines a number of dilemmas that four teachers experienced as they began their teaching career in urban schools in the United States. The dilemmas occurred at the intersection of vision and context—when the visions they had of themselves as teachers and their professional aspirations for the future were not supported by the realities of the classroom, school and districts contexts within which they worked. The chapter examines the ways in which these teachers negotiated the dilemmas in order to sustain their personal and professional identities and discusses implications for pre-service teacher education.

Emotions and Teacher Identity

Emotions as a topic of research have been examined using a range of psychological and sociological lenses. In 1984, Denzin argued that people "are their emotions. To understand who a person is, it is necessary to understand emotion" (1984, p. 1). About the same time, Hochschild (1983) argued that emotions are framed by cultural expectations. Her concept of "emotional labour"—learning to manage and moderate one's emotions in line with the expectations and demands of a job—has been taken up by educational researchers examining the work of teachers, the

[1] All names are pseudonyms.

D. Mayer (✉)
School of Education, Deakin University, Burwood, Australia
e-mail: diane.mayer@deakin.edu.au

C. Day, J. C.-K. Lee (eds.), *New Understandings of Teacher's Work*, Professional Learning and Development in Schools and Higher Education 6,
DOI 10.1007/978-94-007-0545-6_9,

conditions of their work and their professional learning (e.g. Hargreaves 1998a, b). While a lot of the research has focused on teachers' emotions in relation to classroom interactions with students, this chapter explores teacher identity and examines the emotional dimensions of "becoming" a teacher (rather than "being" the teacher) by focussing on dilemmas experienced by beginning teachers.

Teacher identity is a widely researched construct that generally encompasses teachers' beliefs and goals, the ways in which they perceive themselves as teachers and the ways in which they present themselves to others. Lasky succinctly defines professional identity as "how teachers define themselves to themselves and to others" (Lasky 2005, p. 901). Kelchtermans (2005) thinks of "identity" as "self-understanding" and this includes self-image, job motivation, future perspective, self-esteem and task perception. Thus, the concept of teacher identity frames for teachers "how to be", "how to act" and "how to understand" their work and their place in society (Sachs 2003, p. 135). Moreover, a positive sense of identity is fundamental to maintaining self-esteem, commitment to and a passion for teaching (Day 2004).

However, teacher identity is not static. Teacher identities are constructed and reconstructed based on teachers' growing self-knowledge, perceptions of the profession and the workplace, and beliefs about their roles in the profession and workplace. Growth occurs in the space between the structure or context and an individual's agency within that context. Negotiations within this space influence how teachers see themselves both personally and professionally (Day et al. 2006) and involve a discursive dynamic as teachers attempt to address and redress the dilemmas of the job within various contexts (Stronach et al. 2002).

"Teacher identity is often conveyed and expressed through emotions, whether conscious or unconscious. ...the emotions that teachers experience reflect their sense of identity" (Schutz et al. 2007, p. 227). However, in the main, this focus on emotions has not been a significant focus in the research on teacher identity (Day et al. 2006). A key feature of teachers' identities is "purpose for teaching", particularly "moral purpose", and it is this aspect of identity that seems to evoke high levels of emotion, particularly when one's moral purpose is challenged by workplace conditions. According to Hargreaves (1998a), "teachers' emotions are inseparable from their moral purposes and their ability to achieve those purposes". (p. 319) Likewise, in their study of women teachers' anger in school settings, Liljestrom et al. (2007) concluded that anger resulted when teachers felt that they were being impeded in carrying out their moral purposes" (pp. 280–281).

While research like this has investigated teacher and school leader identities in the context of challenges to their moral purposes, their sense of professionalism, and examined the associated emotions (e.g. Day et al. 2006, 2007; Flores and Day 2006), there is much less research on emotions associated with transition from teacher education into beginning teaching even though as far back as 1991, Tickle found in his study of beginning teachers that teachers' emotions were often the focus of regular debriefing meetings (Tickle 1991). More recently, Hargreaves, as part of a study investigating how teachers respond emotionally to educational change at different ages and stages of their careers, found that early-career teachers seemed to experience their work with emotional directness and intensity but that this quickly changed as they learnt to moderate their emotions in line with the demands of the job (Hargreaves 2005, p. 971). Flores and Day (2006), in a longitudinal study of new teachers' professional identities, found that the teachers' personal and professional histories and their pre-service teacher education, along with issues of school culture and leadership, were strong mediating influences on emerging identities.

Investigating Emotions, Identity and Beginning Teaching

Understanding beginning teacher identities and how new teachers negotiate challenges to their moral purposes is especially important given the changing context of teachers' work which often involves greater bureaucratic interventions, closer public scrutiny and tighter accountability. Teachers have a vision about how they think they can best make a positive difference in the lives of students and successfully enacting this vision sustains feelings of agency and purpose. The work context (the classroom resources, the school's collegial environment, the administration and the policy context) is supportive or unsupportive relative to the degree to which teachers feel it is consistent with their vision. The degree to which new teachers can enact their vision—and feel efficacious—is an important predictor of their commitment to teaching and often influences decisions to stay or leave the profession. This is particularly important given the increasing difficulties associated with teacher recruitment and retention (see Ingersoll 2001; Johnson and The Project on the Next Generation of Teachers 2004). As Hammerness suggests:

> The well-documented prospective teachers' experience of reality shock could be the result not only of learning about the bureaucratic nature of schools, the isolation of the profession, and the ambiguous nature of teaching that many have documented (Veenman 1984) but could also result from the gap between teachers' own visions and their current realities (2003, p. 54).

Therefore, this study approaches the emotional dimension of learning to teach through analysis of beginning teachers' dilemmas emanating from the gap between the view they have of themselves as teachers and the realities of their working context. The analysis draws on a set of interviews with four female teachers. These interviews are part of a series of in-depth semi-structured hour-long interviews with nine beginning teachers collected as part of a larger study.

The four teachers were candidates in, or recent graduates of, a master's and credential teacher preparation program that aims to prepare well-qualified teachers committed to working in urban contexts. The program prepares candidates to teach secondary English to both native speakers of English and second-language learners. During the second year of the program, candidates are credentialed and in their first year of full-time teaching while completing the MA teacher research project. At the time of data collection, two of the teachers were in their first year of teaching and completing their MA—Lyn and Beth. The other two had completed all credential and MA requirements and were in their second year of teaching—Cathy and Jo.

Dilemmas Associated with Beginning Teaching

These beginning teachers reported three main dilemmas. Each occurred at the intersection of their visions and the images they had of ideal classroom practice and themselves as teachers, and the realities of beginning teaching in urban schools.

1. *I didn't think I'd be doing this.*
   This type of dilemma occurred when the new teachers found themselves teaching in ways inconsistent with their beliefs and vision. They did this because they felt it was "necessary with these kids". Working through this type of dilemma involved adjusting conceptions of success.
2. *Stepping on others' toes: you're only a second-year teacher.*
   This type of dilemma emerged when the new teacher's vision of herself as a teacher and her future career aspirations collided with the expectations of others. Working through this type of dilemma involved locating communities of support and seeking fulfilment outside the school.
3. *The politics of the school is the tough part.*
   This type of dilemma occurred when the new teacher's vision of appropriate curriculum for her students was stymied by state and district mandates of how and what to teach, and how and what to assess. Working through this type of dilemma involved negotiating the politics of the school and school community.

In all cases, the dilemmas stemmed from a mismatch between the new teachers' visions and the contexts within which they were teaching.

I Didn't Think I'd be Doing This

This dilemma occurred when a teacher's vision of effective classroom practice and the teacher she wanted to be, were different from what she sometimes found to be successful in the classroom. In this case, she seemed willing to accommodate practices that did not fit her vision if those practices were judged to be in the best interests of the students. In this way, she redefined her definition of success. For example, Lyn explained how she needed to focus on:

> …procedures for every single thing. So, how will we take a test? I need to take half a period explaining to everyone what the test taking procedure is. I just spent half a period explaining to everyone what the coming into classroom procedure is, and that is something that I could not have anticipated from being a [student] teacher in [previous practicum school]. But now I'm in a class where half the people are behind grade level and nobody has any idea. I don't know what to tell them about how I'm going to collect their homework today. That's the last thing I'm thinking about, how I'm going to do this miniscule procedure. …So I guess, I would never have wanted to do this whole procedure thing, but I see it as necessary. Clearly, these students need it. (Lyn)

This dilemma is associated with realizing the need to focus on procedural aspects and technical skills of teaching that didn't seem to fit with a vision that had been reinforced by a student teaching experience in a different school. Sometimes the dilemma emerged at the intersection of a perceived need to focus on procedural and technical skills and a vision associated with broader personal and professional goals and ideals informed by literature. Again, conceptions of success were adjusted if it was judged to be in the best interests of the students. Cathy explained:

> I do think that a real issue is seeing your original ideals not realized...because I used to read Paulo Freire...but then you think "oh man, that's not going to keep kids in their seats!" It's really funny...I started out my year last year having this student-centred classroom. They had chairs facing each other and then this year I'm like no way, they're sitting in rows facing the front of the room. And I think that's sort of symbolic. They're going to sit in these rows until they learn to listen to me, and then we'll see about them sitting facing each other. So I think there's that realization that "oh man, you can't have that really democratic classroom immediately until you...." you know, so that is part of the issue—teaching idealism and student centredness. Being an authoritarian figure; you do have to be this really strict authoritarian person and I'm not an authoritarian person but you should see me this year. I'm like, "sit down! Be quiet and sit down in your chair!" and that's not what I dreamed...I did not think that I would be that type of teacher. (Cathy)

However, even though both Lyn and Cathy shifted their vision to accommodate what they believed the students needed, this was not always without feelings of unease and tension. Lyn reflected:

> I have been thinking a lot about urban settings. We read this piece, I want to say it was by Jeannie Oakes, I think it was, where children in the suburban setting at the end of the year said, "I learned how to think critically and I learned how to analyse this and that", and children in the urban setting said, "I learned how to sit down and shut up." You read that and it's shocking and you're like, "Oh my god, I will never teach my students how to sit down and shut up. That is the worst thing. Of course I will teach them how to think analytically." And having started off the year where everyone's in groups and let's all analyse this poetry, but then everybody's like "ahhhhh!" blank stare and then freak out! You know, I feel like I have taken a lot of steps backward, backward. Now I finally have a sense of...now it's December and I finally realize ok what these students can do is sentence starters, fill in blanks. But I don't want them to stay there. So that's a tension that I feel. It's how am I meeting them where they are and also pulling them along. (Lyn)

Even though Lyn adjusted her curriculum in a way that she believed would reach each student, she worried about watering-down the curriculum:

> Sometimes I feel, deep inside, the rumblings of theory...like, "yes, students should be talking to each other because that's how they learn...from each other." But I'm like, every time they talk to each other, they just fight, so I don't want them to, you know? I know that things should be happening but I feel like I cannot...there are too many other things happening so I cannot implement those things. (Lyn)

Thus, dilemmas not only emerged as a result of differences in vision and classroom practice seen as necessary for success, they also occurred when the literature and theory these new teachers had been exposed to in their teacher education (and which seemed consistent with their vision and beliefs) was at odds with the practices they felt they had to use in order to help their students be successful. Like the women teachers in Liljestrom, Roulston and Demarrais' study:

> Learning to negotiate the possibilities for carrying out their teaching purposes appeared to be an important part of these teachers' professional lives. The process of learning to navigate a system that was not always compatible with their own moral purposes and

> expectations was painful for many teachers. Caught in a double bind, women weighed the pursuit of their moral purposes as teachers, while still keeping students' best interests at the centre. (Liljestrom et al. 2007, p. 284)

Stepping on Others' Toes: You're Only a Second-Year Teacher

These new teachers also experienced dilemmas when the expectations that they perceived their colleagues had of them did not match their own view of themselves as teachers and their future career aspirations. For example, Jo's dilemma stemmed largely from her career goals and the steps she took to realize her personal aspirations in an environment that did not support this. She explained how she would like to eventually be an administrator and school leader and she had therefore volunteered for coordinating and training roles in her school and across the school district. However, she noted:

> I have stepped on lots of toes. Our school's very stagnant. There's not a lot of change happening. People are very against anything that is new. So in my position [as school trainer], I just have people simply ignore me. I mean, they just totally ignore me! ...They don't come, they don't answer emails, they don't respond to memos.... Nothing!... I've become this, sort of, vehicle for hatred. ...Within my school, I'm considered a traitor by a number of people because I actually try to work with the administration and not against them. This year, I've received notes, very passive aggressive notes, typed notes from teachers that I'm crossing my boundaries, that I don't seem to understand my place and that I'm only a second-year teacher. ...So it's really frustrating for me...It's frustrating to go to work when you know that you work with people who don't like you. (Jo)

Thus, Jo's vision of her future provided a guiding and sustaining framework for her as she negotiated her school context and the lack of collegiality in that environment. While her actions in the pursuit of enacting her vision prompted these responses from school colleagues, she also drew upon her vision to help her cope with the personal challenges from hostile colleagues.

The Politics of the School is Tough

Many of the beginning teachers in this study learned very quickly about the political contexts of schools and negotiating teaching as a political act. The most prominent example was Beth, a first-year teacher. Beth's school was being monitored by the state and a funded intervention program required them to adopt a scripted curriculum. The English department decided to challenge the directive to teach this curriculum because they believed that students would not be college eligible if they did. Beth found herself in the middle of this very stressful situation:

> ...how much am I willing to risk? Aren't the kids most important? If I stay then I can be with them. Or is it worth making a scene and losing my job and losing the kids too? (Beth)

The essential dilemma centred on Beth's beliefs about how students are motivated to learn, a concern for the students and their futures, and a fear of losing her job, which in addition to being problematic for her career, was fuelled by a concern that if she didn't fight for these kids then who would?

> There are some days when I wake and go, "Oh my god, what's going to happen today?" It's scary because your job has no security. Like the day we gave the principal the letter [outlining the English department's refusal to teach the scripted curriculum]. I was really worried. It was a Friday and we went to school and I was like "What's going to happen when he reads that letter?" (Beth)

Dealing with this dilemma prompted physical symptoms of feeling ill:

> ...when I heard that the principal had said, "If I'm going down I'm going to take everyone with me", I thought I was going to throw up. It made me feel really nervous. (Beth)

However, she did see some humour in the situation:

> I never heard anyone say those things except for in a movie! [Laughter] (Beth)

Beth felt a sense of obligation to the parents who had supported and advocated for her appointment, but she also felt personally and professionally challenged and affronted—"I feel like my own beliefs are being called into question."

This dilemma occurred when Beth's vision of appropriate curriculum for her students was challenged with the imposition of district mandates about how and what to teach. It involved negotiating the politics of the school and school community, and the fear of losing her job and not being able to "protect" her students.

In summary, these teachers experienced three types of dilemmas as they began teaching in urban settings: when they found themselves teaching in ways inconsistent with their beliefs and vision because they believed this was in the best interests of the students; when their visions for themselves as teachers and for their future career aspirations collided with others' expectations; and, when their view of appropriate curriculum for their students was stymied by mandates about how and what to teach.

Negotiating the Dilemmas

The interview data also illuminate ways in which these teachers negotiated the dilemmas when their vision and beliefs about teaching and being a teacher were challenged. In the main, they adjusted their conceptions of success, located communities of support and sought fulfilment outside the school. Interestingly, it seems as though being visionary and having a somewhat idealized notion of professional practice and themselves as teachers, actually assisted these teachers negotiate the challenges associated with beginning teaching in urban schools. As Cathy notes:

> We don't find that a lot of things are changing [in the second year of teaching] and the challenges remain the same but we're much less idealistic than we were last year, so we have less idealism to propel us through the challenges. ...I'm really stressed out. A lot of us in the program are workaholics and very willing to devote our lives to this occupation but I

> don't know how...yeah, I'm getting really tired of working 14-hour days, and not sleeping; having tons of grading to do; it's just never ending because we have 150 papers to grade. So it's very frustrating and I don't feel sustained most of the time but I guess it's the idealism that I still have...that I can sort of, help them [students] make critical choices in their lives, and...you know, view education as something I can provide to allow them to make changes in their own lives and in their community. (Cathy)

Adjusting Conceptions of Success: An Ethic of Care

The teachers' visions are grounded in an ethic of care and it is this that helps them redefine a major criterion of success to "if it is in the students' best interests". As the example of Lyn illustrates, beginning teachers might be able to more easily accept classroom practices that don't fit well with their ideal view of professional practice if they can convince themselves that the practices they adopt are in the best interests of their students, at least in the short term.

As Noddings (1992) pointed out, teachers find the passion and courage to do what they do because they care deeply for the students. This is certainly evident in the case of Beth. Despite the challenges associated with her stance and the possible implications for her career, Beth believed she was doing the right thing for her students:

> I was telling [teacher from the same teacher education program], that I've never been fired from a job and that's scary, but...like, it's not because we're doing something wrong. (Beth)

Her resistance was founded on a concern about students' futures in that the managed curriculum would deny them access to college and the conviction of her beliefs about how these students are motivated to learn:

> And it's really sad because I guess as teachers, you know, you get to know the kids on a personal level. These kids come from really bad neighbourhoods where there's death and loss in their lives. And everyday there's incarceration, there are shootings, there's violence, there's so much stuff that's just not represented [in the scripted curriculum]. These kids are not going to come to school and say "I can't wait till we learn standard number 1.3 in [scripted curriculum] where we read an excerpt of a 300 page book that's cut down to 4 pages." They are just not going to! (Beth)

Moreover, she had made a promise to the students, one that she was reluctant to break:

> I kind of made a promise. I told them that I didn't want to use the book with them and I didn't think that it would help them gain the knowledge that they needed. And now I am told that I have to use it or my job will be at risk, you know. But the thing is, I'm not willing to go back on what I said to my kids. (Beth)

Locating Communities of Support

Like many beginning teachers, the teachers in this study sought communities of support in their school, in their teacher education cohort, and from the administration at their school and within the district.

Support from Teacher Colleagues

Support from teacher colleagues at their school confirmed for these teachers that they were not the only one experiencing difficulties:

> There are a lot of first-year teachers at school. So I hear from other people who are saying the same exact thing. So every time I go "I'm the worst teacher in the world", I hear from someone else, "You will not believe what so and so did in my class today." "Really, they did that? Ooh. How horrible." [Laughter] (Lyn)

As Beth negotiated her dilemma, she spent a lot of time talking with trusted colleagues from whom she got support and moral encouragement:

> I do a lot of talking with [induction mentor] and [teacher educator] who is very supportive…moral encouragement. And [colleague from the same teacher education program] of course. He's in the same boat. He and I talk all the time. (Beth)

It was this support and the collective action of her department that helped Beth negotiate the dilemma.

> Yes, it's the easiest thing to tell you what has sustained me most as a new teacher, it is the collaboration with the teachers, with [colleague from the same teacher education program], with our department chair. She's only a third-year teacher, so she's very new and she's very, very young, but she collaborates a lot and she's one door over from me, so we talk all the time. And she sends me her problem kids and stuff—they sit in my class. Also, having [induction mentor] there. He's very supportive and he's willing to fight and stand behind us. So that's really, really awesome. And of course, the kids. I love the kids—love them! (Beth)

Support from Administration

Many participants like Jo highlighted the lack of support from the administration:

> I wasn't feeling supported. I wasn't being evaluated even though I requested that I be evaluated—I asked the administrator to come into my class to see what I was doing; I was really trying to be proactive—it wasn't working. (Jo)

However, Lyn found great support from the principal in her school. She felt that her professional views and opinions were valued even though she was a first-year teacher.

> The principal is awesome and I love working with her a lot. She's super motivated and involved and cool. She's really into, not leadership by fear of the leader, but really into teamwork and listening to others' perspectives. We're actually working together now. She's started this school improvement, like "What is our vision of our school for the future?" type thing. And she's asked me as a new teacher to give input, which is really cool. (Lyn)

Support from Teacher Education Cohort

The participants talked about the support from the teacher education cohort as they negotiated their first year of teaching. They valued belonging to a community of like-minded teachers:

> [The program] is really good in the fact that it gives you lots of connections to lots of teachers who believe in the same things that you believe in. That's really helpful. (Beth)

Likewise, Cathy valued belonging to a community of like-minded people and she also valued the teaching ideas she had access to through this community:

> So it's belonging to the community of teachers who are very like-minded. They're, yeah, they have good ideas and meeting with them and collaborating with them sustains me. The cohort, having that listserv and getting 15 responses back with email attachments sustains me. (Cathy)

For Jo, the MA cohort was very helpful during her first year of teaching:

> I had this great support network of people who are going through the same thing as you. We were around for each other. We get excited about what we do. We talk about, "oh I did this thing and it really worked." Somebody will come in with a problem and they'll get 20 solutions. It re-energized me every time I came [to class]. I know that's how we all felt. Seeing all these teachers doing really wonderful things, motivated me to want to be as wonderful as they are. It's not the same in my school. It's so isolating and I don't know what's happening. (Jo)

Search for Fulfilment Outside the School

Like the teachers in the Project on the Next Generation of Teachers, Harvard School of Education (Donaldson 2005), some teachers in this study were planning for a teaching career beyond the classroom. As Jo explained:

> …I got more involved in things across the district so that I could feel that I was making a difference. I actually went to one of the administrators that I really like and I told her that I was really frustrated and that I just didn't feel like I was a part of anything that was changing at this school. She suggested that I start going to some of these district meetings. At the same time, we were having this big fight in our district over the standardized curriculum and I heard through the grapevine that there were groups of parents and teachers who were meeting outside the school to talk about what was happening and to see what they could do. So I got involved in going to these meetings. And I went to board meetings because of these connections and spoke up at meetings and it made me see that I could do something. (Jo)

Jo's vision sustained her actions as she negotiated her feelings of being ineffective at her school and the obstructions she perceived from her school colleagues. She took actions to try to make a difference at a broader level. The example of Cathy above also indicates her goal of working towards a broader level of impact outside the school.

Negotiating the Dilemmas: Does Teacher Education Have a Role?

These examples highlight the demands of teaching in urban school settings and the associated dilemmas of negotiating the intersection of the realities of teaching in particular contexts that often challenge their visions. These teachers' visions developed from their own prior experiences, beliefs and moral purposes, and were informed by the theories and literature encountered in the teacher education program as well as their prior student teaching experiences. Dilemmas emerged when they perceived that the contexts of their first teaching appointments (the classroom resources, the collegial environment of the school, administration, the wider policy context) did not support their vision and ideals. They experienced the isolation and bureaucracy often associated with urban contexts (Weiner 1999), but it was the mismatch of vision and the realities of the school and district contexts within which they began teaching that weighed heavily on their thoughts and emotions.

As the examples show, beginning teachers demonstrate much courage and determination as they strive to improve the lives of those for whom they care, often in an environment of increased bureaucratic accountability and reduced teacher control. They deal with identity dilemmas by finding ways to reaffirm their vision, adjust their conceptions of success, locate communities of support and seek fulfilment outside the school. So, does pre-service teacher education have a role in helping new teachers negotiate the emotional context of beginning teaching, particularly in contexts that challenge their moral purposes and visions? Like Hammerness (2003) I believe that teacher education does have a role.

The essential dilemmas for these beginning teachers involved problems of vision match. When this happened, the teachers considered whether to "move on" to a working environment where the match might be closer. Interestingly, the two teachers who were considering this were in their second year but neither was considering leaving the profession. Rather, they were considering career moves that they believed would allow them to enact their vision. However, it was the idealism associated with their vision that kept them going in trying times. As Cathy pointed out, when this idealism diminishes the further one gets from the teacher preparation program, feelings of burnout emerge. Therefore, articulating a vision and finding ways to sustain the ideals associated with the vision is very important in the beginning years of teaching. Teacher educators could help better support and sustain new teachers in their lives and work if they help them articulate a clear sense of purpose for work in their chosen profession. Such a clear sense of purpose is likely to sustain their commitment when they encounter difficult situations in their first years of teaching, by reminding them why they choose teaching as their profession. It might also help them recognize and celebrate their achievements and thus contribute to feelings of efficacy and agency.

Likewise, these examples suggests that if beginning teachers can maintain a vision focus beyond the classroom and keep an eye to the future, they might be able to more easily negotiate the early years of teaching. Therefore, in addition to helping new teachers articulate a clear vision and sense of purpose, teacher education should consider helping prospective teachers plan actions to achieve their visions and also help them to accept the time and determination that may be required to feel success in relation to their ideals.

The importance of communities of support, both in their schools and across the teacher education cohort, is highlighted here as an important component in negotiating the vision-context dilemmas. The participants highlighted the value of the peer support network in the second year and part-time component of their MA program, but as time goes on it is the communities of support at the school level that become more valuable. However, a community of like-minded colleagues was highly valued by these teachers. In Nieto's (2003) study with teachers in the United States, it was also the "emotional stuff" and the value of belonging to a learning community that "kept them going". This highlights the importance of teacher education having a clearly articulated and coherently structured philosophy and purpose, as well as some way of connecting with the candidates as they move into full-time teaching.

In summary, teacher education faces the great challenge of educating teachers whose ideals and vision about teaching can prevail in settings that often actively work against them. This underscores the importance of focusing less in teacher education on giving prospective teachers knowledge about student characteristics and teaching skills and more on the social and political conditions that frame and constrain teachers' work (Liston and Zeichner 1990). Helping prospective teachers identify and examine their specific purpose and vision within the socio-political context of schools and teachers' work and helping them realize that they will experience difficult emotions as they begin teaching and that their visions will be challenged, may help beginning teachers negotiate a less traumatic entry into the profession, may help build resilience.

Sachs (2001) stresses the importance of teachers holding on to the image of the teacher they want to be, of maintaining an identity based on strong values and beliefs likely to sustain them in the face of challenges and ongoing educational reform and change. Teachers' capacities to sustain their commitment—to be resilient—are moderated by their identities, their professional life phases and the contexts within which they work (Gu and Day 2007). However, the expectation that workers follow particular display rules (Hochschild's "emotional labour") has been linked to emotional exhaustion, burnout, reduced job satisfaction and likely separation (Hochschild 1990; Morris and Feldman 1996). Pre-service teacher education may be able to contribute to beginning teachers' resilience and thereby reduce burnout and attrition by close mentoring and guidance in the examination of unpleasant emotional experiences (Martinez 2004).

Therefore, with the need for more and more high-quality teachers in the profession, the importance of examining the role of vision, identity and the dilemmas associated with any vision-context mismatch in the first years of teaching, along with the ways in which teachers negotiate those dilemmas in order to feel efficacious, is very important for the future of the profession. In particular, this study highlights the importance of seeking out and sustaining the idealist, for it is these people who will likely have greatest impact in high needs schools. As Cathy reminds us, "Who else is going to teach besides the idealist?" Teacher education must find ways of sustaining the idealist.

References

Day, C. (2004). *A passion for teaching.* London: Falmer.

Day, C., Kingston, A., Stobart, G., & Sammons, P. (2006). The personal and professional selves of teachers: Stable and unstable identities. *British Educational Research Journal, 32*(4), 601–616.

Day, C., Flores, M. A., & Viana, I. (2007). Effects of national policies on teachers' sense of professionalism: Findings from an empirical study in Portugal and in England. *European Journal of Teacher Education, 30*(3), 249–265.

Denzin, N. K. (1984). *On understanding emotion.* San Francisco: Jossey-Bass.

Donaldson, M. L. (2005, April). *On barren ground: How urban high schools fail to support and retain newly tenured teachers.* Paper presented at the American Educational Research Association annual conference, Montreal, Canada.

Flores, M. A., & Day, C. (2006). Contexts which shape and reshape new teachers' identities: A multi-perspective study. *Teaching and Teacher Education, 22,* 219–232.

Gu, Q., & Day, C. (2007). Teachers resilience: A necessary condition for effectiveness. *Teaching and Teacher Education, 23,* 1302–1316.

Hammerness, K. (2003). Learning to hope, or hoping to learn? The role of vision in the early professional lives of teachers. *Journal of Teacher Education, 54*(1), 43–56.

Hargreaves, A. (1998a). The emotional politics of teaching and teacher development: With implications for educational leadership. *International Journal of Leadership in Education, 1*(4), 315–336.

Hargreaves, A. (1998b). The emotional practice of teaching. *Teaching and Teacher Education, 14*(8), 835–854.

Hargreaves, A. (2005). Educational change takes ages: Life, career and generational factors in teachers' emotional responses to educational change. *Teaching and Teacher Education, 21,* 967–983.

Hochschild, A. R. (1983). *The managed heart: Commercialization of human feeling.* Berkley: University of California Press.

Hochschild, A. R. (1990). Ideology and emotion management: A perspective and path for future research. In T. D. Kemper (Ed.), *Research agendas in the sociology of emotions* (pp. 117–142). Albany: State University of New York Press.

Ingersoll, R. M. (2001). Teacher turnover and teacher shortages: An organizational analysis. *American Educational Research Journal, 38*(3), 499–534.

Johnson, S. M., & The project on the next generation of teachers (2004). *Finders and keepers: Helping new teachers survive and thrive in our schools.* San Francisco: Jossey-Bass.

Kelchtermans, G. (2005). Teachers' emotions in educational reforms: Self understanding, vulnerable commitment, and micropolitical literacy. *Teaching and Teacher Education, 21,* 995–1006.

Lasky, S. (2005). A sociocultural approach to understanding teacher identity, agency and professional vulnerability in a context of secondary school reform. *Teaching and Teacher Education, 21,* 899–916.

Liljestrom, A., Roulston, K., & Demarrais, K. (2007). "There's no place for feeling like this in the workplace": Women teachers' anger in school settings. In P. A. Schutz, R. Pekrun (Eds.), *Emotion in education* (pp. 275–291). San Diego: Elsevier.

Liston, D., & Zeichner, K. (1990). Teacher education and the social context: Issues for curriculum development. *American Educational Research Journal, 27*(4), 610–636.

Martinez, K. (2004). Mentoring new teachers: Promise and problems in times of shortage. *Australian Journal of Education, 48*(1), 95–108.

Morris, J. A., & Feldman, D. C. (1996). The dimensions and antecedents, and consequences of emotional labor. *Academy of Management Review, 21*(4), 986–1010.

Nieto, S. (2003). *What keeps teachers going?* New York: Teachers College Press.

Noddings, N. (1992). *The challenge to care in schools: An alternative approach to education.* New York: Teachers College Press.

Sachs, J. (2001). Teacher professional identity: Competing discourses, competing outcomes. *Journal of Educational Policy, 16*(2), 149–161.

Sachs, J. (2003). *The activist teaching profession.* Buckingham: Open University Press.

Schutz, P. A., Cross, D., Hong, J., & Osbon, J. (2007). Teacher identities, beliefs, and goals related to emotions in the classroom. In P. A. Schutz, R. Pekrun (Eds.), *Emotion in education* (pp. 223–241). San Diego: Elsevier.

Stronach, I., Corbin, B., McNamara, O., Stark, S., & Warne, T. (2002). Towards an uncertain politics of professionalism: Teacher and nurse identities in flux. *Journal of Educational Policy, 17*(1), 109–138.

Tickle, L. (1991). New teachers and the emotions of learning teaching. *Cambridge Journal of Education, 21*(3), 319–329.

Weiner, L. (1999). *Urban teaching: The essentials.* New York: Teachers College Press.

Chapter 10
Stories and Affect in Teacher Education

Nel Noddings

Introduction

In Western thought, affect and emotion have been distrusted, denigrated, or at least set aside in favor of reason. The tendency to distrust—even deplore—emotion has been aggravated by the rise of professions with their insistence on detachment, distance, cool appraisal, and systematic procedures. At a time when teaching is struggling to be recognized as a full profession, there is a temptation to regard emotion and affect as signs of unprofessional demeanor—things to be rooted out as part of the campaign to achieve professional status. However, even from this perspective, one could argue for the inclusion of affect and emotion in the teacher education curriculum, i.e., it could be argued that one has to understand a phenomenon in order to control or eliminate it. But one could also argue that affect and emotion belong in the curriculum because they may enhance a passion for teaching, relieve a sense of isolation, and improve classroom performance. In this chapter, I will concentrate on the use of stories that both induce feeling and help us to understand what we are feeling. The discussion will take place in three parts: First, I will explain very briefly why affect is so often avoided. Second, I will discuss the use of stories in teacher preparation. Finally, I will suggest ways in which teachers can maintain their own enthusiasm for teaching by building a repertoire of stories.

The first part of this was first published in the Cambridge Journal of Education, Vol. 26, No. 3 (1996): 435–448.

N. Noddings (✉)
Lee Jacks Professor of Education Emerita, Stanford University, Stanford, CA, USA
e-mail: noddings@stanford.edu

C. Day, J. C.-K. Lee (eds.), *New Understandings of Teacher's Work,* Professional Learning and Development in Schools and Higher Education 6,
DOI 10.1007/978-94-007-0545-6_10, © Springer Science+Business Media B.V. 2011

The Avoidance of Affect

For the past 200 years, philosophers have emphasized reason over affect. Not only has reason been declared the source of moral knowledge and agency, it has also been identified as the human capacity that deserves respect and moral treatment. Reason has served as the ticket of admission to the moral community. Emotion has, for the most part, been dismissed as unreliable. Kant, for example, insisted that moral feeling could not precede a genuinely moral act; that act, he said, must be preceded and motivated by observance of the moral law. Indeed, a "moral" act motivated by pleasure was branded "pathological" (Kant 1983, p. 34). Kant did allow a measure of happiness to creep in after the moral act, i.e., one is allowed a feeling of satisfaction for having done the right thing.

In contrast, Hume—one of the few "hard-headed" philosophers to give emotion a prominent place in morals—recommended cultivation of the moral sentiments as an important aspect of character development. Recognizing the necessity of both reason and sentiment, he gave sentiment priority:

> The final sentence, it is probable, which pronounces characters and actions amiable or odious, praise-worthy or blameable; that which stamps on them the mark of honor or infamy, approbation or censure; that which renders morality an active principle, and constitutes virtue our happiness, and vice our misery: It is probable…that this final sentence depends on some internal sense or feeling, which nature has made universal in the whole species. For what else can have an influence of this nature? (Hume 1983, p. 15)

If we follow Hume, both moral life and our general happiness depend heavily on the cultivation of appropriate feelings. People are esteemed when they are "sociable, good-natured, humane, merciful, grateful, friendly, generous, beneficent" (Hume 1983, p. 15). Not surprisingly, Hume often uses stories to illustrate his points. For example, he recounts this story of Pericles, told by Plutarch:

> When Pericles, the great Athenian statesman and general, was on his death-bed, his surrounding friends, deeming him now insensible, began to indulge their sorrow for their expiring patron, by enumerating his great qualities and successes, his conquests and victories, the unusual length of his administration, and his nine trophies erected over the enemies of the republic. "You forget," cries the dying hero, who had heard all, "you forget the most eminent of my praises, while you dwell so much on those vulgar advantages, in which fortune had a principal share. You have not observed that no citizen has ever yet worn mourning on my account." (Hume 1983, p. 17)

The social virtues based on fellow feeling are fundamental for Hume.

Unamuno has also called into question the inordinate emphasis on reason:

> Man is said to be a reasoning animal. I do not know why he has not been defined as an affective or feeling animal. Perhaps that which differentiates him from other animals is feeling rather than reason. More often have seen a cat reason than laugh or weep. Perhaps it weeps or laughs inwardly—but then perhaps, also inwardly, the crab resolves equations of the second degree. (Unamuno 1954, p. 3)

Even in the arts, critics and philosophers have been wary of emotion. The music of Tchaikovsky, for example, has been heavily criticized for being overly sentimental.

Some of this criticism is, of course, justified and Tchaikovsky himself discarded some of his compositions as too emotional and trivial (Cross and Ewen 1953). But it came as an enormous relief to many music lovers when Leonard Bernstein confessed publicly that he loved the music of Tchaikovsky—in another critic's words, "pages of music filled with incomparable melody and tenderness that came from the heart and go to the heart" (Cross and Ewen 1953, p. 803).

Everywhere in Western thought—even in the objections raised against the Romanticists—we find a distrust of emotion. But, fortunately, we find also a deep concern about its neglect. C. S. Lewis worried about a particular educational program that put great emphasis on critical thinking and neglected feeling. Recognizing that the educational theorists who produced it emphasized critical thinking to protect students against dogmatism and propaganda, Lewis nevertheless had his doubts:

> My own experience as a teacher tells an opposite tale. For every one pupil who needs to be guarded from a weak excess of sensibility there are three who need to be awakened from the slumber of cold vulgarity. (Lewis 1955, p. 24)

Further, the lack of attention to emotion might very well have an opposite effect to the one intended:

> By starving the sensibility of our pupils we only make them easier prey to the propagandist when he comes. For famished nature will be avenged and a hard heart is not infallible protection against a soft head. (Lewis 1955, p. 24)

One reason for keeping emotion out of morals, aesthetics, the professions and education is concern about rational and professional functioning. In the professions, this concern takes several forms: first, there is a fear that professional judgment will be impaired by emotion; second, it has been widely taught that professionals must learn to protect themselves against the burnout that may result from feeling too much for one's clients; finally, it has become a mark of professionalization to be detached, cool, and dispassionate (Larson 1977; Starr 1982). There is little evidence to support the first concern and both the second and third are coming under more frequent attack. Indeed, both theoreticians and practitioners in nursing and medicine are exploring the efficacy of shared feelings in the treatment of patients (Watson 1985; Candib 1995) and educators have expressed increasing concern about the professionalization of teaching insofar as it requires detachment and the concealment of feeling (Noddings 1984, 1992; Metzger 1987). We may now be entering an era of balance between reason and emotion in professional life. Clearly, both require cultivation through sensitive education.

Stories in Teacher Preparation

Young people in training to teach may suppose that "real professionals" do not allow themselves to feel—that they have conquered their emotions and face the problems of teaching with dispassionate rationality. The use of stories in teacher education could be powerful in dispelling this belief. More and more teacher stories are appearing in educational literature and some of these illustrate how deeply even experienced teachers feel about the inevitable failures that occur in classroom life. Colsant (1995), for example, tells his own story with touching honesty. Attempting to teach French culture to inner-city Chicago students in the same way that he had successfully taught young people in Quebec, he found himself sliding into despair. He admits that he came to hate his first period class. The kids despised him and he despised them. But hate is a repulsive emotion to a good teacher. It moved Colsant to scrap what he was doing, make peace with his students and start over. He began to listen to their problems, to engage them openly about what he was going through and to try new techniques. Still, with all the good will and effort, success eluded him:

> I try to acknowledge my failure and their resistance while giving them a choice, even an invitation to join and work. Instead, I make them feel they are outsiders, wrong if they don't join the rest. I am still pushing French on them. My old self speaks while I try to find my new voice. The dilemma is not resolved. I am not making it. (Colsant 1995, p. 69)

But Colsant did make it. He did not ever teach French to Chicago kids in the way he had previously taught it, but he managed to connect with his students, kids who—more than anything else—needed an adult who would trust, respect, and care for them. And they did learn some French. They began to use French words and phrases to express ideas that were not in the textbook. Further, they learned something about struggle and cooperation, polite modes of interaction, persistence, and concern for the feelings of others. Colsant's story makes clear that teachers feel and that feelings color much of what they do.

Besides suffering feelings of failure for himself and feelings of initial dislike for his students, Colsant experienced the empathic feelings that come when a teacher cares for his or her students. When mutual respect and concern had been established, Colsant suffered when a student suddenly moved away. Why? To where? With whom? And then a former student was shot dead. Colsant experienced the pain that comes from caring. Suffering is one of the costs of relating. Thinking back on what he went through with that difficult class and what they went through—the fear, the losses, the minor triumphs, the moments of shared vexation and humor—he now sees his old students in the new ones who face him:

> New lads are there all right, not remote antagonists, but alive in the toil of listening. New conversations will surely start. (Colsant 1995, p. 89)

Hansen (1995) describes another teacher, Mr James, who has had to compromise what he planned to teach in order to give students what they need. Mr James explicitly recognizes the emotionality of teaching. He says:

> Teachers are always responding to problems and crises with young people. It is a teacher's duty to bring order to chaos, to answer violence with peace, to replace confusion with clarity. These adverse conditions are not defeated by swift strokes, but students focus on the teacher's handling of a crisis. Her [his] choice of a position is crucial; it establishes which values are preferred. While operating as a rational and humane model of values and decorum, however, the teacher is still an emotional, visceral creature. Blatant injustice, for example, calls for outrage, an affective response that must be felt and expressed. (Hansen 1995, p. 67)

Like Mr Colsant, Mr James is heavily guided by how he feels and how his students feel. Without the emotion these two men feel, both might join the ranks of apathetic, burnt-out teachers. Explicit attention to feelings, willingness to share the pain of their students and the decision to risk still more suffering when they come to care for their students characterize these men as teachers.

Other kinds of decisions are made by good teachers, and teachers in preparation should hear about these too. Some teachers make a decision common to professional life; they decide to maintain a wall of separation between themselves and their students. Hansen (1995) describes another fine teacher, Ms Payton, who made such a decision. It is important for beginning teachers to understand that a certain aloofness and formality may be necessary, at least initially. Ms Payton, for example, says that because she was young and looked like her students when she started to teach, she had to set up and enforce a real separation. "I was known as a tyrant" she admits (Hansen 1995, p. 37). But Ms Payton responds generously and effectively when students bring problems to her. She is alert for academic problems and works hard to remedy them. However, she still maintains her distance and wants nothing to do with her students outside of class. She is afraid that familiarity might make her "easier" on her students and, if that were to happen, she would regard herself as a failure as a teacher.

It might be good for beginning teachers to hear these three teacher stories back-to-back. Here are three good teachers—all recognized for their skills and devotion. All three have come to terms with emotion in teaching: one uses it as a driving force to motivate change in his own teaching; another uses it to show students how a rational person controls and employs emotion; a third keeps it at arms length in order to concentrate on subject matter. New teachers can learn from all three.

Stories can also be used effectively as case studies (Clandinin et al. 1993). It is helpful to follow the development of teachers as they move through student teaching, the early years of teaching and mentoring new young teachers. In these stories, we hear not only emotion but also accounts of learning, coping, and being socialized. We also learn that students are not the only source of emotion in teaching. Administrators arouse both anger and appreciation, principals (headteachers) induce respect and contempt, parents cause frustration and sympathy, colleagues promote enthusiasm and disgust. Teacher room (staffroom) talk can raise one's spirits or, more often, drive an idealistic teacher into pessimism and depression.

Then, too, there are thoughtful and deeply moving accounts of particular problems in teaching: coming to a critical understanding of one's ideology (Ellsworth 1989); reconciling authority, caring and evaluation (Pagano 1990); committing oneself to multicultural education (Hooks 1994); finding a constructive outlet for one's political commitment (Ayers 1993); finding a path between the demands of patriarchy and the needs of women (Grumet 1988). All of these writers use personal stories to enhance theoretical discussions of teaching. Sometimes there are stories within stories and readers are encouraged not only to stretch their imaginations, but also to increase their cultural literacy. Pagano (1990), for example, starts a section of one chapter—a section called "A story"—with a line whose author she cannot place: "Man is a creature of passion who must live out that passion in the world"

(p. 105). Who said it? she wonders. It started a story for the writer and it starts one for Pagano. Might it start one for new teachers as well?

Neither teacher educators nor classroom teachers should tell stories just for the sake of telling stories. Narayan (1991) tells the story of a guru, Swamiji, who gave good counsel on the use of stories:

> "When you tell a story", Swamiji said, "You should look at the situation and tell it. Then it turns out well. If you just tell any story any time, it's not really good. You must consider the time and shape the story so it's right. All stories are told for some purpose." (Narayan 1991, p. 123)

"The teacher is an emotional, visceral creature" (Hansen 1995). Stories of teaching can be used to remind us of that. But students are also emotional creatures and teachers should be aware of their possible effects on students. Orwell (1956) told the story of his mistreatment in a British boarding school, Crossgates. Students (except the very wealthy) were regularly beaten for offences ranging from bed wetting to stumbling over Latin translations. Orwell was only eight years old when he started at Crossgates and, although he came to hate both the headmaster, Sim, and Sim's wife, he says he never thought to question their judgment. Thus:

> This was the great abiding lesson of my boyhood: that I was in a world where it was not possible for me to be good....Life was more terrible, and I was more wicked, than I had imagined. (Orwell 1956, p. 423)

Orwell, however, did not give up trying to be good and there were many compensations in his life. What of all the children today who learn roughly the same lesson and find no reason to balance it with hope?

When I read and reread stories like Orwell's, I want to question every act of coercion we use on children. Question, not reject out of hand. Surely some such acts are necessary and I certainly do not advocate a neglectful permissiveness. But why must we choose between the two extremes? Why not use reason, inspiration, persuasion and love to get students to try the things (like algebra and great literature) that we believe might be good for them? Student stories can provide powerful inducements to reflect on our own practices.

Frightened by some of the teacher stories they hear and troubled by student stories, teachers need also to hear stories that remind them of teachers' potentially good effects on the lives of students. Booth (1988) tells the wonderful story of how he felt that he had to decide between chemistry and English as fields of study because he had such fine teachers in these subjects and he dedicated his book, The Vocation of a Teacher, to "Eleven Beloved Teachers." Jackson (1992) recalls his high school algebra teacher with great affection, although he is not quite sure why she was so important to him. I, too, have recounted the story of what teachers meant in my life (Noddings 1996), and Scheffler (1995), now in retirement from teaching at Harvard, has written a book recalling and honoring the teachers of his youth. He writes:

> My book is an effort to revisit teachers of my youth, and to urge them to hold forth once again. I wanted the pleasure of their long lost company: I longed to hear their lessons anew, to profit from their advice, and to observe, with mature eyes, how they taught and what they imparted to their pupils. (Scheffler 1996, p. 360)

Only peculiarly emotionless young teachers would be unmoved by the thought that their students might want to revisit them 50 years later and "urge them to hold forth once again." Perhaps these greatly appreciated teachers looked at the child as Buber did: "This phenomenon of uniqueness, which is more than just begetting and birth, this grace of beginning again and ever again" (Buber 1965, p. 83). If so, it is not surprising that they are remembered for years and years.

Building a Repertoire for Affect

"No tears in the writer, no tears in the reader," said Frost (1949, p. vi). It is also likely that, if there is no feeling for the subject in the teacher, there will be none in the student. Even when teachers are enthusiastic about their subjects, students often fail to follow their example, and this can be a great disappointment for conscientious teachers. However, if teachers can stand back a bit from their own subject-specific enthusiasm, they may see that almost all students seek connections—connections among the subjects they are forced to study, connections to their concrete life situations, and connections to the great existential questions. If this is true, then teachers might try to enhance their own affective responses by looking at their subjects in terms of these connections.

The standard mode of continued learning for secondary school teachers has long been one of linear, hierarchical study. Teachers who pride themselves on their subject matter knowledge often pursue courses of study indistinguishable from those of other graduate students in the subject. What they learn in such courses may increase their enthusiasm for the subject they teach, but it is rarely useful in any direct way. Studying nonlinear differential equations, for example, will probably do little to enhance a high school mathematics teacher's lessons. Indeed, highly specialized teachers may put more and more distance between themselves and their students and other colleagues.

I am not suggesting that we abandon linear, higher learning entirely; it has its uses. But I am suggesting that teachers might broaden and deepen their affective relation to subject matter by exploring its connections to other subjects, individual lives and existential questions. In so doing, they might induce corresponding affective responses in their students. One way to explore such connections is to build a repertoire of stories.

At the beginning of this chapter, I described the pervasive denigration of affect in moral theory, aesthetics, and professional life. Teachers seriously concerned about the lack of attention to affect in these areas can search for stories that provide connections and invite affective response. For example, mathematics teachers might have their students read and discuss Flatland (Abbott 1952). In addition to a fascinating discussion of mathematical topics, Flatland provides an opportunity to talk about sexism, classism, and mysticism. Both sexism and classism are treated in a powerful manner and, in keeping with the best satire, there is a good deal of humor in the story. The treatment of mysticism, however, is appreciative. As a result of this introduction, students may find themselves fascinated by mysticism in their own and other religions.

Imagine a society in which all the males are polygons and class status depends on the number of one's sides. Isosceles triangles are the working poor, so to speak, and those polygons with so many sides that they approximate circles are the priests at the top of the social hierarchy. Every father in Flatland hopes that his sons will have more sides than he has. In this highly classed society, women are mere line segments and special rules govern their behavior. They are, essentially, nonpersons. Because they are line segments—like needles—women are extremely dangerous. The laws of Flatland decree separate entrances for them and insist that they issue a continual "peace cry" so that unsuspecting males will be aware of their presence and escape being pierced. Further:

> Any female, duly certified to be suffering from St Vitus' Dance, fits, chronic cold accompanied by violent sneezing, or any disease necessitating involuntary motions, shall be instantly destroyed. (Abbott 1952, p. 13)

Discussion of the satirical sexism in Flatland might lead to interest in the biographies of women mathematicians, in the contemporary problems of women in mathematics or in further conversations across other disciplines.

In addition to sexism and classism, Flatland introduces a good bit of mysticism. The narrator of the story, an upstanding square, is visited by a three-dimensional entity. Of course, no one believes him and he finishes his tale in prison—treated as either madly or subversively dangerous. In the mystical tradition, he longs for another visitation, something to reaffirm what he knows really happened. But how can one explain a third dimension to people living in a two-dimensional world? How would we describe a four-dimensional entity to our peers? The narrator's story is illustrative of the experience of mystics in history. He knows that he has been visited by three-dimensional beings, but in his psychic suffering, his faith wavers:

> It is part of the martyrdom which I endure for the cause of Truth that there are seasons of mental weakness, when Cubes and Spheres flit away into the background of scarce-possible existences; when the Land of Three Dimensions seems almost as visionary as the Land of One or None; nay, when even this hard wall that bars me from my freedom, these very tablets on which I am writing, and all the substantial realities of Flatland itself, appear no better than the offspring of a diseased imagination, or the faceless fabric of a dream. (Abbott 1952, p. 103)

Clearly, discussion of mysticism could become part of an interdisciplinary unit of study that could be shared by teachers of English, social studies, and science. Collaboration is another means of enhancing teacher affect and, of course, it is also a way of extending each individual teacher's repertoire of stories.

Like mathematics teachers, science teachers often pride themselves on the depth of their scientific knowledge, but they rarely consider developing their knowledge across the disciplines. Yet they too have an opportunity, and perhaps an obligation, to serve as models of educated persons. Consider how absurd schooling must seem to many students when they—who are forced every year to study four or five different subjects—are taught by people who seem to know only one and are often unable to bring that one into focus on anything that really matters in the lives of young people. Science teachers, too, can make connections through the judicious use of stories.

Biology teachers, for example, might collect creation stories and begin the study of evolution with a discussion of how people everywhere through all time have had an interest in origins. Such stories can be gathered from a variety of cultures. The biblical story can be told. The following paragraph from Huckleberry Finn might be read:

> It's lovely to live on a raft. We had the sky, up there, all speckled with stars, and we used to lay on our backs and look up at them, and discuss about whether they was made or just happened—Jim allowed they was made, but I allowed they happened; I judged it would have took too long to make so many. Jim said the moon could a laid them; well, that looked kind of reasonable, so I didn't say nothing against it, because I've seen a frog lay most as many, so of course it could be done. We used to watch the stars that fell, too, and see them streak down. Jim allowed they'd got spoiled and was hove out to the nest. (Twain 1982, p. 742)

Approaching a unit on evolution this way also gives science teachers an opportunity to tell students about the historical (and contemporary) conflicts over evolution and creation. This is itself a fascinating story and should be part of the curriculum. Do scientists and bishops engage in fiery debates? Do they stoop to ad hominem attacks on one another? Students may be amazed to hear that Bishop Samuel Wilberforce (nicknamed "Soapy Sam") demanded to know whether Professor J. H. Huxley's ancestors were descended from apes through his grandmother's or his grandfather's side. Huxley's response was, more or less, that he would rather be descended from apes than from a man who used his considerable talent and influence to ridicule science and reason. At the meeting where this exchange occurred, students shouted profanities, ladies fainted and distinguished gentlemen became irate.

A bit of humor can also be added to the story. The economist/humorist Stephen Leacock commented:

> Once started, the nebulous world condensed into suns, the suns threw off planets, the planets cooled, life resulted and presently became conscious, conscious life got higher and higher up till you had apes, then Bishop Wilberforce, and then Professor Huxley. (Leacock 1956, p. 2463)

I suppose there are science and mathematics teachers who are not "turned on" by explorations in other subjects. But, then, they should easily understand how it is that many students are not excited by mathematics or science. However, it seems likely that most teachers, like their students, can experience renewed enthusiasm for teaching through the use of stories that invite affective responses. Think what it might mean to students when they see their science teacher interested in literature and history and their mathematics teacher interested in the political problems of sexism and classism!

English teachers are involved with stories regularly, but even they miss the kinds of connections discussed here. The school curriculum is so designed that literature is often chosen by author rather than by theme and many teachers spend more time on literary techniques (e.g., metaphor, simile, the meaning of black tresses or a red dress) than on the great existential questions and their meaning in current life. Again, it seems likely that teachers might experience enhanced affect if they were encouraged to choose deeply moving literature organized around a theme. Students are not the only ones bored in schools. Teachers often are too! If different themes are chosen from year to year, teachers might maintain their enthusiasm, and, if the themes are chosen with students' interests in mind, student enthusiasm too might be enhanced. Themes that might interest students include love, friendship, courage, war, evil, the sea and the struggle of growing up.

Literature relevant to a theme may be chosen from the traditional canon, from great modem literature or from popular literature. Quality need not be sacrificed, but connections should be increased. As Frost claimed, "No tears in the writer, no tears in the reader." Teachers should be encouraged to teach literature that meets two basic criteria: the literature should be widely judged as of high quality and the teachers themselves should find it personally moving. It is, at least in part, through the teacher that affect will be produced in the student.

In conclusion, I want to say something about lesson planning and stories. Planning can be an affectively rich part of teaching. It has always been one of my favorite teaching tasks. I do not plan lessons by writing a learning objective and page assignment numbers in a cramped space. Even as a high school mathematics teacher, I could not plan this way. At planning time, the possibilities are endless. I often surround myself with books I love and keep jumping up to get more, as one idea triggers another and memories extend in all directions. I over-plan and much of what I read will not appear in a particular day's lesson. Instead, it will join a collection that provides a wonderful storehouse of material to be used spontaneously over a long period of time.

Planning prepares not just the lesson, but, more importantly, the teacher. The intellectual excitement of too many possibilities is priceless. Of course, there comes the moment of narrowing down, of deciding on exactly what will appear in tomorrow's lesson, but the material left out is not wasted. It has already contributed to the teacher's growth and some day it will contribute to the growth of new students.

Postscript

I have presented an argument for the inclusion of affect and stories in teacher education. First, I gave a brief sketch of reasons why affect is so often dismissed in professional life. Then I tried to show how useful it might be for teachers-in-training to hear the true stories of veteran teachers, what they have felt and still feel and how they embrace, use, or control emotion. Finally, I argued that teachers who take affect seriously can enrich their own lives and those of their students by developing a rich repertoire of stories. Even today, after many years of teaching, developing that repertoire gives zest to my own planning and, I hope, to my classroom performance.

The creative use of stories in all our courses is probably more important today than it was in 1996. As Maxine Greene has reminded us again and again, stories open spaces for us to think, to empathize, and to imagine (Greene 1988, 2007). In contrast, current trends in schooling push us to close things down around specific learning objectives and test preparation. It is almost as if we had joined Thomas Gradgrind and the teacher M'Choakumchild (Dickens 1982) in demanding that our children never wonder—just learn facts and repeat them.

Stories are important not only in arousing interest and inviting imaginative engagement; they should also be highly useful in developing empathy. In the past decade, psychologists and moral educators—especially those working in care ethics—have begun to put great emphasis on empathy. The psychologist Hoffman (2000) defines empathy to include both cognitive and emotional processes, and he takes it as basic in moral development. The philosopher Slote (2007) makes the same move and even titles his book "The Ethics of Care and Empathy."

Historically, however, *empathy* has been firmly rooted in cognitive processes. First used in aesthetics, it pointed to a process by which observers could project themselves into an art object in order to understand it. Even today, most dictionaries define empathy as an intellectual process. When the focus is on feeling with or for others, we usually use *sympathy*. In my earlier work, I avoided the word *empathy* for this reason. However, if the word is understood as Hoffman and Slote define it, it provides a useful shorthand to refer to both understanding and feeling (Noddings 2010). Readers should, however, be aware of the ambiguities in the term.

Stories can be used to teach empathy vicariously. Let's say a character, Bill, was being teased by other boys for his stature, big ears, or some other physical feature. The teacher might ask, "How do you think Bill was feeling?" It is probably better to ask this than to ask, "How would *you* feel in this situation?" We want students to put aside their own feelings temporarily and take on the feelings of others. Next, the teacher should ask students to tell how they know what Bill was feeling. Is the feeling clearly expressed in the episode under discussion, or is there more to be explored in earlier episodes? What we are after here is empathic accuracy. When we are fairly confident that we have accurately discerned Bill's emotional state, we can examine our own feelings—feelings that should resonate sympathetically with Bill's. Finally, the teacher might ask, "If you were present at an episode of this sort, what might you do or say to help Bill?"

One can see that empathy activated in a case like Bill's is bound up with a sense of fairness and social justice. Students who already have a commitment to social justice will find it easy to sympathize with Bill. As they are encouraged to analyze and discuss a great variety of cases, they may find some that do not arouse empathy so obviously.

Consider how we often feel when bad things happen to bad people. At movies, for example, we may cheer when the bad guy gets his just deserts. Should we try to understand and feel—to empathize—with enemies and criminals? Many of us believe that lessons along these lines are among the most important we can teach. Can we (should we) empathize with a condemned murderer when he faces and fears his own death by execution? When we detect psychological pain and fear, should our reaction be one of sympathy? Can we set aside our disgust for the terrible acts the criminal committed and try to relieve his pain? A fully developed empathy will respond to the feeling expressed without regard to the personal history of the one suffering. This does mean that we turn the criminal free or overlook his criminal acts, but our empathic capacity is triggered by the expression of pain or fear. Indeed, many who have a well-developed capacity for empathy are opposed to capital punishment or any punishment that is not strictly needed to protect society. The deliberate infliction of pain is ruled out.

Along similar lines, we might ask whether empathic citizens should have sympathy for the suffering of enemies. Anticipating the fear and pain of enemies (or future enemies) should provide a strong incentive to avoid war. Stories that invite empathic concern for enemies are central to peace studies, but they may be difficult to discuss if the events depicted are current; caught up in our own pain, we find it hard to empathize with those who are hurting us. It might be better to start with the story of Achilles and his cruelty in the *Iliad,* asking how anyone could become so devoid of empathy (Shay 1994; Tatum 2004; Weil 1977). Could this happen to one of us (to *me*)? In an example such as Bill's, empathy may be triggered by a lively sense of justice. In our second examples, however, empathy invited by immediate sensitivity to expressions of pain may promote a newer and more generous sense of social justice. By providing terrible experience vicariously and probing it deeply, we hope to encourage empathic development that will contribute to both social justice and world peace.

References

Abbott, E. A. (1952). *Flatland.* New York: Dover.

Ayers, W. (1993). *To teach: The journey of a teacher.* New York: Teachers College.

Booth, W. C. (1988). *The vocation of a teacher.* Chicago: University of Chicago Press.

Buber, M. (1965). *Between man and man.* New York: Macmillan.

Candib, L. (1995). *Medicine and the family: A feminist perspective.* New York: Basic Books.

Clandinin, D. J., Davies, A., Hogan, P., & Kennard, B. (Eds.). (1993). *Learning to teach, teaching to learn.* New York: Teachers College.

Colsant, L. C. (1995). 'Hey, man, why do we gotta take this?'...Learning to listen to students. In J. G. Nicholls & T. Thorkildsen (Eds.), *Reasons for learning.* New York: Teachers College.

Cross, M., & Ewen, D. (1953). *Milton Cross' encyclopedia of the great composers and their music.* Garden City: Doubleday.

Dickens, C. (1982). *Hard times.* Harmondsworth: Penguin. (Original work published 1854)

Ellsworth, E. (1989). Why doesn't this feel empowering? Working through the repressive myth of critical pedagogy. *Harvard Educational Review, 59*(3), 297–324.

Frost, R. (1949). *Complete poems of Robert Frost.* New York: Henry Holt.

Greene, M. (1988). *The dialectic of freedom.* New York: Teachers College.

Greene, M. (2007). The arches of experience. In L. Bresler (Ed.), *International handbook of research in arts education,* Part I. Dordrecht: Springer.

Grumet, M. R. (1988). *Bitter milk.* Amherst: University of Massachusetts Press.

Hansen, D. (1995). *The gall to teach.* New York: Teachers College.

Hoffman, M. (2000). *Empathy and moral development: Implications for caring and justice.* New York: Cambridge University Press.

Hooks, B. (1994). *Teaching to transgress: Education as the practice of freedom.* New York: Routledge.

Hume, D. (1983). *An enquiry concerning the principles of morals.* Indianapolis: Hackett.

Jackson, P. W. (1992). *Untaught lessons.* New York: Teachers College.

Kant, I. (1983). *Ethical philosophy: The metaphysics of morals* (trans: Ellington, I. W.). Indianapolis: Hackett.

Larson, M. S. (1977). *The rise of professionalism.* Berkley: University of California Press.

Leacock, S. (1956). Common sense and the universe. In J. R. Newman (Ed.), *The world of mathematics* (Vol. 4). New York: Simon and Schuster.

Lewis, C. S. (1955). *The abolition of man: How education develops man's sense of morality.* New York: Collier Books.

Metzger, W. P. (1987). A spectre is haunting American scholars: The spectre of "professionism". *Educational Researcher, 16*(6), 10–21.

Narayan, K. (1991). 'According to feelings': Teaching and healing with stories. In C. Witherell & N. Noddings (Eds.), *Stories lives tell: Narrative and dialogue in education.* New York: Teachers College.

Noddings, N. (1984). *Caring: A feminine approach to ethics and moral education.* Berkley: University of California Press.

Noddings, N. (1992). *The challenge to care in schools.* New York: Teachers College.

Noddings, N. (1996). Accident, awareness, and actualization. In P. Peterson & A. Neumann (Eds.), *Research and everyday life: The personal origins of educational inquiry.* New York: Teachers College.

Noddings, N. (2010). *From maternal instinct to morality: The emergence of care ethics.* Berkley: University of California Press.

Orwell, G. (1956). *The Orwell reader.* New York: Harcourt, Brace.

Pagano, J. A. (1990). *Exiles and communities: Teaching in the patriarchal wilderness.* Albany: State University of New York Press.

Scheffler, I. (1995). *Teachers of my youth.* Boston: Kluwer.

Scheffler, I. (1996). Response to Professors Pekarsky, Yob, & Brown. In A. Neiman (Ed.), *Philosophy of education 1995.* Urbana-Champaign: University of Illinois.

Shay, J. (1994). *Achilles in Vietnam: Combat trauma and the undoing of character.* New York: Scribner.

Slote, M. (2007). *The ethics of care and empathy.* New York: Routledge.

Starr, P. (1982). *The social transformation of American medicine.* New York: Basic Books.

Tatum, J. (2004). *The Mourner's song.* Chicago: University of Chicago Press.

Twain, M. (1982). *Mississippi writings.* New York: Literary Classics of the United States.

Unamuno, M. D. (1954). *Tragic sense of life* (trans: Crawford Flitch, J.E.). New York: Dover.

Watson, J. (1985). *Nursing: Human science and human care.* Norwalk: Appleton-Century-Crofts.

Weil, S. (1977). The Simone Weil reader. In G. A. Panichas (Ed.), The Simone Weil reader. New York: Moyer Bell.

Chapter 11
Emotion, Identity and Teacher Learning: Becoming a Primary Mathematics Teacher

Jeremy Hodgen and Mike Askew

The difficulties of professional development and learning amongst mathematics teachers are well-documented (Clarke 1994). The problem is particularly acute amongst primary (or elementary) teachers (Bibby 1999). For many primary teachers, their relationship with mathematics is a fraught with anxiety and emotion, much of it relating to their negative experiences of school mathematics (Buxton 1981). These negative experiences parallel the experiences of most school students who regard mathematics as dull, boring and irrelevant (Osborne et al. 1997). Even many successful students perceive themselves to have failed at the subject (Brown et al. 2008; Stobart et al. 2006). We believe that, to break this vicious circle, there is an urgent need to teach mathematics differently. But moving beyond teaching mathematics as a set of dull and decontextualised procedures requires developing a different and more positive relationship with the discipline (Noddings 1992). Yet, since Buxton's pioneering study more than two decades ago, and aside from the notable exceptions of Bibby (2002) and Povey (1997), there has been little theoretical or empirical research exploring teachers' emotional relationships with mathematics. In this chapter, we seek to address this by exploring how teachers can become engaged with professional development (PD) in primary mathematics despite these difficulties. Our focus is on how emotion can be understood as having both individual and social dimensions.

This discussion is based on an analysis of our interactions as a researcher (Jeremy) and as a Higher Education teacher (Mike) with a primary teacher, Ursula, as she participated in professional development in mathematics. We focus on how she became drawn to mathematics despite her initial avoidance of the subject and relate this to the social aspects of learning. Our central theme is the developing narrative that Ursula constructed concerning her relationships with school mathematics and mathematics teachers, one of whom was Mike.

This chapter was first published in the Oxford Review of Education, 33 (4), 2007: 469–487.

J. Hodgen (✉)
Department of Education and Professional Studies, King's College London, London, UK
e-mail: jeremy.hodgen@kcl.ac.uk

C. Day, J. C.-K. Lee (eds.), *New Understandings of Teacher's Work*, Professional Learning and Development in Schools and Higher Education 6,
DOI 10.1007/978-94-007-0545-6_11, © Springer Science+Business Media B.V. 2011

Ursula: The Case Study

Ursula[1] was a teacher-researcher in the Primary Cognitive Acceleration in Mathematics Education (CAME) Project between November 1997 and July 2001 (Johnson et al. 2004). As part of this project, Jeremy studied Ursula's professional development (alongside that of five other teacher-researchers) (Hodgen and Johnson 2004). Eighteen months previous to this, she had attended a 20-day mathematics course that had been taught by Mike.[2]

Our interest in Ursula is as a "telling" rather than a "typical" case (Mitchell 1984). When we first met her in the mid-1990s, Ursula was a primary class teacher and Mathematics Co-ordinator at Parkway School, a primary school in outer London. Ursula trained as a primary teacher in the early 1990s. Later, in the second year of the Primary CAME Project, she became a Numeracy Consultant. In many respects, Ursula's professional development in mathematics was somewhat unusual for a primary teacher. First, whilst the 20 days scheme was a substantial PD programme, only a minority of English primary teachers, mainly school mathematics co-ordinators, took part directly in the training. Second, Primary CAME was an exceptionally extended and intense PD experience, involving one-day release every fortnight for three years. Moreover, as part of the project, she co-wrote curriculum materials, led PD sessions for other teachers and gave research presentations to teachers and academics. Finally, Ursula's PD was unusual in that it was substantial. Initially, Ursula described her feelings about mathematics as follows:

> It is just a whole negative thing. I assume that I can't do anything, I have a complete mental blank. Whenever I see anything like that I just get a mental blank and I just think—I can't do that. [...] As, Bs, Xs and Ys, all mixed together, put in a few brackets and I'm gone, I'm away with the fairies.

By 2001, she had moved from this position of disconnection in mathematics to one in which she (both as a Numeracy Consultant and a Primary CAME teacher-research) had led many PD sessions focusing on algebra (including several sessions in which Jeremy observed her successfully and confidently responding to questions involving "As, Bs, Xs...Ys...[and]...brackets.") More significantly perhaps, she identified herself positively as a teacher of mathematics:

> I like being a specialist. I like having one subject. I like being a maths teacher.

In relation to mathematics, Ursula shifted from what Povey (1997) describes as a position of silence, or disconnection with mathematics, to a position of *author/ity*, a belief in her own active role in the construction of mathematical knowledge. Whilst the success of Ursula's professional change may seem unsurprising given the level

[1] Ursula and the name of her school mathematics teacher, Miss Barker, are pseudonyms.

[2] The 20-day course was part of a scheme funded by the then Department for Education and Science for primary mathematics teachers aimed at increasing their subject knowledge and pedagogical skills as well as their ability to support other teachers in improving their teaching of mathematics (McNamara et al. 2002).

of PD that she engaged in, this degree of change is unusual amongst primary teachers in relation to mathematics teaching. Indeed, even a substantial amount of PD does not guarantee learning (e.g. Spillane 1999) and we note that of the six teachers in Jeremy's study only Urusla and one other teacher appeared to change substantially in relation to mathematics (Hodgen 2003).

Methodology and Context

This paper arose in the first instance from analysis conducted for Jeremy's doctoral study. In this study, data were qualitative and included observations of seminars, lessons and PD sessions led by Ursula and other teacher-researchers, semi-structured interviews with individuals and groups, and structured mathematical interviews.[3] Jeremy's role was as a participant observer. Analysis was conducted using techniques drawn from grounded theory (Strauss and Corbin 1998), but adopting the more theory-driven approach that Charmaz (2000) describes as constructivist grounded theory. In addition, Kvale's (1996) technique of narrative structuring was used to understand the teachers' trajectories of participation. These on-going analyses were shared and discussed with the six teachers. (See Hodgen 2003, for a more detailed discussion of the methods and methodology.) Our analysis draws mainly from the seminars, PD sessions and the interviews. This reflects the way in which emotion emerged in the study. Essentially, Ursula talked about her emotional engagement in these settings, although we note that her participation in PD sessions was that of a teacher rather than a participant.[4]

The focus of Jeremy's study was the professional development associated with Primary CAME. Ursula's identification of the importance of Mike's 20-day course in her development as a mathematics teacher led us to analyse and compare this to Mike's own recollections of this course.[5] This later analysis was conducted largely through an extended conversation between ourselves drawing again on Kvale's (1996) methodological approach.

---

[3] The main data set for Jeremy's doctoral study consisted of 39 day seminars, 41 lesson observations, 16 PD sessions and 25 interviews. Of these, 4 lesson observations were of Ursula's lessons, 6 of the interviews involved Ursula, whilst she was involved in all the day seminars and all but 1 of the PD sessions. Seminars, lessons and PD sessions were taped and partially transcribed. Excerpts for transcription were identified as potential critical incidents using participant fieldnotes as in previous research. Interviews were fully transcribed. This data set was supplemented by records of more informal discussions, general fieldnotes and project documentation, in particular drafts of lesson materials.

[4] We acknowledge the point made by one anonymous reviewer that the classroom is a crucial community in understanding teacher identity. However, we note that, after the first year when she became a Numeracy Consultant, the majority of Ursula's teaching was in leading PD sessions.

[5] Ursula gave permission for the data to be shared between us.

The Context: Primary CAME and the National Numeracy Strategy (NNS)

Primary CAME was itself one element of a large five-year research programme investigating primary mathematics in England, the Leverhulme Numeracy Research Programme (LNRP). (See Millett et al. 2004, for an overview of LNRP, the context in which it took place and the aspects of the programme focusing on teachers' professional development.) Primary CAME drew on a substantial body of work in secondary education focusing on the development of students' thinking informed by Vygotskian and Piagetian psychology (Shayer and Adey 2002). Secondary CAME has been shown to have substantial long-term effects on student achievement (Shayer and Adhami 2007) and aimed to extend this approach for upper primary school students.[6] One result of the project is a series of 24 "Thinking Maths" lessons specifically for primary (Johnson et al. 2003).

This research took place alongside the introduction of the NNS, a substantial policy initiative in primary mathematics education in England. To support the implementation of the NNS, a national training programme was introduced supported by a cohort of newly appointed Numeracy Consultants. Although the NNS was not strictly mandatory, the vast majority of schools in England and Wales, including all those involved in Primary CAME, adopted the NNS.

Ursula and the other teacher-researchers' professional development in Primary CAME was somewhat unusual in that it was integrated within the project's wider work. During the first year of the project the research team met fortnightly for day-long seminars. A typical meeting included one- or two-lesson simulations, a session reflecting on lessons taught and discussion on an aspect of the CAME approach or theory, taking an approach that Shayer and Adhami (2007) describe as "a constructive criticism of normal instructional teaching in mathematics" (p. 287). The seminar agendas were flexible and much of the discussion was open-ended, lively and wide-ranging with at times heated debates about the nature of teaching and learning. Alongside the research seminars, Ursula and the other teacher-researchers taught CAME lessons. Initially, these lessons were taken exclusively from the secondary materials, in order to communicate key aspects of the CAME approach. As the project developed, the teachers themselves suggested new contexts for lessons. Many of these lesson development trials were either team-taught or taught with other research team members observing.

Identity, Learning and Professional Change

Central to our analysis is Wenger's (1998) conception of identity as located in communities of practice and his understanding of learning in terms of identity construction:

[6] Primary CAME focused on Year 5 and Year 6 primary school students (aged 9–11).

> Building an identity consists of negotiating the meanings of our experience of membership in social communities. The concept of identity serves as a pivot between the social and the individual, so that each can be talked about in terms of the other. It avoids a simplistic individual-social dichotomy without doing away with the distinction. The resulting perspective is neither individualistic nor abstractly institutional or societal. It does justice to the lived experience of identity while recognizing its social character—it is the social, the cultural, the historical with a human face. (p. 145)

Here, Wenger highlights the role of both human agency and social structure in the construction of identity. Learning involves individuals acting within and on social structures. Similarly, Carr (2001) argues that learning is a negotiation between the individual learner and the social context in which "a culturally and personally located social schema" may be "transacted, redefined…resisted and, like discourse, called upon when the moment is opportune" (p. 527). Schifter (1996) conceives of teacher change in terms of teachers constructing "narratives of professional identity" that draw on their experiences in different communities (p. 2). She stresses the plurality of teacher professional identity:

> These teachers enact multiple identities: as mathematical thinkers, as managers of classroom process, as monitors of their students' learning, as colleagues, and as members of the wider education community. 'Identities' in this sense—more a matter of what one does than who one thinks one is—are constructed in and realised through practices. (p. 2)

It is important to note here that, whilst Schifter sees these different aspects of identity as constructed through practices, these identities cut across the communities of practice a teacher participates in. Thus, in contrast to the notion of identity simply as membership of a distinct community, this conception of a primary teacher's identity might be as a mathematics teacher, for example, which could be enacted in a variety of distinct communities, including the classroom, planning sessions with colleagues, the wider school, community, professional communities and more. Similarly, Wenger (1998) argues that an individual's identities within different communities, whilst distinct, are not wholly separate:

> An identity is thus more than just a single trajectory; instead, it should be viewed as a nexus of multimembership. As such a nexus, identity is not a unity but neither is it simply fragmented. …Considering a person as having multiple identities would miss all the subtle ways in which our various forms of participation, no matter how distinct, can interact, influence each other and require co-ordination. (p. 159)

Confronted by tensions between the different aspects of their identities, individuals are compelled to negotiate and reconcile these different forms of participation and meaning in order to construct an identity that encompasses the membership of different communities. This process of identity reconciliation is central to an individual's ability to make connections and transfer meaning and knowledge between practices.

Holland et al. (1998) take the idea of identity and agency further by using the notion of co-development to emphasise the ways in which the change of individuals, practices and communities are inter-linked and interdependent. They point to the space for human agency in inventing and authoring new practices and ideas. Thus, they conceive of teachers not only actively making sense of new situations, but also constructing new meaning in the process. Drawing on Anderson's (1983) work on nationalism, they refer to two aspects of identity, which they describe as follows:

> We make an analytic distinction between aspects of identities that have to do with figured worlds—story lines, narrativity, generic characters, and desire—and aspects that have to do with one's position relative to socially identified others, one's sense of social place, and entitlement. These figurative and positional aspects of identity interrelate in myriad ways. Sometimes they are completely coincident; sometimes one dominates over the other. (p. 125)

We find this distinction between a grounded positional identity and a figured, or imagined, identity to be very useful. Whereas positional identity is grounded in specific communities and describes how people "comprehend and enact their positions in the worlds in which they live" (Boaler and Greeno 2000, p. 173), figured identity focuses on the ways in which individuals enact the less-localised identities, such as being a mathematics teacher, that Schifter (1996) refers to.

Identity and Emotion

> [Mathematics] SUCKS and I wouldn't want to spend any more of my time looking at algebra and other crap. (13 year old student quoted in Brown et al. 2008)

> I hate maths INSET. [I feel] very threatened—there have been times when I've wanted to go out but I end up sitting with [the headteacher] sometimes—we both giggle our way through because I think she feels as bad as me but she is certainly very uncomfortable doing it—I feel everyone knows that I can't do it—I think automatically when something turns up—I think I can't do this—I can't do it—and it's like being 13 again and I've never got over that and I don't think I will. (Primary Teacher quoted in Bibby 1999, p. 227)

Mathematics generates stronger emotive reactions than other school subjects (Hoyles 1980).[7] As we have already noted, for many primary teachers these reactions are negative. Professional change any subject is difficult (Hawley and Valli 1999). Professional change in mathematics is thus doubly difficult (Clarke 1994). The notion of identity provides a way of understanding this difficulty. Fundamental changes in teachers' beliefs and knowledge necessitate fundamental changes to teachers' identities involving far more than "fixing" or "topping up" teachers' "inadequate" knowledge. Professional change, then, involves at least in part becoming a "different" teacher and a "different" person. Becoming "different" involves letting go of what one has been at the same time as maintaining the more fundamental aspects of one's identity. Drawing on Hollway and Jefferson's (2000) notion of the defended self, Barton et al. (2005) highlight how learning and change may be perceived as deeply emotionally threatening to a teacher's identity. Alternatively, becoming "different" can be intensely attractive. (See, for example, the stories of teachers in Schifter 1996.) In order to conceptualise this deep interconnection between emotion and identity, we draw on three sources.

---

[7] It is important to note that Hoyles (1980) found that mathematics was unusual amongst school subjects in the intensity of both positive and negative attitudes reported by learners.

First, we see emotion as deeply connected to the figured aspects of identity and to the role of imagination and desire. Lacan conceives of identity in terms of the desire for an unattainable completeness: "as an individual I am forever trying to complete the picture I have of myself in relation to the world around me and the others who also inhabit it" (Brown and Jones 2001, p. 10). Lacanian theory is particularly appropriate, because of the way in which pleasure is seen as dialectically linked to pain. Thus, it provides a way of locating the motivation to sustain change in relation to the very real difficulty of this for teachers.

Second, we see emotion as grounded in an individual's positional identity—enacted and constructed within specific communities:

> [L]earning is perceived as a form of engagement that enables [learners] to actualize their identity through participation in activities situated in a specific context. Their understanding of and behaviour in the mathematics classroom is function of the interplay between who they are (their identity), and the specific classroom context. Who they are, what they value, what matters to them in what way in this situation is revealed to them through their emotions. (Op 't Eynde et al. 2006, p. 194)

Op't Eynde, De Corte, and Verschaffel's emphasis on values points to the ways in which positional and figured aspects of identity interact. An individual's figured identity as a mathematics teacher, for example, can only be enacted in particular local communities.

Third, we draw on DeBellis and Goldin's (2006) analysis of knowledge and emotions in which they highlight the relationship between cognition and emotions and the importance of developing a personal relationship with mathematics. DeBellis and Goldin highlight both mathematical intimacy and mathematical integrity as central features to developing positive relationships with mathematics:

> Mathematical intimacy refers to deep, *vulnerable* emotional engagement an individual may have with mathematics. Mathematical integrity refers to the individual's fundamental commitment to mathematical truth, search for mathematical understanding, or moral character guiding mathematical study. (p. 132, our emphasis)

We note here DeBellis and Goldin's focus on the vulnerability associated with such mathematical intimacy—intimacy of whatever kind involves some degree of threat to one's identity. (See Singh 1998, for an example of this vulnerability in an extremely successful mathematician.) This focus on the relationship between how mathematics is known and emotion resonates strongly with the work of Bibby (2002) and Povey (1997) and is an issue we explore further in the following discussion.

Ursula's School Experience: Disconnection with Mathematics

We begin by analysing the origin of Ursula's disconnection with mathematics. Our focus here is on an incident at secondary school to which she attributed her negative relationship with mathematics. This incident was clearly pivotal to Ursula since she told and re-told it to Jeremy several times. Prior to the incident described below, she had been identified as mathematically able. She was in a small top set group who were taking a mathematics extension examination, an O/A, aimed at high attainers in mathematics at the same time as GCSE.[8] This O/A course was taught in after-school sessions by her mathematics teacher, Miss Barker:

> that [the O/A] was after school, and that was with Miss Barker. And Miss Barker was actually, in retrospect, I think she was probably a very good teacher, because she did try to stand at the front and teach us. But I remember going from what I considered to be things that were really easy, drill and practice things, to this lesson where there was just this enormous algebraic equation going across the board. Absolutely enormous, and I'd walked in late because it was after school and I wasn't really over-keen on this, and I'd missed the first lesson, and I couldn't come to grips with this at all. And that was that. Walked out the classroom and didn't go back again. [...] Supposed to work something out from it and everybody else in the room seemed to be able to do it except me. Because I'd kind of missed out on what I was meant to be doing with it. [...] In fact, I could quite happily probably tell you for the last two years I probably didn't go to any maths lessons because I can't remember them at all, apart from the after school one. [...] The only good thing about it was I kind of looked around the room and thought—mm, this is an interesting group to be in. But that's it. [...] Yeah, there were some exceptional high fliers in that. It was a very small group. There must have only been about six of us. But most of them were the exceptional high fliers that just don't bear thinking about, you know, in your school year, they don't exist. They just get everything right, and you assume they do, and they don't exist as people. [LAUGHS.] But, only two girls [...] But I can remember the room as well. I can remember the room in minute detail. It obviously had huge impact because I could remember everything about it. [...] And knowing how well I didn't get on with Miss Barker it's quite likely that she made some derogatory comment that I didn't understand. Although I don't remember her doing it. It wouldn't have surprised me if she did.

There are a range of fascinating and important issues in this powerful account that resonate with the literature on attitudes to mathematics: the construction of mathematical ability and failure (Boaler et al. 2000); the link between ability in mathematics and a lack of effort (Bartholomew 2000); the gendered nature of the subject (Mendick 2006); the labelling of what one can do as "really easy" common sense and what one cannot do as incomprehensible (Coben 2000); and identification of those who can do mathematics as different and alien (Picker and Berry 2000). For our current purposes, we highlight Ursula's sudden incomprehension of mathematics in the form of the "enormous algebraic equation", her shame and the personalisation of both of these with her teacher, Miss Barker. Student's difficulties with algebra are well-documented (Hart 1981) and indeed many people's negative attitudes to mathematics are also associated with algebra (e.g. Mullis et al. 2004; Osborne et al. 1997). It seems likely that at least some other students in the O/A group had some difficulty with the "enormous algebraic equation". Yet, her perception that "everybody else in the room seemed to be able to do [mathematics] except me" is common amongst secondary school students (Brown et al. 2008). Here, Ursula experienced what Bibby (2002) describes as a strong sense of shame.

---

[8] The General Certificate in Secondary Education (GCSE) in England. GCSE examinations are generally taken at the end of compulsory schooling (age 16). Almost all students sit GCSE mathematics. The O/A is no longer available. Only a relatively small proportion of students took the O/A and it was not available in all schools.

In seeing herself "suddenly through the eyes of others" (Giddens 1991, p. 65), she experienced a threat to her identity:

> Shame bears directly on self-identity because it is essentially anxiety about the adequacy of the narrative by means of which the individual sustains a coherent biography. (Giddens 1991, p. 65)

The "huge impact" of this shame is evident not only in the language that Ursula used and in her repeated re-telling of the incident but also the "minute detail" of her recall. The role of Miss Barker's likely "derogatory comment" is a significant feature of Ursula's shame. In her study of primary teachers, Bibby (1999) also highlights the frequent personalisation of mathematics failure with a secondary teacher. Ursula's resultant disconnection with mathematics is evident in the physical distancing: "Walked out the classroom and didn't go back again." Finally, we note that Ursula's account is of a very familiar and recognisable classroom situation with the "enormous algebraic equation going across the board", the "drill and practice" and the teacher "stand[ing] at the front and teach[ing]".

Ursula's Professional Development: Re-connecting with Mathematics

Here we focus on two key moments in Ursula's professional development as a mathematics teacher: the 20-day course taught by Mike and Primary CAME. We note that there were other important aspects to Ursula's professional learning, in particular her close collaborative relationship with another teacher (Hodgen 2003; Hodgen and Johnson 2004).

The 20-Day Course: An Opportunity to Challenge the Authority of the Teacher

We now turn to a consideration of the 20-day course that Mike taught. Ursula was something of a reluctant attendee. She had been "sent on" the course because she "became a maths co-ordinator by accident [...] and the maths co-ordinator at our school left [...] and I'd written [...] the only schemes of work that the school had at the time". Despite this reluctance Ursula identified this course as crucial in her professional learning as a mathematics teacher, describing it to Jeremy as follows:

> it was just a good, a good course. It was a very inspirational. [...] this is good maths practice, here some ideas you can go back and try. [...] But it was all about, it was maths at adult level, I suppose, and maths at children level, [...] He [Mike] did it well, 'cos we, we went back and we tried things but we also wanted to do things. So we were doing things on the train on the way home and we were phoning each other up and comparing how things had gone.

However, our focus here is on an incident in which she got frustrated with Mike about doing "maths for maths sake". This incident is particularly significant because each time she told the story of Miss Barker and the "enormous algebraic equation", she immediately recounted her frustration with Mike:

> The other person who got me very frustrated because I didn't understand was Mike. [...] I obviously hadn't been listening and didn't know where it came from, and he was asking people to work out...about tangents...and there was something about it. But again it was using the vocabulary that I couldn't remember quite. And I got really cross with him and I kept saying—why do you want to put a line on a circle? For God's sake, why does anybody want to work this out with a line on a circle? I couldn't understand why anybody wanted to do it. [...] You had to work something out around this, but I don't know what you had to work out because I'd given up by that point. And I just got cross with him. But again, I think it was into the realms of maths for maths sake. [...] I just remember being very frustrated and feeling like I could have quite happily just sat there and cried, or screamed at him, one or the other. So I shouted at him instead.

The repeated narrative connection of Miss Barker with Mike as the "other person I got frustrated with" suggests that Ursula was in some way working through her difficulties with the previous teacher. Further, given the way in which Ursula's negative attitude to mathematics was so personalised in this teacher, we suggest that this incident had helped her to find her voice mathematically and, thus, move on from the position of silence that we referred to earlier.

In fact, Ursula had made a very strong impression on Mike, but his perception was that she had not enjoyed the 20-day course and he had failed to inspire her about mathematics and mathematics teaching. Mike does not recall an incident involving tangents. But he does remember Ursula questioning him on many occasions about doing "maths for maths sake". For example:

> Ursula called me over.
> "My 5 quid calculator has got a 1/x button on, so why doesn't this expensive one?"
> "Well, it does," I replied " it's that x^{-1} button."
> This seemed an opportunity to explore powers and so I stopped everyone to go through the argument as to why, for consistency, mathematicians had decided to define x^{-1} as 1/x. While the teachers' nods during my explanation suggested that they were following me in the logic, afterwards there was quite a lot of muttering going on at Ursula's table.
> "Is there anything you are not clear about?" I enquired.
> "No, we follow your argument," Ursula replied. "But we were just saying to each other, 'why would anyone ever want to do that in the first place?'"

Whilst Ursula's and Mike's recollection of this incident do differ, they are similar in that they relate to issues of purpose and motivation for doing mathematics. Whilst our analysis here is to some extent more speculative than elsewhere, this does highlight an importance of allowing space for learners' own voices. Facilitating space for learners to express doubt, dissent, interest, disinterest can enable them to develop understanding of why people might do mathematics, the very question that Ursula asked. But, as Amit and Fried (2005) note, such a practice is rare in mathematics classrooms.

We emphasise that this emotional space was not an explicit element of the course. Unwittingly, or at least implicitly, Mike provided such a space within which

Ursula could challenge the authority figure of the teacher thus beginning to repair her own emotional relationship with mathematics and to develop a different and more positive image of mathematics teaching (Bibby 2002). We suggest that this in turn enabled Ursula to begin to understand the attraction of mathematics and the possibility of developing Debellis and Goldin's (2006) mathematical intimacy, issues that we turn to in the next section.

Engaging with CAME: Creating a Desire to Be a Mathematics Teacher

Unlike the 20-day course, Ursula positively volunteered to participate in CAME. Nevertheless, the experience was at times extremely difficult: "I just can't do this"; exasperating: "I'm so annoyed, I'm I feel like smacking him [one of the researchers]"; painful: "this meeting is a nightmare"; and confusing, "What is special? I'm doing this already." Despite this, Ursula persevered with the project working "past midnight" at times. In this section, we examine what motivated her engagement despite these difficulties and frustrations.

CAME, like many reform initiatives in mathematics education, places considerable emphasis on talk and argument about mathematics. This is very different to the norm in most mathematics classrooms. Ursula focused on this in a description of an early CAME lesson:

> They were really noisy. I had stand up arguments between children about the maths, shouting at each other. If anyone had come in, they'd have thought it was chaos, but I loved it.

The image presented here was certainly an exciting one in which children were engaged in mathematical talk. However, the way in which Ursula expressed this message is very significant. Schools and classrooms are generally characterised by order, control and turn-taking. "Chaos" and children "shouting at each other" are the very antithesis of what classrooms are expected to be like. Certainly, Ursula used these descriptions in order to emphasise that mathematics in this incident was different to ordinary primary mathematics lessons. But, this went beyond mere emphasis. Her description of the children's mathematical talk was framed in language that implicitly challenged her own authority as the teacher. Indeed, she presented the children as arguing about mathematics without apparent teacher intervention. This is in marked contrast to the culture of many mathematics classrooms—including Miss Barker's secondary mathematics classroom described above—where authority for what is right or wrong, together with what counts as mathematics, rests with the teacher and the textbook. Thus, in this brief description Ursula pointed to three inter-related issues in relation to school mathematics: the children's control of the mathematics; the contrast with other people's mathematics lessons; and, her own strongly expressed belief in this way of working. This combination was typical of the descriptions she gave of CAME lessons during the early stages of the project.

However, equally important to these messages was the form in which she presented them. In particular, she presented the fractions lesson not simply as an alternative to the norm, but in terms that emphasised this event's status as a deviant case. These points about authority, and the marked contrast with ordinary mathematics lessons, were emphasised by her statement that "anyone", implying anyone who taught in the ordinary way, would have judged the episode as chaotic. This highlights the intuitive and undeveloped nature of Ursula's beliefs in relation to mathematical authority at this stage. Ursula believed that, contrary to her own experiences, authority should be dependent not on the teacher but on mathematical discussion. However, whilst she believed this to be the case, she did not know it to be the case and would have had difficulty justifying this belief to others. So, despite her presentation of these beliefs as strongly held, they were not strongly warranted. Indeed, Edwards and Potter (1992) argue that strong and emotive claims like Ursula's "I loved it" are typical of the way such contested and weakly warranted beliefs are presented. Contested and uncertain beliefs need such strong support. The more consensual and certain beliefs are, the less they need such support.

Eighteen months later, writing a paper for an academic conference with another teacher-researcher, Ursula described the same incident very differently:

> There followed a brief silence and then uproar. Many of the children made intuitive guesses but the result was that of an equal split between the whisky glass, the water glass and them both holding the same amount of liquid. Very quickly the pupils attempted to explain their answer and the majority of them instinctively began to draw their various glasses. Some children used colour, others used fractions, a few used ratio.

The contrast with Ursula's earlier description of the lesson is striking. In this later writing, she was certainly celebrating the children's excitement and linking this to positive changes in children's attitudes towards mathematics. However, in this extract she explicitly emphasised the mathematical activities of explanation and representation. The earlier "chaos" and "stand up arguments" have been replaced with the "uproar" of "intuitive guesses" and "pupils attempt[ing] to explain their answer" using a range of different approaches to tackling the problem. This description was preceded with a general explanation of the CAME approach of which the following is an excerpt:

> One of the outstanding features of Thinking Maths lessons…is the enthusiasm with which classes tend to greet them. …For several children these lessons have changed the way in which they view maths, engendering a far more positive attitude to the subject than previously held. …In many ways this excitement reflects not just the content and structure of the lessons but, equally importantly, the fact that one important feature is the dialogue that is central to this way of teaching and learning, not just between teacher and pupil but also between pupil and pupil. The lessons are about all members of the class, including the teacher, exploring mathematical ideas and challenges together in a climate in which everyone's views are valued.

Here, the children's excitement was related explicitly to the central importance of mathematical dialogue and to the climate of the mathematics classroom. Here, unlike the earlier quote, she explicitly included the teacher in the dialogue. This intense engagement of teachers and children is evident in the notes of another lesson (team-taught and recorded jointly by Ursula and another teacher-researcher):

> Whole class (teachers n'all) spontaneous applause. All the children know that they have succeeded—right on the dot of lunchtime. Loads of praise given. We told them we were going to stop after they had found a suitable method of grouping, thinking they would be unable to cope with the rest.

Of course, these descriptions had both different audiences and different purposes. The writing of an academic paper is of a different genre and requires greater crafting than a contribution to a seminar discussion. However, a key difference here is that Ursula was able to write in this academic genre, to craft the description and to provide the necessary justifications to her position. Moreover, this fluency and confidence featured widely in her later more developed discourse. The following quote, in which Ursula looked back on her earlier confusion, exemplifies this:

> To begin with the confusion with me was the lessons seem relatively closed. You seem to be closing down on children when, you know, I understand from courses, the 20 day course and looking at investigative ways of doing things where you're trying to open things up all the time. The big confusion for me with CAME is you're closing things down for children and narrowing it down all the time. Whereas now I think in any maths lesson, I think I see the questions in two ways and I can choose now which one I want to do. I can quite happily close down the children and focus in a little more. Or I can open it up wider. So I've got more the repertoire of both things, I think.

Here, in contrast to her earlier comment in which she invoked her existing open-ended and investigative teaching and the CAME approach as binary opposites, she saw them rather as complementary parts of her mathematics teaching repertoire: the investigative approach seeking breadth; and, CAME seeking depth. Her earlier confusion was that in seeking depth, CAME appeared to be "closing down on children". Despite the presentation by the academics of CAME as progressive and open, this apparently more closed approach seemed to her to be at times closer to the normal practice in school mathematics than to the investigative approach she had been developing.

A crucial difference in these accounts was the way in which Ursula contrasted CAME with ordinary primary mathematics teaching. In both the later accounts, rather than as deviant to the norm, she presented CAME not only as a viable alternative but also as one that encompassed and developed ordinary primary practice. The descriptions were presented less emotively and more neutrally. Moreover, in integrating the importance of mathematical dialogue with explicit mathematical behaviours, the later comments demonstrate the confidence and fluency explanations that Berliner argues are characteristic of experienced, expert teachers' discourse (cited in Brown and McIntyre 1993). Ursula had resolved her earlier confusion about the CAME approach and her earlier intuitive ideas about authority in school mathematics were more strongly held, and, more significantly, were more strongly warranted.

The use of the strong emotive term of "love" in these extracts is of further significance or Ursula's identity. Within the constraints and affordances of the past and present, an individual can "explore, take risks and create unlikely connections" (Wenger 1998, p. 185). Indeed, an individual's identity, and ultimately legitimacy, within a community depends not simply on their acceptance by existing participants as in Lave and Wenger's (1991) early work, but on the individual's identification with the community. In expressing "love" for her image of the chaotic and different practice of CAME, a practice which as a newcomer she could only imagine, Ursula was articulating a desire not only for this different way of teaching but also to be a different teacher herself.

We use the term desire deliberately to emphasise not just the personal and emotional investment in professional change but also the compulsion to change that Ursula experienced. There is considerable evidence in the literature that the process of professional change is confusing and painful. (For example, see the teachers' stories in Schifter and Fosnot 1993). Indeed, Ursula herself expressed extreme pain and confusion at various times during the first year of the project. Yet, at the same time, Ursula found the possibility of change deeply attractive in terms of her teaching, through excitement and interest, and beyond the classroom in terms of her professional status and future career. Despite the pain of this process, Ursula was driven to engage with CAME, a drive she expressed as love. Thus, she experienced what Lacan calls "jouissance…which simultaneously attracts and repels" (Zizek quoted in Brown et al. 1993, p. 14). Ursula's motivation to change was not simply that she perceived the need nor even an active choice because the new practices were interesting: it was rather that she was compelled to change through this powerful emotive and motivating force of desire.

Yet, this desire was not simply an external force acting on Ursula. Indeed, she actively created and maintained this compulsion to change:

> There are bits sort of similar, but I have to make myself convinced that it is different—somehow. But I don't know why I have to do that, but I do. I have to make it seem different. The kids notice a difference. They seem to feel a difference, but I think that's because we do a whole thing in one lesson. And there aren't bits coming right from other, you know, it's not a rolling programme. You know there aren't bits coming in from here, there and everywhere. We're not going off at a tangent. We're not doing this, that and the other.

The difference that Ursula had difficulty perceiving is something more than the surface features of the lessons, because she has to convince herself not to do her normal teaching practices of "bits coming in from here, there and everywhere" and "going off at a tangent". Ursula had to convince herself about CAME's difference to ordinary closed school mathematics and of the similarities to her investigative approach.

Ursula's Identity as a Mathematics Teacher: Concluding Comments

We have focused on how Ursula created an identity as a mathematics teacher by, first, engaging and challenging traditional norms of teacher authority, and, second, by constructing a strong and powerful image of a different mathematics teaching. Significantly, this image was at least initially only partially grasped and Ursula's engagement and identity construction was "facilitated by fantasy" (Evans 2000,

p. 224). Our analysis has focused largely on Ursula's role in actively constructing this identity. Yet, this individual activity was itself located socially—Ursula's individual activity could not have taken place without the opportunities afforded by the 20-day course and Primary CAME.

Discussion

Ursula's negative experience of secondary school mathematics is commonplace amongst primary teachers (Bibby 1999). One common belief amongst primary teachers is that a teacher's difficulties with mathematics enables her to better empathise with and understand children's difficulties (Goulding 2007). This can lead to teachers protecting pupils from—or defending them against—mathematics (Barton et al. 2005; see also, Nimier 1993). Often such "protection" focuses on making mathematics "simple" and "easy" by emphasising step-by-step and procedural techniques. Despite intentions otherwise, such a position is likely to reproduce the negative attitudes of mathematics as boring and irrelevant (Boaler and Greeno 2000). Whilst Ursula's case that teachers can reconnect with mathematics whilst maintaining an identity as a primary teacher, we do think that becoming more proficient at mathematics may be in tension with currently dominant conceptions of the caring aspects of a teacher's identity as a primary teacher. We are certainly not arguing here that a "caring" notion of a teacher is necessarily at odds with a care for the discipline, but we note that Ursula was intensely aware of her "difference" to other teachers in her school (Hodgen 2003). There are many descriptions of teaching that demonstrate that such an expanded notion of care can be achieved (e.g. Lampert 1990; Escalante and Dirman 1990), although many of these are located in secondary school mathematics. Our point is that currently the identities most easily and readily available to primary teachers are not associated with such an expanded notion of care. Ursula's case strongly suggests the importance of developing a more positive relationship with mathematics itself and "build[ing] a bond between the personal knowledge constructed and the mathematical content" (DeBellis and Goldin 2006, p. 138). As McLeod and McLeod (2002) note, there are very few resources suggesting (or research investigating) *how* teachers might develop beliefs and attitudes. Professional development in primary mathematics in the UK has generally focused on cognitive and pedagogic issues: teachers' mathematics subject knowledge, how children learn and teaching approaches. These issues are, of course, important. Indeed, our own professional development initiatives have focused on these issues. But, given the high emotional stakes for mathematics, such an approach is, in our view, doomed to failure unless placed within an affective frame in which teachers have space to question mathematics and mathematics teaching. We wonder how possible it is for the majority of primary teachers to resolve the tensions between the caring and nurturing aspects of primary teaching identity and a strong disciplinary focus in mathematics. For both of us, mathematics is interesting and engaging because it is inherently difficult and challenging. We believe that enabling all children (of whatever attainment level) to experience this difficulty and challenge is essential in avoiding children's perceptions of mathematics as boring and irrelevant. Developing such a strong disciplinary focus is particularly difficult for primary teachers in the UK who currently teach many other subjects aside from mathematics.

Ursula's case demonstrates the possibility of primary teachers confronting and challenging negative attitudes to mathematics and, thus, developing a mathematical voice. The professional development experiences that enabled her to achieve this were, however, unusually intense and extended. It is unlikely that such intense experiences could be replicated on a wider scale in formal professional development initiatives, although in our view considerably more resources could and should be devoted to the professional development of teachers than is currently the case in England. The challenge then is how to create both such space and opportunity for primary teachers within much less intensive professional development initiatives. Spillane (1999) argues that a necessary condition for significant professional change is the opportunity for "rich deliberations" with knowledgeable experts. Our analysis suggests that, in addition to the development of mathematical and pedagogical expertise, such rich deliberations should provide opportunities for teachers to explore their identities as mathematics teachers and learners. Creating such opportunities is far from simple. We emphasise again that emotional and identity construction activity that we have described above was not planned. Indeed, at the time of the 20-day course, Mike felt that he had been unsuccessful in teaching Ursula. We speculate that it may be that such radical change as Ursula's requires an extended period *after* a formal course for any changes to become apparent. Certainly, our work highlights the need for further research investigating the ways on the affective aspects of teacher education.

We have already pointed to the emotional difficulty for teachers engaging in professional change (Clarke 1994). Hence, in order for change to take place, teachers need what Goldsmith and Schifter (1997) describe as "a compelling reason to undertake the task of transforming their practice" (p. 46). For Ursula, this motivation was inextricably linked to her identity—her desire to be a mathematics teacher and the opportunities she had to develop a different and more positive relationship with mathematics. Ursula's case demonstrates the complexity of "creating" such motivation in that it is a construction of both individual and social activity. A crucial factor for Ursula was the space afforded to question and challenge the nature of disciplinary and teacher authority in mathematics coupled with the opportunities afforded by CAME to explore the teaching of mathematics. Elsewhere, one of us argues that the opportunity to develop, or author, lesson materials is particularly crucial (Hodgen and Johnson 2004).

Finally, whilst mathematics and primary teaching is in many ways an extreme case, our analysis has relevance for the professional development of teachers more generally. It is our belief that developing a strong disciplinary bond is central to the teaching of any subject and as such teachers need space to develop both disciplinary intimacy and integrity. Yet, as with mathematics, there is an urgent need to investigate how professional development can facilitate teachers' emotional development.

References

Amit, M., & Fried, M. N. (2005). Authority and authority relations in mathematics education: A view from an 8th grade classroom. *Educational Studies in Mathematics, 58*(2), 145–168.

Anderson, B. (1983). *Imagined communities*. London: Verso.

Bartholomew, H. (2000). *Negotiating identity in the community of the mathematics classroom*. Paper presented at the British Educational Research Association Annual Conference, Cardiff University, 7–10 September.

Barton, B., Paterson, J., Kensington-Miller, J., & Bartholomew, H. (2005). *Dodging the dragon: Strategies for professional development in low socio-economic areas*. Paper presented at the 4th International Mathematics Education and Society Conference, Gold Coast, Australia.

Bibby, T. (1999). Subject knowledge, personal history and professional change. *Teacher Development, 3*(2), 219–232.

Bibby, T. (2002). Shame: An emotional response to doing mathematics as an adult and a teacher. *British Educational Research Journal, 28*(5), 705–721.

Boaler, J., & Greeno, J. G. (2000). Identity, agency and knowing in mathematics worlds. In J. Boaler (Ed.), *Multiple perspectives on mathematics teaching and learning*. Westport: Ablex.

Boaler, J., Wiliam, D., & Brown, M. (2000). Grouping—Disaffection, polarisation and the construction of failure. *British Educational Research Journal, 26*(5), 631–648.

Brown, S., & McIntyre, D. (1993). *Making sense of teaching*. Buckingham: Open University Press.

Brown, T., & Jones, L. (2001). *Action research and postmodernism: Congruence and critique*. Buckingham: Open University Press.

Brown, T., Hardy, T., & Wilson, D. (1993). Mathematics on Lacan's couch. *For the Learning of Mathematics, 13*(1), 11–14.

Brown, M., Brown, P., & Bibby, T. (2008). 'I would rather die': Attitudes of 16 year-olds towards their future participation in mathematics. *Research in Mathematics Education, 10*(1), 3–18.

Buxton, L. (1981). *Do you panic about maths? Coping with maths anxiety*. London: Heinemann Educational Books.

Carr, M. (2001). A sociocultural approach to learning orientation in an early childhood setting. *Qualitative Studies in Education, 14*(4), 525–542.

Charmaz, K. (2000). Grounded theory: Objectivist and constructivist methods. In N. K. Denzin & Y. S. Lincoln (Eds.), *Handbook of qualitative research* (2nd ed.). London: Sage.

Clarke, D. M. (1994). Ten key principles from research for the professional development of mathematics teachers. In D. B. Aichele & A. F. Coxford (Eds.), *Professional development for teachers of mathematics: The 1994 Yearbook of the National Council of Teachers of Mathematics*. Reston: National Council of Teachers of Mathematics.

Coben, D. (2000). Mathematics or common sense? Researching "invisible" mathematics through adults' mathematics life histories. In D. Coben, J. O'Donoghue, & G. E. Fitzsimons (Eds.), *Perspectives on adults learning mathematics: Research and practice*. Dordrecht: Kluwer.

DeBellis, V., & Goldin, G. A. (2006). Affect and meta-affect in mathematical problem-solving: A representational perspective. *Educational Studies in Mathematics, 63*(2), 131–147.

Edwards, D., & Potter, J. (1992). *Discursive psychology*. London: Sage.

Escalante, J., & Dirman, J. (1990). The Jaime Escalante Mathematics Program. *Journal for Negro Education, 59*(3), 407–423.

Evans, J. (2000). *Adults' mathematical thinking and emotions: A study of numerate practices*. London: RoutledgeFalmer.

Giddens, A. (1991). *Modernity and self-identity*. Cambridge: Polity.

Goldsmith, L., & Schifter, D. (1997). Understanding teachers in transition: Characteristics of a model for developing teachers. In E. Fennema & B. S. Nelson (Eds.), *Mathematics teachers in transition*. Mahwah: Erlbaum.

Goulding, M. (2007). *Mathematical subject knowledge in primary teacher training—A view from England and Wales*. Paper presented at the Nuffield Mathematical Knowledge for Teaching Seminar Series, 11–12 January, Cambridge. http://www.maths-ed.org.uk/mkit/seminar1.html. Accessed 10 Jan 2007.

Hart, K. (Ed.). (1981). *Children's understanding of mathematics: 11–16*. London: John Murray.
Hawley, W. D., & Valli, L. (1999). The essentials of effective professional development: A new consensus. In L. Darling-Hammond & G. Sykes (Eds.), *Teaching as the learning profession: Handbook of policy and practice* (pp. 127–150). San Francisco: Jossey-Bass.
Hodgen, J. (2003). *Teacher identity and professional development in primary school mathematics*. Unpublished PhD thesis, King's College, University of London.
Hodgen, J., & Johnson, D. C. (2004). Teacher reflection, identity and belief change in the context of primary CAME. In A. Millett, M. Brown, & M. Askew (Eds.), *Primary mathematics and the developing professional*. Dordrecht: Kluwer.
Holland, D., Lachicotte, W., Skinner, D., & Cain, C. (1998). *Identity and agency in cultural worlds*. Cambridge: Harvard University Press.
Hollway, W., & Jefferson, T. (2000). *Doing qualitative research differently*. London: Sage.
Hoyles, C. (1980). *Factors in School Learning – the Pupil's View: a study with particular reference to mathematics*. Unpublished PhD thesis, University of London, London.
Johnson, D. C., Adhami, M., Shayer, M., Hodgen, J., Hafeez, R., Dubben, S., et al. (2003). *Primary CAME thinking maths: Teachers' guide*. London: BEAM Education.
Johnson, D. C., Hodgen, J., & Adhami, M. (2004). Professional development from a cognitive and social standpoint. In A. Millett, M. Brown, & M. Askew (Eds.), *Primary mathematics and the developing professional*. Dordrecht: Kluwer.
Kvale, S. (1996). *Interviews: An introduction to qualitative research interviewing*. London: Sage.
Lampert, M. (1990). When the problem is not the question and the solution is not the answer: Mathematical knowing and teaching. *American Educational Research Journal, 27*(1), 29–63.
Lave, J., & Wenger, E. (1991). *Situated learning: Legitimate peripheral participation*. Cambridge: Cambridge University Press.
McLeod, D. B., & McLeod, S. H. (2002). Synthesis—Beliefs and mathematics education: Implications for learning, teaching and research. In G. C. Leder, E. Pehkoken, & G. Törner (Eds.), *Beliefs: A hidden variable in mathematics education?* (pp. 115–123). Dordrecht: Kluwer.
McNamara, O., Jaworski, B., Rowland, T., Hodgen, J., & Prestage, S. (2002). *Developing mathematics teachers and teaching: A research monograph*. http://www.maths-ed.org.uk/mathsteachdev/index.html. Accessed 10 Jan 2007.
Mendick, H. (2006). *Masculinities in mathematics*. Buckingham: Open University Press.
Millett, A., Brown, M., & Askew, M. (Eds.). (2004). *Primary mathematics and the developing professional*. Dordrecht: Kluwer.
Mitchell, J. C. (1984). Typicality and the case study. In R. F. Ellen (Ed.), *Ethnographic research: A guide to general conduct*. London: Academic.
Mullis, I. V. S., Martin, M. O., Gonzalez, E. J., & Chrostowski, S. J. (2004). *TIMSS 2003 international mathematics report: Findings from IEA's trends in International Mathematics and Science Study at the fourth and eighth grades*. Chestnut Hill: TIMSS & PIRLS International Study Center, Boston College.
Nimier, J. (1993). Defence mechanisms against mathematics. *For the Learning of Mathematics, 13*(1), 30–34.
Noddings, N. (1992). *The challenge to care in schools: An alternative approach to education*. New York: Teachers College Press.
Op't Eynde, P., De Corte, E., & Verschaffel, L. (2006). "Accepting emotional complexity": A socio-constructivist perspective on the role of emotions in the classroom. *Educational Studies in Mathematics, 63*(2), 193–207.
Osborne, J., Black, P., Boaler, J., Brown, M., Driver, R., & Murray, R. (1997). *Attitudes to science, mathematics and technology: A review of research*. London: King's College, University of London.
Picker, S. H., & Berry, J. S. (2000). Investigating pupils' images of mathematicians. *Educational Studies in Mathematics, 43*(1), 65–94.
Povey, H. (1997). Beginning mathematics teachers' ways of knowing: The link with working for emancipatory change. *Curriculum Studies, 5*(3), 329–342.

Schifter, D. (Ed.). (1996). *What's happening in math class? Volume 2: Reconstructing professional identities*. New York: Teachers College Press.
Schifter, D., & Fosnot, C. T. (1993). *Reconstructing mathematical education: Stories of teachers meeting the challenge of reform*. New York: Teachers College Press.
Shayer, M., & Adey, P. S. (Eds.). (2002). *Learning intelligence*. Buckingham: Open University Press.
Shayer, M., & Adhami, M. (2007). Fostering cognitive development through the context of mathematics: Results of the CAME project. *Educational Studies in Mathematics, 64*(3), 265–291.
Singh, S. (1998, August 31). The monday interview: The cleverest man in Britain? *Guardian*.
Spillane, J. P. (1999). External reform initiatives and teachers' efforts to reconstruct their practice: The mediating role of teachers' zones of enactment. *Journal of Curriculum Studies, 31*(2), 143–175.
Stobart, G., Bibby, T., & Goldstein, H. (2006). *Moving to two-tier GCSE mathematics examinations, An independent evaluation of the 2005 GCSE Pilot and Trial*. London: QCA.
Strauss, A. L., & Corbin, J. (1998). *Basics of qualitative research: Techniques and procedures for developing grounded theory* (2nd ed.). London: Sage.
Wenger, E. (1998). *Communities of practice: Learning, meaning and identity*. Cambridge: Cambridge University Press.

Part IV
Emotions in Leadership

Chapter 12
The Dynamic Nature of Emotions in Educational Leadership: Lessons from the Career Stories of Israeli Late-Career Principals

Izhar Oplatka

Introduction

The study of emotion in organisations and leadership has been receiving increasing attention in recent years as more and more researchers argued that understanding the emotions at work is a *sine qua non* of understanding leadership and of leading effectively (e.g. Goleman 1998; Stein 2005), and criticised the long-year conjecture that emotions are irrational and unproductive (e.g. Hartel et al. 2005). For many researchers nowadays, emotions are intertwined with, and embedded in, all aspects of organisational life, as individuals and groups deal daily with issues of anger, disappointment, frustration, fear, guilt, love friendship pleasure, and so forth (Brotheridge and Lee 2008; Fineman 2000; Kunda 2006).

The term "emotion" is defined as "an awareness of four elements that we usually experience at the same time: appraisal of a situation, changes in bodily sensations, the free or inhibited display of expressive gestures and a cultural label applied to specific constellations of the first three elements" (Hochscild 1990, pp. 118–119). Yet, there is a distinction between feelings, emotions, emotion work, and emotional labour. According to Gronn (2003), feelings are subjectively experienced physiological and psychological sensations or states (e.g. anger, frustration). When the feelings are expressed interpersonally, either spontaneously or intentionally, they become emotions. Emotions are expressed publicly, and are associated with a specific stimulus, as opposed to "mood" which is more enduring, more diffuse and less related to specific stimuli (Frijda 1993).

Given the central place of emotions at the workplace, there is a growing recognition of the role of emotions on leader and follower behaviours (e.g. Ashkanasy

This research was supported by THE ISRAEL SCIENCE FOUNDATION (grant No. 181/07). A special gratitude is endowed to Debby Yanku-Haddad for her research assistance in this study.

I. Oplatka (✉)
School of Education, Tel Aviv University, Tel Aviv, Israel
e-mail: oplatka@post.tau.ac.il

C. Day, J. C.-K. Lee (eds.), *New Understandings of Teacher's Work,* Professional Learning and Development in Schools and Higher Education 6,
DOI 10.1007/978-94-007-0545-6_12,

and Tse 2000; Brotheridge and Lee 2008). The literature in management and business administration abounds with empirical reports on various emotional and social aspects of leader behaviours, the nature of the emotions that managers display, the role of the leader in managing the emotional impact upon employees of disruptive change (Paulsen et al. 2005), and the key role of leaders in building positive psychological states in highly competitive environments (Seligman 2002). Other reports examine the relationship between leadership and common concepts in the study of emotion such as emotional display and rules (Brotheridge and Lee 2008), emotional labour (Harris 2002), emotional regulation (Clarke et al. 2007), and the ways by which leaders are becoming emotional managers (George 2000).

The conclusion arising from these studies highlights the importance of emotions for the effective management of organisations (Fineman 2000; Stein 2005). Managers who are more emotionally expressive are more likely to be perceived as being charismatic and are more likely to generate a positive emotional climate in the workplace (Riggio 2007), which in turn contributes much to organisational effectiveness. Failure to understand the emotional aspects of organisational behaviour and the significance of handling damaged relationships means that the manager is unlikely to realise pathologic and disruptive aspects in the organisation (Brotheridge and Lee 2008; Hartel et al. 2005).

The realisation that effective organisation is strongly related to emotional leadership has penetrated the literature in educational administration (Blackmore 1999; Beatty 2000; Gronn 2003), at least in part, due to the central place of human relationships and human needs at successful schools (Day 2008; Jacobson and Bezzina 2008; Toremen et al. 2006). There is a broadening of inquiry in the field of EA that now includes studies on the passions and emotions of leadership (e.g. Day 2004; Oplatka and Mimon 2008; Sugrue 2005), as well as on teacher–principal emotional relations (e.g. Blackmore 1999; Oplatka 2007).

In light of the emergent research on emotions of educational leadership, I would like to display in this chapter a developmental view of emotions in school leadership through life stories of late-career Israeli principals who have been interviewed in-depth about their professional identity and career experiences during their career cycle. From their accounts we gain much knowledge about the dynamic aspects of origins, qualities and effects of emotions in educational leadership. Briefly, it is apparent that school principal's emotional understanding, empathy, trust, and emotionality develop throughout the years in post to a point in which emotions play a key role in lives and career of the late-career principals.

Taking a dynamic, developmental perspective of emotions in educational leadership can enlarge our understanding of the changing nature of major concepts such as emotional understanding and display throughout the career cycle. Besides, this may provide insights into leaders' ability to express certain emotions and understand their followers' emotional needs and experiences in diverse career stages (e.g. early career, mid career). After all, the research on emotions in organisations is argued to help leaders increase the happiness of their workers and assist employees to achieve positive outcomes for themselves even when painful events are encountered, as Hartel et al. (2005) commented. This chapter may shed light on leaders' career stage and their emotional engagement in school.

The Research on Emotions of Educational Leadership

Emotion and leadership is now a growing part of the educational leadership field and the literature pays increasing attention to the social and organisational aspects of emotions in educational organisations, in general, and in educational leadership, in particular (e.g. Hargreaves 2001; Harris 2004; Zorn and Boler 2007). Researchers take the view that leadership is an emotional practice involving intensive personal interactions that are publicly displayed, yet this view, as Harris (2004) indicated, is mainly normative, tending to focus on what leaders should be doing rather than on the emotional labour of their work. Consequently, the emotional practice and processes of educational leaders remain, as Beatty (2000) commented, under-explored, and virtually uncharted territory.

Underlying this emergent research is the conjecture that emotion is inherent to the practice of leadership rather than separate from it (Crawford 2007; Day 2004; James and Vince 2001). Life in schools is complex substantially because emotion is integral to the processes of teaching and learning and, therefore, school leaders need to manage emotionally as well as rationally (Fullan 1998), i.e. leadership is a combination of cognition and emotion. Both emotions and cognition are equally important in guiding, facilitating or inhibiting leadership capability (Beatty 2002; Harris 2004). The social activities of schools coupled with major place of teacher–students and principal–teachers interactions produce and reflect emotions, passions, feelings, and so forth (Crawford 2007; Oplatka 2004a; Sachs and Blackmore 1998).

In conjunction with this assumption, past research has identified a wide variety of emotions and emotional engagements among school leaders, including passion, empathy, excitement, satisfaction, intuition, relief, joy, trust, adrenaline rush, and care (Beatty 2000; Blackmore 1999; Oplatka et al. 2001). In contrast, and presumably due to large-scale Neo-Liberal reforms introduced during the 1990s (e.g. school-based management, privatisation, marketisation, choice) in many countries, the literature focuses on negative emotions of school leaders, such as fear of failure (Gronn 2003), a sense of emotional "woundedness" (Johnson et al. 2005), anxiety, fear, pain, demoralisation, anger, frustration, despair, dissatisfaction, distress (Blackmore 2004; James and Vince 2001), disempowerment, threatened self, and disillusionment with the system (Beatty 2000). Note, however, that female principals found themselves split between social scripts that perceive the display of negative emotions as non-feminine (Blackmore 1999; Oplatka and Atias 2007).

Educational leaders were found also to help others manage their emotions (Crawford 2007), mainly in times of accountability, commercialism, and competition. For example, Australian principals increasingly had to manage teachers' sense of alienation and anger arising from a dissonance between what they referred to as their "real work" and the type of work required by new reformers (Blackmore 2004). Beatty's (2000) findings bring strong support to the need for leaders to understand their emotional selves and how these insights shape their leadership behaviours and actions with others in school.

Related to the above are studies that have pointed to a positive connection between emotions of leadership (e.g. trust, understanding, appreciation) and teachers' professionalism, commitment, self-efficacy, improvement, and self-confidence (Rizvi 2008). School leaders who offer emotional candour, conveying their own sense of vulnerability as basis for mutual understanding, may promote creativity and collaborative improvement among their staff (Leithwood and Beatty 2008) and improve the running and the change management in their school (Crawford 2007; James and Vince 2001). Interestingly, emotional displays presented by staff members and colleagues, that are often negative, can help school leaders to realise their own sense of disempowerment and inability to exercise control over their subordinates' sense of frustration and anger (Johnson et al. 2005). But, in many times the emotional price school leaders have to pay in order to be successful in the era of accountability and commercialism is related to early retirement and retention in post (Beatty 2000).

The current study reports on the place of emotions in the life stories of school principals who reached their late career in this emotional energy-consuming role. As emotional understanding and intelligence received a prominent place in their story, I turn now to display briefly these and related theoretical concepts.

Emotional Intelligence and Understanding

Three similar concepts can be found in the literature on emotion in organisations that refer to one's ability to not only to deal with one's emotions but with those of others: "emotional intelligence" (EI), "emotional understanding" (EU), and "empathy". Salovey and Mayer (1990) are said to have coined the first term, EI, but its popularisation is associated with Daniel Goleman's book emotional intelligence. According to the former authors, EI is defined as "the subset of social intelligence that involves the ability to monitor one's own and others' feelings and emotions, to discriminate among them and to use this information to guide one's thinking and actions" (Salovey and Mayer 1990, p. 189). Later, the two authors redefined the term to refer to "a set of interrelated skills concerning the ability to perceive accurately, appraise, and express emotion; the ability to access and/or generate feelings when they facilitate thought; the ability to understand emotion and emotional knowledge; and the ability to regulate emotions to promote emotional and intellectual growth" (Mayer and Salovey 1997, p. 10). In other words, EI includes the abilities to perceive emotion in the self and in others, use emotion to facilitate performance, understand emotion, and regulate emotion in the self and in others (Cote et al. 2006).

EI involves abilities that can be categorised as self-awareness, managing emotions, empathy, and handling relationships. (Wong and Law 2002), and results from experience and learning in the domain of emotions (Goleman 1995, 1998), i.e. may be developed through experience and learning (Cooper and Sawaf 1996; Goleman et al. 2002). Individuals who are emotionally competent can accurately assess and express emotions in themselves and towards others and integrate emotions with other cognitive processes to solve problems (Goleman et al. 2002; Johnson et al. 2005).

The second term, EU, was discussed elaborately by Denzin in his book from 1984. He defines EU as "an intersubjective process requiring that one person enter into the field of experience of another and experience for herself the same or similar experiences experienced by another" (Denzin 1984, p. 137). The subjective interpretation of another's emotional experience from one's own standpoint is central to EU, as interpretation precedes understanding. Persons seeking to understand and interpret the emotional experience of another must make the other's experience their own and experience that experience from their own standpoint (Mead 1982).

Denzin (1984) further distinguishes between emotional and cognitive forms of understanding, claiming that:

> Cognitive understanding is devoid of feeling and emotionality. Thoughts interrelate with feelings. The person must cognitively interpret a situation as he builds up, checks and calls out in himself inner self-feelings and thoughts. All emotionality involves thoughts and cognitions about the feelings one is feeling. (p. 142)

Thus, emotional misunderstanding occurs when peoples' emotional scanning goes awry where "they mistake their feelings for the feelings of others" (Zorn and Boler 2007, p. 139). If a person is incapable of bringing the other's experience into his own frame of reference, one-sided, empty, spurious EI may be produced (Denzin 1984).

The last concept, "empathy", defined as "the process of putting oneself in the place of another person, seeing matters from the other's perspective, perceiving the other's feelings and thoughts and conveying this awarding to that person" (Toremen et al. 2006, p. 2), resembles, by and large, the two previous terms. Thus, being an empathic manager requires some affective, cognitive, and communicative skills, such as communication skills, perception of feelings within self and others and hidden feelings, self-awareness, paying attention to nonverbal responses, and being accepting and open (Baillie 1996; Cooper 2004; Wiseman 1996). Profound empathy entails a rich understanding of others in their social, historical, and relational contexts (Cooper 2004).

Employees with high levels of EI are those who can make use of the antecedent- and response-focused emotional regulation effectively, and master their interactions with others in a more effective manner (Wong and Law 2002), which in turn lead to a high likelihood of success at work (Ashkanasy and Hooper 1999), as well as high levels of job performance (Goleman 1998). As far as leadership is concerned, Goleman (2000) argued that more emotionally intelligent leaders are more able to alter the leadership styles due to their higher levels of self-awareness, self-management, ability to read a situation, and adaptability. In addition, one important aspect of EI is the capacity to develop realistic evaluations about oneself as a leader, as well as an understanding of dominant negative emotions at the workplace such as jealousy, envy and interpersonal rivalry (Stein 2005). Emotionally intelligent leaders display sets of behaviour that demonstrate self-awareness (i.e. self-confidence, realistic evaluations of their strengths and weaknesses), self-management (i.e. self-control, trustworthiness, conscientiousness, adaptability, initiative), social awareness (i.e. empathy, ability to build networks), and social skills (i.e. developing others, conflict management) (Goleman 1998).

The research on emotions in educational leadership is replete with explicit and implicit clues about EI, EU, and empathy in reports on school leadership. It is evident that successful school leaders clearly had better empathic skills (e.g. active listening, sensitiveness, calming, facilitation, consideration and discernment, and behaving compatibly with teachers' moods) than their unsuccessful counterparts (Crawford 2007; Toremen et al. 2006). In this sense, educational leaders who recognise the differing needs of teachers, according to the ages and stages of their careers, are more likely to gain loyalty and solid commitment to whatever the school and its children may need, as Leithwood and Beatty (2008) maintained. They further elaborate on this point:

> Gaining emotional knowledge is engendered by dynamic emotional engagement on both sides, which fosters the ethic of mutuality, shared humanness, and the discovery of emotional common ground…the notion of the leader as merely thinking about other's feelings, rather than *feeling with others*, is a critical distinction. (p. 148)

An empathic, emotionally intelligent leader makes teachers feel supported and cared about, influences and renders their unbearable feelings more bearable and makes them feel understood, valued and their needs to be satisfied (Toremen et al. 2006). This capability is an indicator of leader's success in many educational systems.

The conceptual framework of the study presented in this chapter was adopted from Salovey and Mayer (1990) who conceptualised EI as composed of four distinct but inter-related dimensions, of which three are used to analyse the career-stories of the late-career principals in this study: (1) *Appraisal and expression of emotion in the self that* relates to the individual's ability to understand their deep emotions and be able to express these emotions naturally. (2) *Appraisal and recognition of emotion in others that* relates to peoples' ability to perceive and understand the emotions of those people around them. People who are high in this ability will be much more sensitive to the feelings and emotions of others as well as reading their minds (Wong and Law 2002). (3) *Regulation of emotion in the self* that relates to the ability of people to regulate their emotions, which will enable a more rapid recovery from psychological distress.

Methodology

The study described in this chapter represents one part of a wider study of the career experiences of principals in their late career, using a qualitative paradigm (Paton 2002), because the late-career stage encompasses a number of relevant variables that interact with each other, with no appropriate conceptual framework to describe its characteristics and determinants in principalship.

Context: Before moving to present the research findings, some information about Israel and the Israeli educational system is warranted to help readers understand how this study may relate to other educational systems. Thus, Israeli ideological values tend to emphasise the importance of collectivism, i.e. preference for group goals attainment and social cohesiveness (Gardinger 1993), as well as the central place of "emotions" in social life. For example, Israeli pre-service teachers expected their first school principal to develop friendly relationships with them, and refrain from formality and remote connections (Oplatka 2004b), a cultural expression given the different expectations reported by Chinese pre-service teachers (Lee et al. 2000).

Although gradually changing, the Israeli educational system is relatively centralised both in structure and procedure (Iram and Schmida 1998). The government is the provider of education for almost everyone and education is geared towards matriculation exams that usually take place at the end of high school and are necessary to gain entrance into higher education institutions (Goldscheider 1996). All schools are required to follow a basic national curriculum, although at the same time the Ministry of Education (MEO) encourages schools to specialise and offer unique subjects out of a predetermined list of subjects.

The effectiveness of the Israeli centralised system has been questioned in the 1990s onwards as new educational themes became important, such as educational diversity, decentralisation, and the encouragement of excellence (Iram and Schmida 1998). Furthermore, the traditional relationship between parents and schools has changed; parents and community are now conceived as a core element of the school environment. The involvement and participation of parents in school life and activities have been legitimised, and parents are entitled, and sometimes encouraged, to participate in social events, fund-raising, and decision-making forums.

Participants and Sampling: The source of information for this chapter was 15 late-career principals from elementary schools. Yet, due to the controversy in the literature on career development as to the appropriate criterion to measure career stage, the current study used two criteria: age (over 55) and positional tenure (over 10 years in principalship). These criteria have been used in several studies to operationally define career stages (e.g. Gibson 2003) and coincide with Super's models of career development that incorporate Levinson's adult development model into career stage theory (Super 1992).

The participants were selected solely from elementary schools for two reasons. Firstly, the "culture of care" that characterises elementary schools (Nias 1989) makes the management of this type of school unique in that it includes emotional commitment and a focus on instruction. Secondly, since the research is explorative and qualitative in nature, it aimed to use sites that are as homogenous as possible. The similarities (e.g. curriculum, instructional organisation, structure) and differences (e.g. culture, personnel, and contexts) among elementary schools might assist in the generation of patterns of late career in principalship.

Procedure: A life-story, semi-structured interview with the principal was conducted in this study. This kind of interview is based on the assumption that people create stories that manifest their self and their social identity; the life-story is thus a personal narrative told by the interviewee himself/herself (Sarbin 1986). The life-story strategy allowed the researcher to trace the principals' internal career experiences, problems and needs, as well as to connect their subjective constructions of their late career and contextual, biographic, and organisational factors manifested within their accounts. Additionally, this strategy permits the late-career principals to compare their experiences and behaviour at this career stage with their own experiences in earlier career stages. To this end, the interview guide comprised both biographical and perceptual questions to answer.

The analysis of the interview transcriptions followed the four stages described by Marshall and Rossman (1995), i.e. organising the data; generating categories, themes and patterns; testing any emergent hypothesis; and searching for alternative explanations. This analysis aims at identifying central themes in the data, i.e. searching for recurrent experiences, feelings, and attitudes, so as to enable us to code, reduce, and connect different categories into central themes. The coding is guided by the principles of "comparative analysis" (Strauss and Corbin 1998). It includes the comparison of any coded element in terms of emergent categories and subcategories. Finally, comparisons are made among the data comprising the entire data set, leading to the identification of patterns of late career in principalship.

The analysis was strengthened by structured analysis and by a critical colleague, who played devil's advocate in questioning the research processes and outcomes, two common indicators used by qualitative researchers to build confidence in their analytic procedures (Marshall and Rossman 1995). However, consistent with most qualitative researchers who assume that those they study interpret reality from multiple perspectives for varying purposes (LeCompte and Preissle 1993), I am interested in revealing participants' subjective ideas about reality, rather than finding some objective reality.

Findings

The central theme arising from the interview transcripts refers to the dynamic nature of emotions in educational leadership. It seems that emotions play a greater role in late career rather than in earlier career stages of school leaders, especially in areas of emotional understanding and empathy, trust in teachers, and the development of positive emotions among others. This is accompanied by a greater cognitive awareness among the late-career principals of diversity in the staff room.

Cognitive Consciousness to Teacher Diversity

The late-career principals in this study pointed to the internal modifications they had experienced since they entered principalship that made them more cognitively aware of teachers' diverse needs. A male principal (59, 13[1]) expressed his new attitudes towards the staff:

> ...I have teachers with a complicated personality, with many sensitivities, and I manage to manoeuvre between them in recent years without raising my voice...so I have never had severe conflicts or breakdowns, I mean, now I posses the skills to do all these things and lead them in a way I believe in.

The principal–teachers relations are claimed to be in harmony, mainly due to the late-career principal's understanding of diversity among teachers, or in a female principal's (55, 11) words, "people have different characters, and I always try to compromise, to enable the teachers work together". This kind of understanding seems to have developed during the career cycle, as arising from the next two quotes:

> I think that I'm more flexible, less obsessive, less controlling than in the past because I understand that everything takes time. I am more patient towards processes...in the past I used to be very energetic, wanted to do everything at once, but now I understand that every teacher has her own tempo, more time, less time, and I have no longer use a stopper.... (A female principal, 57, 22)
>
> I feel I am different in respect to staff empowerment, I feel I am different today, I decentralise authority, the way I look at every teacher's development is different, and I am able to see the differences between teachers and find the strengths in every teacher without giving up my aims or ideas. (A female teacher, 56, 12)

Understanding and acknowledging diversity is devoid of feeling and emotions, as Denzin (1984) maintained, and is chiefly connected to thoughts, awareness, and cognition. Yet, in line with the cognitive modifications the late-career principals reported on, their accounts are replete with many examples of increased emotional understanding as the next section displays.

Emotional Understanding and Empathy

The most prominent shift in the principal's emotional engagement in late career seems to refer to their higher ability to perceive and recognise the emotions of their staff. Their sensitiveness to the feelings and emotions of their teachers is highlighted against their relatively lack of such abilities in earlier career stages, as is echoed from a female principal's (56, 15) account:

> ...I'm very sensitive to people, in my character I'm sensitive, I listen to everyone, very tolerant, compromising...I am less aggressive than in the past, I think that today, I listen more, trying to approach the other person, to bring her to my side rather than be in conflicts...

Having said that, she continued:

> But I don't think that this is because of my role only, I think this is because of my age...I know how I would react to my partners when I was twenty two years old, and how I react

[1] The first number refers to the principal's age and the second to the length in principalship.

> today to my husband, or what would I say to my son [in the past], and what I'm telling him today. I think that the older we are, the more we gather much personal experiences and knowledge about the world…so I am more open to peoples' needs.

When asked how late-career principals differ from their younger counterparts, a female principal (56, 12) displayed a similar view:

> I think that they are first of all more patient, holding a holistic view of the person. With your experience you can see beyond the words that a person sitting next to you is saying. You can express much more empathy to her difficulties, you can understand them, and you can look deeply and from there to promote the person. This is the advantage of senior principals…

Emotional understanding and empathy encompass also listening to others' needs, an element intensified in late career because principals at this stage have already developed a managerial expertise that leaves them much time for non-management tasks. A principal (57, 11) confessed that he "can listen now to people, to stakeholders, to the staff, to pupils, to parents and to many other things". Yet, this listening is likely to be more complex and profound as it seems to be accompanied by immersion in one's emotional world and caring for one's particular needs. Due to their senior age, the late-career female principals reported being "the mothers" of their staff "caring for them, accompanying them in the delivery, in their personal life, a lot, in crises…" (56, 9).

The consideration in teachers' needs coupled with much empathy towards their unique personal needs is associated with the late-career principal's experience and maturity, as is echoed in the subsequent quotes:

> …In the past, if a teacher had to take her ill son to the doctor I would be very angry at her, telling her off for leaving the school, but today I tell her: "first go, and I will take care of the class". So I am doing things that I must not do, but this year I had a burned-out teacher who had a baby, and it's very hard for her. So, she asked for a day-off and I told her "go", even though I can't say that…because I do care about her condition…she will make up for the missing lesson…. (63, 11)
>
> …We shall not be too difficult (with the staff), we have to be open, if a teacher has to go out during the school day to her son's birthday, you should be happy with that and let her go, because this kind of gesture contributes to warm interpersonal relations in school…I don't let her do that all the time, but in recent years I'm more flexible, more human I would say…. (58, 8)

The late-career principal's ability to appraise teachers' emotions and regulate his/her own accordingly has some personal price, such as personal distress or lack of clear boundaries between the personal and professional. One female principal (63, 8) "takes things very personally and cries a lot and alone", while another regulates her emotions in order to refrain from personal distress:

> …I don't think we have to involve our personal problems here, I have some reservations about it, I had some dramatic events in school, and I took it very personally and I realised it wasn't good, and we need to separate it from the school, I have to be empathic, supportive, and helpful, but I must not identify emotionally, I have to be in distance.

Then, she provides more details about these events:

> Look, a certain teacher, her son committed a suicide during his army service, and my deputy, she got a divorce, her husband suddenly left the house, so it is so dramatic, and I took

> it so personally, I was emotionally involved, very strongly...so at a certain moment I felt I can't contain it anymore, to take it on my back...I have my own personal problems at home, my sister got sick, so I'm taking her now to the hospital...so we are all empathic, we try to help, but I feel I can't hold it anymore...

A Greater Trust in Teachers

The meaning of trust between school members is becoming a major topic in the study of educational leadership resulting in new insights into the culture of trust and its contribution to school effectiveness and teacher moral (e.g. Hoy et al. 2006). It is evident that teachers and stakeholders emphasise the creation and sustained building of productive, participative community relations. Teachers, particularly, want their principal to trust them and let them deal with professional issues autonomously (Day 2008).

Interestingly, our interviewees reported, explicitly and implicitly, on the dynamic nature of "trust" in their career cycle, from low levels of trust in their staff's efficacy and competence to higher ones. When asked if her leadership views had changed throughout the years, a female principal (57, 22) replied:

> Yes, no doubt, I trust teachers more than in the past, I don't think that what I am doing is the best way to do it, and I can trust others and be flexible, [but] anyway the flexibility is a matter of experience. At the beginning it is very frightening to lose control...but along the years you are becoming more flexible...

In this sense, while reflecting upon their career cycle, most of the late-career principals in this study used the word "trust" to demonstrate the alterations they have experienced in their leadership perspectives and styles. The meaning of "trust" arises in the interviews to present many aspects of principal–teachers relations, as is illustrated in the following quotes:

> ...and I have a skilful staff that I trust and consult with. A teacher can tell me she had a bad lesson...she is not afraid I would tell her off. We are together for so many years, so I don't even think to reprimand her, just to guide, to explain her. I can open every class door when I want, just to sit there, listen and give advices.
>
> Interviewer: Is that different from what was in the past?
>
> Interviewee: Yes, of course, of course. I am more confident today, so I can more easily see if the way we are going is good or not good and act accordingly...I am not threatened so fast, so I am more relaxed with the teachers, parents, students. (A female principal, 63, 11)

> ...Today I know that even if I make a mistake, someone from my staff will solve it at once, sometimes even better than me...when I entered principalship the staff was very young... but today I can sit with closed eyes. In the past, I used to order the textbooks of the first grade, today I can sit calmly, telling the teachers to go to the head of library, and she will report me on budget, future purchases....(A female principal, 56, 15)

The higher levels of "trust" are subjectively connected to high self-confidence and self-efficacy, two self-concepts that have been developed among the interviewees throughout the years in principalship. Yet, high levels of "trust" are also strongly associated with the model of "participative leadership". Feeling high levels of trust towards their teacher's competency to work effectively and take on middle management roles seems to encourage the late-career principals to decentralise their authority more considerably than in the past, nominating both young and senior teachers to management positions in school. The next citation, narrated by a female principal (55, 11) manifests this transition explicitly:

> …I can divide my leadership style in this school into three parts. The first part was the more central part, that I thought from the beginning that I'm going to be very centralist…just to be familiar with the school, so as to create an order and organisation at work…I had to be centralist in order to be familiar with every aspect of such a large school, everywhere, be it the staff meetings, parties, events or just in class observations, I mean, to enter every place, to see every draft, I had to build the administrative, the pedagogical and the didactic frames of this school as nothing was here…and I was aware of what I am doing…

Then, when she reaches the recent years, her tone is changing:

> But after three years there were some teams, slowly slowly, teachers started to take on roles, so I became half centralist…somehow between centralism and decentralism, but I didn't rely on them completely…but in the last three years the staff works autonomously, very nicely. We have a team of middle management, I divided the school into three divisions, and I have a head of k-2, a head of 3–4, and a head of 5–6…

Another female principal (56, 12 in post) expressed the professional change she had experienced in a slightly different way:

> …I am ready not to be centralistic anymore, I am ready to decentralise roles without being afraid of losing my status, or that someone will be successful than me…I'm very proud when someone from my staff succeeds, I see it as part of the large work I do with them.
>
> Interviewer: Have this pride characterised you before?
>
> No, I think that in the past I was more centralistic, I didn't trust the staff very much, and I looked at the school from a different point of view.

The higher levels of trust are not only associated with higher levels of self-confidence and self-efficacy but also with the teachers' dominant career stage at school. Senior staffs with whom the principal have undergone many years in post is likely to increase the late-career principal's levels of trust, and in contrast. In case the staff is composed almost entirely of young and novice teachers the late-career principal is less likely to trust the teachers, and "can't nominate them to middle management roles, so naturally I am more centralistic than in past years, and also because I have to be a mentor of the novice teachers", as a female principal (57, 22) confessed.

Developing Positive Emotions Among Teachers

The late-career principals' ability to understand the emotions of their staff is likely to be manifested also in their propensity to express their own emotions naturally and openly in order to develop positive emotions in the school. This tendency is expressed, first and foremost, by attempts to create a positive atmosphere in the school. Most interviewees ardently claimed for having good inter-relations in the staff room, a kind of a "family" in one of a female principal (63, 11). In this positive climate the principal plays a key role as exemplified in the next quote:

> I always tell my teachers, it is true that we had a hard day, very complex day, but just as you want the child to come to the school smiling, you also should smile. It's over, I know there are phones at nights, but tomorrow is a new day, and we have to begin it differently, anew, in a pleasant atmosphere.... (A female principal, 55, 11)

Another female principal expressed her contribution to the positive school atmosphere in a slightly different way, emphasising her role of "a peace keeper":

> My door is open, open...if there is a misunderstanding between two teachers, as happened last week, I take everyone to my room, talk with her separately, without telling the other about our conversation, compromising and bridging between them, and each one of them is coming to me individually to say "thank you", so the atmosphere is great here. (58, 20)

The conversations between the principal and the teacher are used also to provide the teacher with a feedback on her performances in the class, a very stressful part of principal–teachers relations. In the case of the late-career principals, this sort of conversation is used to develop positive and constructive emotions in the observed teacher, because as a female principal (55, 11 in post) said, "when I comment, I take it to a positive direction, not to the negative one, so I build a platform on which a good and productive communication is created". All in all, the late-career principal highlighted a "culture of care" (Nias 1989) in which they, as the senior persons, care for the teacher's lives holistically, i.e. both to his/her personal and professional aspects. This can be a genuine interest in the condition of a pregnant teachers, consideration in an ill teacher, calling to a woman in the delivery room and so on. All these emotional displays are assumed, by our interviewees, to promote a good atmosphere and climate in the staff room, and in turn, better performances in the class.

Concluding Messages

The late-career principal's accounts are embedded with many words describing the path they have undergone from an emphasis on "rational", cognitive constructions of educational leadership to more emotional, less rational ones. Their higher emotional awareness of teachers' emotional needs is manifested by many words and phrases during the interview conversation such as sensitiveness, flexibility, respect, harmony, listening, immersion, trust, and identification. These and similar words are related by the principals to "compromise", "bridging", or "patience" to illustrate their new emotion-attuned leadership style, that is underpinned by their self-confidence, a sense of professional expertise, and high self-efficacy in late career, and results in a better school climate and good atmosphere in the staff room.

What has come to light, then, is the likely emergence of passionate leadership in later career stages, a model of leadership defined by Davies and Brighouse (2008) as follows:

> Passionate leadership is about energy, commitment, a belief that every child can learn and will learn, a concern with social justice and the optimism that we can make a difference. (p. 1)

This emergence draws support from past research in non-education organisations suggesting that adults have significantly higher EI than adolescents, because it develops with age (Cote et al. 2006; Mayer and Salovey 1997). For the late-career principals, however, passionate leadership is not oriented towards students solely, but also towards the teachers. They display a fundamental empathy, i.e. basic characteristics and means of communication needed to initiate empathic relationships (Cooper 2004), and seem to understand their staff's emotional experiences even without participating in them per se, a kind of emotional engagement which is, according to Denzin (1984), is part of "emotional understanding".

Traditionally, rationality was prized as a mark of effective management, and emotionality was seen as a weakness and an inability to control oneself (Brotheridge and Lee 2008; Kunda 2006), a belief supported also by a senior headteachers in Crawford's (2007) study. While this kind of conjecture still exists in some organisations, and even supported by some educational policy-makers nowadays, the late-career principals' accounts seem not only to contest this kind of traditional assumption, but also to advocate an alternative model of emotional leadership.

This sort of emotional, passionate leadership is believed, by our interviewees, to be compatible with major educational values and norms contributing much to a better school climate and effectiveness. A support for this kind of belief we gain from past research both in educational and non-educational organisations. For example, Goleman (2000) found that priming good feeling in subordinates positively impacts on an organisation's emotional climate and brings out the best in them. Executives' display of positive emotions and encouragement of such emotions in their employees have also been found to influence expectancy motivation, creativity, goal-directed behaviour, altruistic intentions, and emotional well-being (Brotheridge and Lee 2008). Sometimes, nevertheless, emotional expression is viewed as calculated in order to accomplish goals, and the authenticity of performances is therefore regarded with suspicion (Kunda 2006), a potential staff's response also in school.

In educational institutions, Beatty (2000) contends that there is an "emotional economy" and that educational leaders need to be "emotionally accountable" in order to take responsibility for what they do. Analysing "trust", it is likely that creating a climate of trust in school, as our interviewees claimed to do, is essential to foster positive feelings of involvement, to help solve problems on a continuing basis, to encourage teachers to engage in extra-role activities, and create normal and healthy responses to the principal's initiatives (Harris 2004; Oplatka 2007; Sachs 2000).

Perhaps, the including theoretical message of this study is twofold. Firstly, more attention should be given in the research on emotions of educational leadership to personal characteristics and contextual elements. As this study showed, the career stage of school leaders may have some implications about our understanding of emotions, emotional understanding, emotional display, and emotionality. Secondly, scholars from the career-stage perspective (e.g. Day and Bakioglu 1996; Ribbins 1999) may want to consider adding emotional elements to their constructions of career stages in principalship, in general, and some references to EI or EU, in particular. Needless to say, theoretical developments in these areas may contribute much to the inclusion of emotion-based contents in leadership preparation and development programs.

References

Ashkanasy, N. M., & Hooper, G. (1999). *Perceiving and managing emotion in the workplace: A research agenda based on neurophysiology.* Paper presented at the 3rd Australian Industrial and Organisational Psychology Conference, Brisbane, June.

Ashkanasy, N. M., & Tse, B. (2000). Transformational leadership as management of emotion: A conceptual review. In N. M. Ashkanasy, C. E. J. Hartel, & W. J. Zerbe (Eds.), *Emotions in the workplace: Theory, research and practice* (pp. 221–235). Westport: Quorum.

Baillie, L. (1996). A phenomenological study of the nature of empathy. *Journal of Advanced Nursing, 24*(6), 1300–1308.

Beatty, B. (2002). Emotion matters in educational leadership: Examining the unexamined. Unpublished PhD thesis, University of Toronto.

Beatty, B. R. (2000). The emotions of educational leadership: Breaking the silence. *International Journal of Leadership in Education, 3*(4), 331–357.

Blackmore, J. (1999). *Troubling women: Feminism, leadership and educational change.* Buckingham: Open University Press.

Blackmore, J. (2004). Leading as emotional management work in high risk times: The counter-intuitive impulses of performativity and passion. *School Leadership and Management, 24*(4), 439–459.

Brotheridge, C. M., & Lee, R. T. (2008). The emotions of managing: An introduction to the special issue. *Journal of Managerial Psychology, 23*(2), 108–117.

Clarke, C., Hpe-Hailey, V., & Kelinher, C. (2007). Being real or really being someone else? Change, managers and emotion work. *European Management Journal, 25*(2), 92–103.

Cooper, B. (2004). Empathy, interaction and caring: Teachers' roles in a constrained environment. *Pastoral Care in Education, 22*(3), 12–21.

Cooper, R. K., & Sawaf, A. (1996). *Executive EQ: Emotional intelligence in leadership and organisations.* New York: Perigee.

Cote, S., Miners, C. T. H., & Moon, S. (2006). Emotional intelligence and wise emotion regulation in the workplace. In W. J. Zerbe, N. M. Ashkanasy, & C. E. J. Harter (Eds.), *Individual and organisational perspectives on emotion management and display* (pp. 1–24). Amsterdam: Elsevier.

Crawford, M. (2007). Emotional coherence in primary school headship. *Educational Management, Administration and Leadership, 35*(4), 521–534.

Davies, B., & Brighouse, T. (Eds.). (2008). *Passionate leadership in education.* London: Sage.

Day, C. (2004). The passion of successful leadership. *School Leadership & Management, 24*(4), 425–437.

Day, C. (2008). Successful leadership: An intelligent passion. In B. Davies & T. Brighouse (Eds.), *Passionate leadership in education* (pp. 75–90). London: Sage.

Day, C., & Bakioglu, A. (1996). Development and disenchantment in the professional lives of headteachers. In I. Goodson & A. Hargreaves (Eds.), *Teachers' professional lives* (pp. 123–139). London: Falmer.

Denzin, N. (1984). *On understanding emotions.* San Francisco: Jossey-Bass.

Fineman, S. (2000). *Emotions and organisations* (2nd ed.). New York: Sage.

Frijda, N. H. (1993). Moods, emotion episodes and emotions. In M. Lewis & I. M. Haviland (Eds.), *Handbook of emotions* (pp. 381–403). New York: Guilford.

Fullan, M. (1998). Leadership for the 21st century: Breaking the bonds of dependency. *Educational Leadership, 55*(7), 45–51.

Gardinger, M. (1993). Thoughts toward the formation of an Israeli management model. In A. Shenhar & A. Yarkoni (Eds.), *Israeli management culture* (pp. 99–108). Tel Aviv: Cherikover. [In Hebrew.]

George, J. M. (2000). Emotions and leadership: The role of emotional intelligence. *Human Relations, 53*(8), 1027–1055.

Gibson, D. E. (2003). Developing the professional self-concept: Role model construals in early, middle, and late career stages. *Organisational Science, 14*(4), 591–610.

Goldscheider, C. (1996). *Israel's changing society: Population, ethnicity, and development.* Colorado: Westview.

Goleman, D. (1995). *Emotional intelligence.* New York: Bantam.

Goleman, D. (1998). *Working with emotional intelligence.* New York: Bantam.

Goleman, D. (2000). Leadership that gets results. *Harvard Business Review, 2000*(March–April), 78–90.

Goleman, D., Boyatzis, R., & McKee, A. (2002). *Primal leadership.* Cambridge: Harvard Business School Press.

Gronn, P. (2003). *The new work of educational leaders: Changing leadership practice in an era of school reform.* London: Chapman.

Hargreaves, A. (2001). Emotional geographies of teaching. *Teacher College Record, 103*(6), 1056–1080.

Harris, B. (2004). Leading by heart. *School Leadership and Management, 24*(4), 391–404.

Harris, L. C. (2002). The emotional labour of barristers: An exploration of emotional labour by status professionals. *Journal of Management Studies, 39*(4), 553–584.

Hartel, C. E. J., Zerbe, W. J., & Ashkanasy, N. M. (2005). *Emotions in organisational behaviour.* Mahwah: Erlbaum.

Hochscild, A. (1990). Ideology and emotion management: A perspective and path for future research. In T. Kemper (Ed.), *Research agendas in the sociology of emotions.* Albany: State University of New York State.

Hoy, W. K., Quincy-Gage, C., & Tarter, C. J. (2006). School mindfulness and faculty trust: Necessary conditions for each other? *Educational Administration Quarterly, 42*(2), 236–255.

Iram, Y., & Schmida, M. (1998). *The educational system of Israel.* Westport: Greenwood.

Jacobson, S. L., & Bezzina, C. (2008). Effects of leadership on student academic/affective achievement. In J. Lumby, G. Crow, & P. Pashiadris (Eds.), *International handbook on the preparation and development of school leaders.* New York: Routledge.

James, C., & Vince, R. (2001). Developing the leadership capability of headteachers. *Educational Management, Administration & Leadership, 29*(3), 307–317.

Johnson, R. G., Aiken, J. A., & Steggerda, R. (2005). Emotions and educational leadership: Narratives from the inside. *Planning and Changing, 36*(3–4), 235–252.

Kunda, G. (2006). *Engineering culture: Control and commitment in a high-tech corporation.* Philadelphia: Temple University Press.

LeCompte, M. D., & Preissle, J. (1993). *Ethnography and qualitative design in educational research.* San Diego: Academic.

Lee, J. C. K., Walker, A., & Bodycott, P. (2000). Pre-service primary teachers' perceptions about principals in Hong Kong: Implications for teacher and principal education. *Asia-Pacific Journal of Teacher Education, 28*(1), 53–67.

Leithwood, K., & Beatty, B. (2008). *Leading teachers with emotions.* Thousand Oaks: Corwin.

Marshall, C., & Rossman, G. (1995). *Designing qualitative research.* Thousand Oaks: Sage.

Mayer, J. D., & Salovey, P. (1997). What is emotional intelligence? In P. Salovey & D. Sluyter (Eds.), *Emotional development and emotional intelligence: Educational implications* (pp. 3–34). New York: Basic.

Mead, G. H. (1982). *The individual and the social self: Unpublished work of George Herbert Mead* (D. L. Miller, Ed.). Chicago: University of Chicago Press.
Nias, J. (1989). *Primary teachers talking: A study of teaching at work.* London: Routledge.
Oplatka, I. (2004a). Women teachers' emotional commitment and involvement: A universal professional feature and educational policy. *Education and Society, 22*(2), 23–43.
Oplatka, I. (2004b). Prospective teachers' constructions of leadership: In search of an 'androgynous' style. *Leadership and Policy in Schools, 3*(1), 37–57.
Oplatka, I. (2007). Managing emotions in teaching: Towards an understanding of emotion displays and caring as non-prescribed role elements. *Teacher College Record, 109*(6), 1374–1400.
Oplatka, I., & Atias, M. (2007). Gendered views of managing discipline in school and class. *Gender and Education, 19*(1), 41–59.
Oplatka, I., & Mimon, R. (2008). Women principals' conceptions of job satisfaction and dissatisfaction: An alternative view? *International Journal of Leadership in Education, 11*(2), 191–210.
Oplatka, I., Bargal, D., & Inbar, D. (2001). The process of self-renewal among women headteachers in mid-career. *Journal of Educational Administration, 39*(1), 77–94.
Paton, M. Q. (2002). *Qualitative research and evaluation method.* Newbury Park: Sage.
Paulsen, N., Callan, V. J., Grice, T., Rooney, D., Gallois, C., Jones, E., Bordia, P., & Jimmesion, N. (2005). Job uncertainty and personal control during downsizing: A comparison of survivors and victims. *Human Relations, 58*(4), 463–496.
Ribbins, P. (1999). Understanding leadership: Developing headteachers. In T. Bush, L. Bell, R. Bolam, R. Glatter, & P. Ribbins (Eds.), *Educational management: Redefining theory, policy, practice* (pp. 77–89). London: Chapman.
Riggio, R. E. (2007). The emotional and social intelligences of effective leadership: An emotional and social skill approach. *Journal of Managerial Psychology, 23*(2), 341–360.
Rizvi, M. (2008). The role of school principals in enhancing teacher professionalism: Lessons from Pakistan. *Educational Management, Administration & Leadership, 36*(1), 85–100.
Sachs, J. (2000). The activist professional. *Journal of Educational Change, 1,* 77–95.
Sachs, J., & Blackmore, J. (1998). You never show you can't cope: Women in school leadership roles managing their emotions. *Gender and Education, 10*(3), 265–279.
Salovey, P., & Mayer, J. D. (1990). Emotional intelligence. *Imagination, Cognition and Personality, 9*(3), 185–211.
Sarbin, T. R. (1986). *Narrative psychology: The storied nature of human conduct.* New York: Praeger.
Seligman, M. E. P. (2002). *Authentic happiness: Using the new positive psychology to realise your potential for lasting fulfillment.* New York: Free.
Stein, M. (2005). The Othello conundrum: The inner contagion of leadership. *Organisation Studies, 26*(9), 1405–1419.
Strauss, A. L., & Corbin, J. (1998). *Basics of qualitative research: Techniques and procedures for developing grounded theory* (2nd ed.). Thousand Oaks: Sage.
Sugrue, C. (Ed.). (2005). *Passionate principalship: Learning from the life histories of school leaders.* London: Routledge Falmer.
Super, D. E. (1992). Toward a comprehensive theory of career development. In D. A. Montross & C. J. Shinkman (Eds.), *Career development: Theory and practice* (pp. 35–64). Springfield: Charles & Thomas.
Toremen, F., Ekinci, A., & Karakus, M. (2006). Influence of managers' empathic skills on school success. *International Journal of Educational Management, 20*(6), 490–499.
Wiseman, T. (1996). A concept analysis of empathy. *Journal of Advanced Nursing, 23*(6), 1162–1167.
Wong, C. H., & Law, K. S. (2002). The effects of leader and follower emotional intelligence on performance and attitude: An exploratory study. *The Leadership Quarterly, 13,* 243–274.
Zorn, D., & Boler, M. (2007). Rethinking emotions and educational leadership. *International Journal of Leadership in Education, 10*(2), 137–151.

Chapter 13
Rationality and Emotion in Education Leadership—Enhancing Our Understanding

Megan Crawford

In the educational leadership literature, rational models of leadership and management are often presented as the only way to look at effective organisations. Sometimes these same models are presented with an emotional twist, and perhaps a reference to Emotional Intelligence (EI). Yet, for those that work in education, the reality of organisation life means that there is much more to the study of emotion and leadership than such stark dividing lines between the so-called rational and the emotional side of the organisations. This aspect is also, I suggest, going to become even more of an issue as educationalists move into more social care settings as part of the children's agenda. In this chapter, I will be discussing the various ideas behind any discussion of emotion and rationality, and looking for how they can enhance our understanding of teachers' careers as they progress into leadership roles. This chapter also invokes the wider field of study, of emotion in organisations, and how the insights gained from there can be applied to educational leaders. I also link this to the personal side of a leader's life and his own autobiography, or personal leadership narrative.

Background

This chapter intends to examine what for many is the dilemma of rationality and emotion for the educational leader. It will suggest that it is not so much a dilemma but a developing understanding of how the two ideas are linked, both in conceptual and practical terms. It will ask how leaders might use theory to inform practice; ultimately not only improve their own leadership skills but also confront some of the unsaid issues of the modern performative culture. This will be done by discussing educational leadership and the wider field, followed by suggestions for the way in which emotion and leadership could be further theorised. My particular view is that a better understanding of the concept of emotion and leadership can enhance leaders' knowledge both of themselves and others (Crawford 2009). Knowing that

M. Crawford (✉)
Oxford Brookes University, Oxford, UK
e-mail: mcrawford@brookes.ac.uk

C. Day, J. C.-K. Lee (eds.), *New Understandings of Teacher's Work*, Professional Learning and Development in Schools and Higher Education 6,
DOI 10.1007/978-94-007-0545-6_13, © Springer Science+Business Media B.V. 2011

the emotional and rational are linked can also enhance our understanding of the part leaders take in leadership. A good starting point is the concept of leadership as an organisational quality. Ogawa and Bossert (1997, p. 19) suggest that: "leadership flows through the network of roles that comprise organisations,...with different roles having access to different levels and types of resources." One of the tasks of those in leadership roles is to create the climate in which people will want to work to the optimum levels of their energy, interest and commitment (Whitaker 1997) to enable those roles in the organisations to have access to leadership resources. All this is driven by emotion. This approach views emotion as inherent to the practice of leadership rather than separate from it (Crawford and James 2006). In particular, I will draw mainly on the social approach to emotion which sees social reality as made up of multiple realities which include the uniqueness of every person: their personality and life history, the context in which they work, and the people they work with. In understanding emotion and leadership, and its role in the organisation, we need to understand how these multiple realities intertwine with each other, form meaning and enable leadership to be part of the flow of the organisation.

The educational leadership literature has expanded over recent years to include emotion (Beatty 2000; Gronn 2003; Day 2004; Crawford 2009) and this has been a stimulus for writers to re-discover emotion and the organisations and what this has to offer leaders. We would do well to re-focus on ideas associated with organisations, as Glatter suggests (2006), so that we see how emotion and the organisation are linked to leadership. When discussing rationality and emotion, this approach has many benefits, as can be seen in much of the business literature (e.g. Briner 1999; Fineman 2008). In her ground breaking book looking at school organisation, Richardson (1973, p. 36) makes the point that an essential part of leadership is to seek understanding of the interplay between rational and emotional forces in any organisation. Through the leader's growing understanding, all those who have to exercise authority in a leadership role should seek to help others to understand this interplay as well. A key insight from my own research is that emotion is encircled and interpreted through human understandings. In other words, the biological and psychological aspects of emotion are mediated both by the social setting, and the life history and careers of the people involved. Locating teachers' lives in a more holistic framework, means that teachers themselves can have a clearer understanding of the emotional in their work lives, and ultimately how this relates to leadership. This framework also means that leaders can begin to develop their own leadership practices in line with what we already know about effective organisations as well as schools specifically.

Teachers' Lives and Careers

It is in social relationships, and the stories that are told about such relationships, that the emotions of leadership can be productively examined (Crawford 2009). Teachers' lives and their careers are in turn affected by these social relations and the role of the leaders within the organisation (Crawford 2008). This is turn relates to the idea of leadership flowing throughout the organisation. Indeed, Kemper (2004, p. 46) argues that:

> A very large class of human emotions results from real, anticipated, imagined, or recollected outcomes of social relations.

The social relations side of organisations is clearly important, as is the leader themselves. Lupton's twin frameworks of "emotion as inherent" and "emotion as socially constructed" is a way to look at the importance of the personality sides of emotion, whilst at the same time not sidelining as unimportant the social interactions between leaders and followers. Whilst more general research into emotion has signposted the importance of "emotion as inherent" (Lupton 1998), much of educational leadership studies have shied away from considering "leadership as inherent" because this may wrongly suggest trait theories where leaders were seen as "born not made" (Law and Glover 2000, pp. 21–22). This approach makes new interpretations of the rational/emotional in leadership interesting because it could mean that some people may be inherently more inclined towards certain types of leadership, which may or may not be effective in different contexts. This approach also highlights how their inherent characteristics interact with the social arena of the school and how leaders may want to portray leadership actions as rational because it is more comfortable emotionally to do so. Organisation structures may unwittingly assist in, or even collude with, peoples' portrayal of events as rational when told in retrospect.

Emotions as socially constructed feeds into a culture of schooling that suggests that emotional labour (Hochschild 1983) is to be taken for granted by leaders, until, of course, they suffer some sort of health breakdown. She defines emotional labour as: "the management of feeling to create a publicly observable facial and bodily display" (Hochschild 1983, p. 7). Managing feeling is an aspect of the role play of leadership which some find much easier than others. For example, one head teacher told me the following story as part of a discussion about the emotions of leadership. This example can be viewed as revealing the juxtaposition of the inherent and the social in any emotional event.

> Earlier this year the school administrator made a written formal complaint about the caretaker. I had to see the caretaker and I found it upsetting as I sort of felt it was in some ways a complaint about me. I knew that that the interview with the caretaker would be difficult, and in fact he stormed out! I just had to deal with it. Later he did apologise, but it left a…nasty taste. There's still an aftermath of the incident within the school—the governors sorted it by giving the caretaker a verbal warning. It was an uncomfortable feeling and I was only able to share it with the Chair of Govs and my husband. Who else is there? It's difficult to get hold of other Heads during the day.

Even on first reading, the inherent (how she reacted internally "upsetting", "uncomfortable", "terrified", "worried and frightened" physically) and the socially constructed (the aftermath within the school which she had to deal with, difficult people) stand out clearly.

This incident also highlights other facets of leading and the rational/emotional interface. The event was unique as it was the first time she had to deal with an incident involving such emotion. Looking back, she noted what she might have done differently, but was new and not confident of her knowledge of the teacher. She said that she had learnt that it is really important to keep a calm front (emotional labour), and use a measured tone, especially with parents. The look on your face is important, she suggested, or as she put it: "Must make sure you are not leaking!" This is a clear example of emotional labour from a leader. Those who interact with the public professionally, such as staff in schools, and especially in leadership positions need to have a "professional/rational" part of themselves on display most of the time. This containment and regulation is necessary for the smooth running of schools, and how leaders present themselves, and how they manage the emotions and feelings that occur in everyday interactions. It is deceptively easy to describe, and much more difficult to manage over long periods of time, and especially in times of great emotional upheaval.

'Acting the part' for leaders is crucial for many leadership activities, e.g. when they wanted to raise the spirits of others, or alter the mood in a specific setting. This is a rational decision. Extreme feelings can initially be handled in an "acting the part/rational way", to help others manage their emotions initially (e.g. death, serious illness of a child in school), but it may also be important for leaders to let others know when they felt such distress. Emotions, such as shame and anxiety, which might reflect on their own leadership judgements, are more difficult to handle, especially as many leaders in education do not have a non-judgement emotional outlet. Accountability and personal responsibility for the schools results are issues that were adding to this burden. It is difficult for leaders to express concern about the way they have handled particular incidents without being judged as ineffective as a leader.

Leaders in schools can often act as a conduit for others' emotions (Beatty 2002; James 2003). Both men and women can be constrained by the educational leadership literature's focus on rationality to the detriment of understandings and expressions of emotionality as important for effective leadership. This can be viewed at several levels in schools. Although displays of emotions can be "real", they can also be managed to influence others. For example, leaders can use emotional displays to assert their power, whether the emotions shown are real or put on for the benefit of the other party. It is in this everyday practice where the intertwining of rationality and emotion can be seen clearly. No one wants to be seen as out of control emotionally, but should the context demand it, leaders can utilise the power of emotional expression. This is very much conscious emotional management. Lewis (2004) argues that there are some emotions that are managed more self-consciously than others. There are, for example, particularly self-conscious emotions which are difficult to describe or handle because only the individual who feels the shame can identify the events that cause them. When head teachers are no longer able to manage and regulate their emotions, then stress and ultimately breakdown are the more likely to occur. Lewis also notes that all such self-conscious emotions have at their centre the notion of self (p. 623). This leads into the part that personal histories play in emotion and leadership, in particular in terms of understanding the self. To look at why this may maybe, it can be useful to consider the individual's life story.

Individual Biographies and Emotional Well-Being

One of the less explored areas in leadership is the idea of a leadership narrative, within which leaders frame their working lives (Crawford 2009). It is often through life story research that researchers can shed light on individuals and their emotional well-being. At the same time, leaders can find aspects of autobiographical work illuminating to their own practice. By developing a narrative of their own leadership journey, they can look in a reflective, perhaps rational way, at emotional events that have occurred along their career route.

Personal histories are powerful. During my initial research (Crawford 2009), I was surprised by the power of story and the social context to move my respondents, and, in particular, their memories of childhood, and also what Denzin calls "emotional epiphanies" in the workplace and their personal lives (Denzin 1984). Autobiographical knowledge (Hargie and Dickson 2004), knowing "where you come from", and "who you are", is clearly important in most professions, but may be particularly important in such a value-based profession as education. I would argue that the educational leadership literature generally downgrades the importance of identity, self and emotion. As a field we need to unravel the connections between leadership, emotion and the head teacher's life story, as part of the understandings generated from the newer emotional perspectives on leadership, through realising that leadership experiences are inseparable from our relationships with others. It is through these relationships that many emotional experiences are played out in schools.

A leader's personal leadership narrative also frames their practice. How a head teacher conceptualises his or her own leadership will have an impact on the way that their leadership is then practised. The personal leadership narrative highlights the idea of emotions being both inherent *and* socially constructed. The telling of the leadership narrative to others can help leadership understand their own leadership practices and how they relate to their own identity and to their management of emotion. Personal narratives also reveal some of the complex relationship between emotion and rationality as they are opportunities to look back in a rational manner at what may have been emotional experiences.

Emotional Themes of Leadership

In terms of rationality and emotion, the popularity of EI should be mentioned to contextualise the discussion. EI has been criticised for becoming too focused on emotional competences, and therefore a way to discover easily if one is competent emotionally in a work context. Fineman (2000a) suggests that emotion has become a management commodity. He argues that it has always been known that certain work relationships require emotional skills (p. 102), but with EI, such competences are linked explicitly to business success, and by extrapolation to effective schools. Fineman suggests that such management ideas become popular because of "psychological, cultural and rhetorical factors" (p. 103). EI may give business a competitive edge, so it is something that business and educational leaders should take note of. Again Fineman notes (p. 105):

> Presenting emotional intelligence as a learned competence or set of competences is a key ingredient of the sell [...] emotional intelligence is stripped of any "irrational", "feminine", even "feeling" connotations that could worry or alienate managers. It is less a celebration of feeling than a resource to enhance managers' "intelligent", rational control.

Leadership in schools requires emotional skill, and EI has taken its place amongst other leadership strategies. However, Fineman sounds a warning note (p. 109):

> The search for key, universal, characteristics of managerial success has a long history of futility. If emotionally intelligent managers succeed, so do/have managers who seem to make no conscious choice about how to express their emotions—be they typically kind, charismatic, impassive, volatile, aggressive, autocratic, even ruthless. On this basis it would, at times, be emotionally intelligent to be uncompromising, inflexible, angry or pessimistic.

Both the popularity and the plausibility of EI may be because it reminds leaders what they intuitively knew already; that emotion and thinking do work together. Also, rational discussion of emotional competences through EI is emotionally safe, and does not require or suggest a change in internal personal feelings.

If leadership is an organisational quality, then so is emotion. To paraphrase Ogawa and Bossert from earlier in this chapter, emotion flows through the network of people who comprise schools, but at the same time, emotion in educational leadership resides not only in the organisation, and makes up the emotional context of the school. It would seem that leaders have to balance the rational and emotional in many direct ways. For example, it may be that for an effective school they have to build a climate where acceptance and trust are key, and others not only want to follow them as leaders, but feel able to become leaders themselves—the task of emotionalising organisations (Fineman 2000b, p. 278). Thus positive emotion could be a necessary condition of distributed leadership. At the same time, the dark side of emotion with shame and embarrassment used to push the performativity agenda may also be a true picture of some schools. Emotionalising schools for good or bad allows new understandings of emotion to inform leadership, and allows leaders to ask how and why emotions shape these processes.

Emotional ways of knowing about what educational leadership is do allow for the rational and emotional to overlap in a practical manner for leaders. Aristotle suggested that practical wisdom is about being able to deliberate well about the things that are good and helpful, so school leaders can use their own understandings of emotion and rationality to inform their practice. By asking what enables successful organisations to succeed and thrive, one of the answers may be that the emotional narrative of the organisations leaders will influence that context so others can be effective. There is a complex social interaction taking place at all times within the organisation. As Whitaker (1997, p. 140) notes:

> It is through the countless interpersonal transactions of the school day that people's lives are changed, organisational improvements are made, dreams are realised and needs are met. We need more understanding of those snatched moments in corridors. [...] Life-centred leadership is essentially a catalytic process, helping others to bring about changes in themselves.

What Whittaker calls "Life centred leadership" is essentially about emotion and about every leader in a school. The catalytic process enables the emotional networks of schools to function effectively.

Southworth has argued (2004, p. 22) that the literature on headship, particularly in primary schools is far too preoccupied with seeing leadership through the lens of the head teacher, and casting heads as "pivotal, proprietorial and powerful", whilst in fact the landscape is changing towards distributed and "learning-centred leadership". Although the rhetoric of the landscape may well have altered, the head teacher is still an emotional pivot in many schools, especially small primary schools. Their own emotional well-being is still vital to create the conditions in which other sorts of leadership can develop and thrive. This could then be extrapolated to senior leaders in larger schools, as often the secondary head can shield him-/herself from day-to-day emotional interactions, This pivotal emotional role was summed up by one head teacher I spoke to in a large primary school:

> Somebody who has clear sense of what they are trying to do and has a firm grip on what's happening and what others are doing. I aim to have open lines of communication—so that staff know what I am thinking and why I am thinking it; a spider in the centre of a web, but not aggressive one!

Her knowledge of her own emotional self enabled her to visualise how she wanted others to relate to each other within the school (staff, parents and children), within an emotional coherent context.

More research needs to be done in schools to clarify the interaction between biological, social and cultural issues in the lives of leaders, to uncover relationships which signpost the links between life history, relationships at home and work, and socialisation. This also has links to leadership development programmes.

Leadership Development

I have already noted that one of the important emotional roles of a school leader is to create the conditions in which people will want to work to the optimum levels of their energy, interest and commitment (Whitaker 1997). Hay McBer calls this sort of commitment, discretionary effort, where people are willing to "go the extra mile" for others in the team or group within which they work: Emotional bonds are often key to this as well.

As I noted above, leadership training has usefully developed EI and the idea of emotional competences, and this has proved helpful to many people. In this section, I want to sketch good practice from research, and then suggest what other areas could be explored. In terms of the personal, emotional side of leadership mentoring and coaching, are often available in both courses from private providers and the National College. Emotion and leadership can be viewed as difficult territory, methods such as storytelling and drama, reflection and journals could be used in relation to emotion and educational leadership. The Lupton (1998) categorisation is a useful aid to thinking, and helps leaders understand that there may well be a cognitive rationale for actions, but there might also be underlying and probably stronger affective rationale. Dillard (1995) convincingly suggests that leaders lead from themselves as people, their past experiences and their personalities and life experiences. For some head teachers, due to any of all of these factors, any display of emotion, either in themselves or others, may be perceived as inappropriate for a head teacher. Møller (2005) suggests that viewing emotion as dangerous reflects a western set of values which split reason from emotion. She notes:

> Rationality has almost been considered sacred and holy, while emotions have been perceived as being more or less inappropriate to talk about and thus devalued in organisations. Nevertheless, it has been recognised that emotions serve essential needs in organisations because they contribute to the development of community, commitment and collective morality [...] however, they (writers) have tended to treat emotions as an instrumental means towards the goals set by organisations. (2005, p. 89)

Moeller argues that this has begun to alter over the last ten years as writers view teaching as an emotional practice, which has been partially reflected in the leadership literature.

Another thematic area that is closely allied to emotion is that of context. Educational leadership research consistently notes the importance of context. In creating greater understanding of the role of emotion in leadership, Howe (1993, p. 140) suggests that leaders draw on three key ingredients in emotional transactions that are relevant to any discussion of context:

- Acceptance (a secure emotional base for the relationship)
- Understanding (an appreciation of the other person's felt experience)
- Dialogue (the communication of understanding and meaning)

More understanding of such aspects of emotional context could draw on present work about context, bringing together the personal and the socially constructed perspectives. Developing leaders' conceptual knowledge of emotional labour through discussion of both the conceptual and the practical side could enhance their own leadership practice and also act as a warning in terms of their own management of emotion. This has implications for long-term sustainability, for building networks, perhaps carried out through group work with cohorts of leaders at different times in their career. Helpful, positive epiphanies could be shared as well as more emotionally wounding experiences. The personal leadership narrative could also be expanded upon as leaders grow and develop. The high accountability framework within which school leadership is situated means that there are very few "safe" emotional spaces for leaders. Creating safe spaces is a challenge for both leaders in schools and those involved at a more systemic level in Local Authorities and networked schools.

Rational or Emotional?

This chapter has been a discussion of the relevance of emotion to leadership in schools and whether there the rational/emotional discussion adds to our developing conceptualisations of emotion and leadership. "Being rational" treats feelings and emotions as "objects" that are separate from organisational practice. Acknowledging the place of the rational within an emotional conceptualisation of an organisation, means that leaders can view both aspects as inherent to leadership. The somewhat restricted view of feelings and emotions in the educational leadership literature, which often limits discussion to conscious experience (EI) can be expanded into a focus on personal narrative and the rational/emotional interface. Leaders can be enabled to understand how their own personal emotional coherence is related to a healthy emotional context, and with (perhaps?) less emotional labour for the head teacher. This aligns with what Senge (1990) calls "the by-product of a lifetime of effort to develop conceptual and communication skills, to reflect on personal values and to align personal behaviour with values, to learn how to listen and to appreciate others and others' ideas". There is still only a partial understanding of both "emotion and leadership", and how this relates to teachers' lives and career paths. Especially at a time of recruitment difficulties, there is an urgent need to develop such understandings by carrying out further research into the area. To paraphrase Leadership cannot, and does not function without emotion. Over the next few years as the Every Child Matters (ECM) agenda is implemented, this emphasis on the personal and social relations is even more crucial. Educational leadership is about people, and people necessarily work in an emotional context, intra-personally and inter-personally. As Glatter (2006, p. 82) states:

> We should consciously seek to contribute to [...] the broader field of organization and management studies, in which [...] schools and universities can be viewed—along for example with churches, counselling agencies, hospitals and prisons—as *human service organizations* whose core task is transforming humans. That is not the core task of (for example), either H.M. Revenue and Customs, in the public sector, or of Tesco in the private sector.

Human service organisations are fundamentally about people. Where people are the core business, then an understanding of emotion and leadership is clearly crucial.

Conclusions

I have argued that the educational leadership field has only begun to discover how research into emotion can enrich educational leadership. Loader (1997, p. 3) wrote a rare example of deeply personal reflections on emotion and educational leadership from someone who has held senior leadership positions. He argues for a more personal, inherently emotional approach to leadership. In particular, he notes the emotional reality of life for those whose careers take them into leadership positions. He writes: "Leadership has its highs and lows, its successes and failures. Principals cry, laugh, dream and become suspicious. There are times when principals do want the fairy godmother to come and save them." Understanding that leadership involves this much self-realisation may be one of the rational points that truly effective school leaders have to face, and learn to manage.

References

Beatty, B. (2000). The emotions of educational leadership: Breaking the silence. *International Journal of Leadership in Education, 3*(4), 331–357.

Beatty, B. R. (2002). *Emotion matters in educational leadership: Examining the unexamined.* Doctoral thesis, Graduate Department of Theory and Policy Studies in Education, Ontario Institute for Studies in Education, University of Toronto, Toronto.

Briner, R. (1999). The neglect and importance of emotion at work. *European Journal of Work and Organizational Psychology, 8*(3), 323–346.

Crawford, M. (2008). Emotional coherence and the team. In E. Samier (Ed.), *Emotions in education.* London: RoutledgeFalmer.

Crawford, M. (2009). *Getting to the heart of leadership.* London: Sage.

Crawford, M., & James, C. (2006). *A new paradigm of emotion and educational leadership.* Paper presented at BERA conference, Warwick.

Day, C. (2004). The passion of successful leadership. *School Leadership and Management, 24*(4), 425–438.

Denzin, N. (1984). *On understanding emotion.* San Francisco: Jossey-Bass.

Dillard, C. B. (1995). Leading with her life: An African Feminist (re) interpretation of leadership for an urban high school principal. *Educational Administration Quarterly, 31*(4), 539–563.

Fineman, S. (2000a). Commodifying the emotionally intelligent. In S. Fineman (Ed.), *Emotion in organizations.* London: Sage.

Fineman, S. (Ed.). (2000b). *Emotion in organizations.* London: Sage.

Fineman, S. (2008). *The emotional organisation: Passions and power.* Oxford: Blackwell.

Glatter, R. (2006). Leadership and organization in education: Time for a re-orientation? *School Leadership and Management, 26*(1), 69–84.

Gronn, P. (2003). *The new work of new educational leaders: Changing leadership practice in an era of school reform.* London: Paul Chapman.

Hargie, O., & Dickson, D. (2004). *Skilled interpersonal communication.* London: Routledge.

Hochschild, A. R. (1983). *The managed heart: Commercialization of human feeling.* Berkley: University of California Press.

Howe, D. (1993). *On being a client: Understanding the process of counselling and psychotherapy.* London: Sage.

James, C. (2003). *The work of educational leaders in building creative and passionate schools and colleges.* Paper presented at the BELMAS conference, Milton Keynes, England.

Kemper, T. D. (2004). Social models in the explanation of emotions. In M. Lewis & J. Haviland-Jones (Eds.), *Handbook of emotions.* New York: Guilford.

Law, S., & Glover, D. (2000). *Educational leadership and learning.* Buckingham: Open University Press.

Lewis, M. (2004). Self-conscious emotions: Embarrassment, pride, shame and guilt. In M. Lewis & J. Haviland-Jones (Eds.), *The handbook of emotions.* New York: Guilford.

Loader, D. (1997). *The inner principal.* Falmer.

Lupton, D. (1998). *The emotional self.* London, Sage.

Møller, J. (2005). Coping with accountability. In C. Sugrue (Ed.), *Passionate principalship; learning from the life history of leaders.* London: RoutledgeFalmer.

Ogawa, R. T., & S. T. Bossert (1997). Leadership as an organisational quality. In M. Crawford, L. Kydd, & C. Riches (Eds.), *Leadership and teams in educational management*. Buckingham: Open University Press.

Richardson, E. (1973). *The teacher, the school and the task of management*. London: Heinemann.

Senge, P. (1990). *The fifth discipline*. London: Century Business.

Southworth, G. (2004). *Primary school leadership in context; leading small, medium and large sized schools*. London: RoutledgeFalmer.

Whitaker, P. (1997). *Primary schools and the future*. Buckingham: Open University Press.

Chapter 14
Leadership and Teacher Emotions

Brenda R. Beatty

This chapter presents a discussion of theoretical and practical implications from the author's research into the emotions of teaching, leading and learning. Discussed are explorations of impact from programmatic approaches to leadership development that have been grounded in the author's theoretical framework of emotional epistemologies. This framework was derived from empirical studies with 50 Ontario teachers and 35 school principals in six western nation states (Beatty 2002a, b). Impact studies from applications of this framework in Masters level school leader preparation courses in the United States and Australia reveal the transformational power of breaking the silence on emotion and positioning inner leadership as foundational to educational professionalism. In a collaborative project 3,000 secondary school student survey responses allowed co-researchers to validate an instrument to measure student sense of connectedness with school (Beatty and Brew 2005). Structural equation modelling with these data provided plausible evidence of linkages among student trust in leaders, trust in teachers, sense of belonging with peers, academic engagement, confidence in self at school and academic performance. These findings echo linkages between student performance and trust factors identified by Bryk and Schneider (2002) who focused on trust among adults in schools. Leadership preparation programmes grounded in leaders' emotional preparedness, personal resilience and well-being, fostered by transcending the normative professional silence on emotion, are providing evidence of impact from this approach. Challenging traditions of isolation and self-denial, emerging evidence confirms that leaders who learn how to do the inner work of emotional meaning making (Beatty 2002a) for emotional understanding (Denzin 1984) are able to create school cultures that revitalise their own, as well as teachers' and students' learning. Conclusions reflect the position that reconnecting with the power of emotions benefits all concerned, including and especially the students.

B. R. Beatty (✉)
School of Graduate Studies in Education, University of Melbourne, Melbourne, VIC, Australia
e-mail: bbeatty@unimelb.edu.au, brendabeatty@brbconsulting.ca

C. Day, J. C.-K. Lee (eds.), *New Understandings of Teacher's Work,* Professional Learning and Development in Schools and Higher Education 6,
DOI 10.1007/978-94-007-0545-6_14,

Social Emotional Factors in Learning, Teaching and Leading[1]

In his argument for developing leaders for their future not our past, Dean Fink reminds us,

> Learning for understanding is not just a cognitive and psychological matter…It involves more than constructivism, multiple intelligences, metacognition, or problem-based learning. Deep learning and teaching are also cultural and emotional processes. (Fink 2005, p. 1)

We know about the power of social interaction in learning (Vygotsky 1978); and the importance of the "gift of confidence" when teachers provide support and guidance for learners who are entering the zone of their proximal development (Mahn and John-Steiner 2002, p. 46). We also know that for adults especially, there is an important impact upon epistemological perspectives from interactive learning with peers (e.g. Perry 1970; Belenky et al. 1986, 1997; Baxter Magolda 1992). The shift from external to internal knowledge authority is catalysed through meaningful collaboration with one's learning peers. Thus it should not surprise us that among the most important conditions for school success are the qualities of relationships; that is, whether they create or fail to engender a sense of safety and belonging that supports genuine inquiry and willingness to risk.

The presence or absence of social protective factors is well known to be predictive of pro or anti-social behaviours and learning outcomes (Dean et al. 2007). However, we are just beginning to understand how intertwined are the relationships among adults in schools with the social emotional conditions for student learning. There is empirical evidence that trust among adults in schools is predictive of student performance (Bryk and Schneider 2002). In a study in which co-researchers developed and validated an instrument to measure student sense of connectedness with school (Beatty and Brew 2005), structural equation modelling provided evidence of plausible connections among student trust in leaders, trust in teachers, sense of belonging with peers, academic engagement, confidence in self at school and academic expectations.

Leaders influence the relative sense of safety and openness to collaboration in the cultures of their schools and correspondingly, the learning conditions of their students (Silins and Mulford 2002) and teachers (Leithwood and Beatty 2008). The need for a secure foundation from which to experiment and take learning risks is as important for adults as it is for children. School leaders figure largely in the picture of teacher learning in this respect. When leaders model ways of being that acknowledge vulnerability and earn trust, all adults in schools can have a constructive impact upon each other, as well as the children and their parents, through flow-on effects that are most accurately envisioned in exponential terms. Correspondingly, the all too common distance and disconnection among adults, among children and between adults and children, especially in secondary schools (Brady 2008), can

[1] Much of the early part of this chapter has appeared in Leading & Managing, Vol. 13, No. 2, 2007, pp. 44–65.

create conditions far from ideal for learning, with proportionally similar ramifications.

Leading Edge Leadership Development

The agenda for learning in schools has shifted dramatically. It is no longer enough to teach and learn only the things that are already known. Schools of today need to promote an ethic of learning to learn, of embracing the unknown with curiosity and confidence. By re-culturing for conditions of social and emotion safety, schools can encourage creativity, bold self-critique, rigorous reflective practice and genuine collaborative inquiry, so as to release powerful potential for transformation at all levels. Correspondingly, leading edge principles for leadership development programming, wisely involve the creation of learning communities, enquiry into real issues, familiarity with research, theory and practice, focus on improved pedagogy and renewed interest in ongoing professional learning (e.g. Paterson and West-Burnham 2005).

In their thorough review of the literature on successful school leadership, Leithwood et al. (2007) present "seven strong claims" supported by empirical evidence both qualitative and quantitative from small and large-scale studies. These authors echo others' findings that classroom teaching has the greatest influence on pupil learning. They link leader practices to classroom practices through their influence on school culture, noting that it is the ways in which leaders demonstrate responsiveness to their contexts more than the practices themselves that powerfully influence teacher motivation, commitment and working conditions. Their review notes that different models of distributed leadership abound, some more effective than others. Finally, they feature a small handful of leaders' personal traits that seem to explain most of the variation in leader effectiveness:

> The most successful school leaders are open-minded and ready to learn from others. They are also flexible rather than dogmatic in their thinking within a system of core values, persistent (e.g. in pursuit of high expectations of staff motivation, commitment, learning and achievement for all), resilient and optimistic. Such traits help explain why successful leaders facing daunting conditions are then able to push forward when there is little reason to expect progress. (Leithwood et al. 2007, p. 14)

The persistent leader who pushes forward despite resistance, to establish dynamic collaborative inquiry, action learning and integrated interdisciplinary thinking has experienced border crossings. The insistence upon new ways of learning and teaching can be confronting and emotionally discomforting. School leaders who promote change in their schools inevitably traverse this terrain, and are regularly wounded in the process (Ackerman and Maslin-Ostrowski 2002, 2004). Without support systems to assist with the healing, wounded leaders can become discouraged, scarred and thus compromised in their overall capabilities. This is especially likely if they remain unsupported with the inner work required to remain personally and professionally whole (Beatty 2005, 2006). Ackerman and Maslin-Ostrowski (2002) suggest the real wound is the loss of the feeling function. Untreated woundings of children, parents, teachers and leaders alike, and the attendant symptoms of emotional numbness can undermine the best laid plans for improvement.

Conversely, the embrace of a "pedagogy of discomfort" (Boler 1999) is a place to begin so that silent suffering is acknowledged and worked through, rather than denied and buried. The openness to exploring one's inner emotional world helps to build resilience. Persons maintain their recuperative powers through the emotional preparedness to explore and learn from the pain.

Persistence in the face of setbacks and disappointments is particularly critical to leadership success which ideally involves facing into and working through these emotional challenges. While the normative administrative culture may tend to deny or dismiss emotions as pesky interlopers (Beatty 2000a), emotions are not optional. They are influential regardless of our consciousness of them. School Leadership preparation program designs that address this social/emotional territory help to develop resilient leaders who will not only survive but also thrive in the role. In leading edge programs cohort structures that emphasise collaborative reflection are creating places within which inner leadership and emotional meaning making (Beatty 2002b) for emotional understanding (Denzin 1984) can help to reframe successful school leadership for the future.

Facing the Future by Understanding and Challenging the Status Quo

"Persistent" is also as good a word as any to describe school cultures especially in high schools, which tend to remain highly bureaucratic with all of the usual fragmentation, compartmentalisation and hegemony that regularly resist well-intended efforts to develop dynamic learning communities. According to Max Weber, there is inertia in bureaucracies whose iron cage qualities can be attributed to depersonalisation.

> …the more fully realized the more bureaucracy "depersonalizes" itself, i.e., the more completely it succeeds in achieving the exclusion of love, hatred, and every purely personal, especially irrational and incalculable, feeling from the execution of official tasks. In the place of the old-type ruler who is moved by sympathy, favor, grace, and gratitude, modern culture requires for its sustaining external apparatus the emotionally detached, and hence rigorously "professional" expert. (Max Weber as cited in Coser 1977, p. 230)

A reinforcing spiral of cause and effect appears: depersonalisation through the exclusion of emotion ensures the endurance of the bureaucratic culture, which in turn ensures continued exclusion of emotion and further depersonalisation. By co-maintaining the silence on emotion, teachers and leaders become part of this self-replicating mechanism of bureaucratic hierarchy. The key is to interrupt the cycle. Successful emotionally grounded school leadership does just that, by transcending the cultural imperative for depersonalisation.

In the educational discourse the call for a departure from traditional bureaucratic hierarchies has been heard for some time; for instance, in the advocacy for teacher empowerment in shared decision-making (e.g. Malen and Ogawa 1988; Blase and Blase 1994; Peterson et al. 1995; Short and Greer 1997) and the associated necessity of different, more collaborative relationships (e.g. Dunlap and Goldman 1991). However, the focus on the emotional dimension of leader–teacher relationships is a relatively recent arrival. Blase and Blase (1994, 2001) note some of the emotional effects on teachers from the process of being empowered. Desirable qualities of leaders who employ transformative, facilitative styles that involve engaging in 'power with' their teachers are reflected in positive emotional indicators, conceptualised as micro-political phenomena (Blase and Anderson 1995).

Instructionally focused leadership implicitly involves acknowledging expertise and establishing developmental processes for teachers and leaders (Glickman et al. 1998). The professional domain of the classroom is emotionally sensitive territory for teachers. Understandably, sensitivity to these emotion matters is foundational to effective instructionally focused leadership.

The need to build a more humane and interpersonally connected professional culture in schools has been well argued (see, for example, Nias et al. 1989; Lieberman 1996; Hargreaves 1998a, b; Fullan 1999). When such collaborative cultures are developed, they are enjoyed and celebrated in their effectiveness for teaching and learning. Such cultures are also reportedly more emotionally comfortable (Nias et al. 1989).

Yet, despite the encouraging evidence from a minority of exemplary collaborative schools, in the main, the teacher–leader relationship remains problematic (Blase and Anderson 1995; Blase and Blase 2003). While we may be able to envision that school cultures need to evolve as the teachers and leaders within them become energised by the spirit of creative cooperation in dynamic learning communities, if depersonalisation persists, the envisioned evolution is unlikely.

What Is It About the Teacher–Leader Relationship?

Starratt (1991) characterises the traditional teacher–principal relationship as one of antagonism. By contrast, he describes a constructive teacher–principal relationship as open and trusting. The gap between the normative pattern and that described below represents a gap in emotional understanding.

> The administrator who is concerned with nurturing the growth of teachers will have to ensure that teachers experience the relationship with the administrator as one of regard, mutual respect, and honest contact between two persons. Even though their traditional organisational roles have conditioned administrators and teachers to an antagonistic relationship, in a school intentionally restructuring itself and concerned about issues of empowerment, it is possible to move toward a relationship based on caring. For relationships of caring to develop, administrators will initially explore with their teachers those

> conditions necessary to initiate and maintain trust, honesty, and open communication (Starratt 1991, p. 196).

The capacity for organisational change is defined by the extent to which emotionally significant matters can be openly addressed (Fineman 1996). With current pressures for educational change and accountability regimes that threaten principals' and teachers' very jobs, Starratt's statements become even more loaded with emotional implications for leaders and for teachers. If they are to accomplish a change in the nature of their relationship—from antagonistic to collaborative—likely to be a prerequisite of survival—trust, so hard won and easily lost, will be the deciding factor.

Trust is reflected in "an individual's or group's willingness to be vulnerable to another party based on the confidence that the latter party is benevolent, reliable, competent, honest, and open" (Hoy and Tschannen-Moran 1999, p. 189). There is no room for antagonism in one who would be nurturing and open, respectful, and trustworthy, honest and caring. All of these actions and qualities on the part of an educational leader involve shifts into a praxis that is philosophically and emotionally different from the status quo in most schools.

To re-culture our schools for the future, we need to understand the patterns of the past. The silencing of individual emotion happens in the midst of an insidious social emotional phenomenon—the adherence to organisational feeling rules (Hochschild 1983), such that "…the altruist is more susceptible to being used—not because her sense of self is weaker but because her 'true self' is bonded more securely to the group and its welfare" (Hochschild 1983, p. 196). This has a disturbingly familiar ring to it for teachers and school leaders, who are professional altruists in the end, using their inner resources for professional service. If emotions are treated as organisational assets, such that "the company offers the worker's true self for sale, the more that self risks seeming false to the individual worker, and the more difficult it becomes for him or her to know which territory of self to claim" (Hochschild 1983, p. 196). The cultural norms that drive emotions underground by exchanging silence for membership can, ironically, rob the entire organisation of any chance at authenticity.

It is one thing to call for the re-culturing of schools (Fullan and Hargreaves 1996) and the repositioning of priorities in leader praxis. It is another to provide workable ways of helping leaders to redefine their professional selves and begin to practice with new priorities. What would it take? And how might whatever it takes be applied in leadership preparation? These questions have formed the impetus for a research agenda that has held me in its grip for over a decade.

To understand the existing patterns in teacher–leader relationships, it has been helpful to explore the lived experiences of teachers and leaders to learn more about the spaces they occupy together, in schools and in each other's minds. Given that emotional silence is taken to be synonymous with professionalism (Beatty 2000a), the first step was to break the silence by creating opportunities for teachers and leaders to take us into their inner worlds. This research agenda has assisted me in discovering the role of emotional understanding in healthy relationships and those characterised by disconnection and antagonism.

This challenging territory calls for the development of a legitimate place for the language of emotion. The studies discussed in the remainder of this chapter have contributed to a growing number of efforts to explore the meaning of emotions in education and to contribute to our developing understanding of emotion's place in the lexicon of leadership.

Teachers Talk About Their Emotional Memories of School Leaders

As one of a team of researchers,[2] I was privileged to have responsibility for the analysis of a powerful data base drawn from a project on *The Emotions of Teaching and Educational Change* funded by the Social Science and Humanities Research Council of Canada which provided transcribed interviews with 50 teachers in Ontario from 15 schools of various sizes, at primary and secondary levels within rural, urban and suburban communities. Principals were asked to identify up to four teachers including oldest and youngest, a gender mix, a range of subject specialist areas and at least one person from an ethno-cultural minority. Interviews were one to one-and-one-half hours in duration and considered a range of aspects of teachers' work. Within these interviews, teachers recounted their personal stories of both an emotionally positive and an emotionally negative experience with school administrators. This method of emotional recall is a procedure used by Hochschild (1983) in her foundational work on the subject, entitled, *The Managed Heart: The Commercialization of Human Feeling.* Although one-time interviews that focus on critical episodes cannot provide definitive evidence of overall frequencies of occurrences, they do provide a window upon the things that teachers find emotionally significant and memorable. Data were coded in a series of iterations that yielded three levels of analysis with theorisable patterns. Inferential statistical explorations provided evidence from which it was possible to conceptualise unique relationships among the various teacher emotional ways of knowing their leaders. All data were accounted for in these grounded theoretical processes. Featured here are results and conclusions from leader-related accounts within interviews from the larger study.[3]

In the first level of analysis the domains of convergence and associated concerns over which teachers had recalled their leaders were represented in the following categories: career, students, and associations between leadership type/style and emotional climate, with matters concerning colleagues, organisational procedures and parents appearing far less frequently. According to the frequency distribution of the

[2] In Beatty's doctoral thesis (winner of the CASEA Thomas B. Greenfield Dissertation of the Year in Canada award), the teacher interview data that related to their experience with leaders were provided by a project entitled *The Emotions of Teaching and Educational Change*, funded by the Social Science and Humanities Research Council of Canada as Grant No. 418699; the online leader data were collected with the support of the University of Waikato, New Zealand.

[3] For other detailed discussions of this study, see also Hargreaves (2000), Schmidt (2000), Lasky (2000).

categories, leaders matter most to teachers in terms of how they can and do affect their careers. For some, just being hired or rehired was the most emotionally positive recollection they could muster, and in some accounts it was clear that the principal had gone to great lengths to keep them on. Being allowed to move schools without recrimination was a great relief to one teacher, and being encouraged to grow professionally was highly valued by others. On the other hand, damaging job references, the blocking of a transfer and interference with professional plans, along with non-consultative decisions about timetable and other responsibilities, damaged teachers' trust and led them to feel anger, frustration and fear. Distrust of their leaders' intentions and the threat of potential danger in teachers' professional lives were clear.

Those teachers who felt supported by their administrator with respect to their career aspirations appreciated the extra effort that leaders made to assist them in maintaining or upgrading their positions. This reportedly made them feel valued and acknowledged for their professional worth. This level of analysis allowed me to see the connections among occasions of leader teacher convergence, the kinds of concern and qualities and frequencies of emotions. The concerns teachers had about their careers and their students as well as their overall sense of the emotional climate associated with demonstrations of openness and honesty, or the lack thereof, were strongly represented.

While the first level of analysis allowed me to discover the intersubjective patterns in their interactions, the second level of analysis allowed me to explore in more detail, the intrasubjective territory of emotional meanings that their leaders had acquired in these teachers' memories, and how they had come to matter to the teacher's self. Indications of different emotional needs, and different kinds of leader effects relative to these needs were apparent. Each positive and negative story was coded for teacher inferences about their leaders' predispositions toward them. Across the positive and negative stories inferences of respect/disrespect, care/lack of care and professional support/lack of professional support were apparent.

Leaders emerged as emotionally significant to teachers for their ability (1) to *affirm* or *invalidate* their professional self by conferring thanks, praise or recognition and thus *respect* upon them or by withholding thanks, praise or being overtly disrespectful—with female administrators more often associated than male administrators with affirmation and respect; (2) to *create* or *destroy* the sense of *care* in relationship, with the teacher's self experiencing a sense of safety and welcome from leaders' openness to teachers' personal needs and intellectual ideas or undermining the sense of safety by disregarding teachers. Male administrators more often than female administrators were remembered for creating an ethic of care. This departure from the reported associations between males and bureaucratic controlling styles (Collard 2001) is noteworthy; (3) to *provide* or *neglect* to provide professional support with student discipline, colleague conflicts, timetabled responsibilities and opportunities for professional growth. For this area of concern, there was no evidence to suggest that male and female administrators were remembered as tending to deal with these issues differently.

An examination of distribution patterns among the respect/disrespect, care/lack of care and professional support/lack of professional support categories, suggested

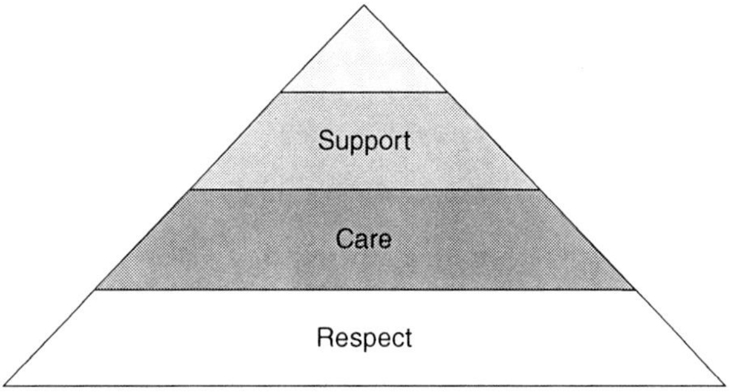

Fig. 14.1 Relationships among respect, care and professional support

a relationship among these categories. While stories of respect and disrespect were fairly evenly distributed, stories of care were overrepresented in the positive with notably low frequencies for lack of care. To interpret this pattern I wondered, could it be that there are low expectations of leaders to demonstrate care for teachers? It would seem that a Maslovian (Maslow 1954) hierarchical relationship exists among the three categories, as illustrated in Fig. 14.1. Respect is essential; care and support are revered.

The third level of analysis involved the assessment of communication type, according to medium and quality. Among the positive stories there was a definite preference for face-to-face as opposed to written communication, with *engaged* two-way communication being held as the ideal. The teachers' positive emotional stories about their leaders stood out for their association with teacher satisfaction and sense of security and optimism. From these stories, it was clear that teachers valued the opportunity for meaningful mutual engagement and learning reciprocity (Little 1982) with their leaders. Correspondingly, among the negative stories, while face-to-face interactions predominated here too, a full 20% of these accounts had involved no communication at all and a range of relationship-damaging interpretations of leaders' "silence".

Among the negative interaction subset, a pattern of discontinuous emotional meanings and emotional misunderstandings suggested that these teachers and their leaders may have had parallel, but non-intersecting perspectives on matters of career, students, school climate, organisational procedures and colleagues. Long-standing career effects such as the loss of confidence for stepping up to leadership and alienation from professional self-efficacy had resulted from unresolved issues. Prolonged distress had been exacerbated by the professional blackout on discussing how these teachers were really feeling. Emotionally wounding experiences revealed a sense of teachers feeling trapped behind a barrier of emotional silence which had isolated them from these influential professional colleagues.

Relationship Requires Interaction

The results of the teacher study affirmed the positive power of an emotional connection between teachers and their leaders. Indeed, the potential for what Beattie

(1995) calls interacting narratives, deserves attention in strategic restructuring so as to provide encouragement and regular opportunities for teachers and leaders to reconstruct and reconstitute their relationships.

The collaborative schools in particular were emotionally comfortable places, but they were also tough-minded. Their staff could confront and attempt to resolve differences, not least because they were able to deal constructively with the personal and professional aftermath of any disagreements that might occur (Nias et al. 1989, p. 182).

The emotional implications of facing fears and moving toward emotionally challenging, even professionally dangerous (Maurer 1996) terrain point to a need for courage and counter-intuition (Beatty 2002b) on the part of both teachers and leaders if they are to challenge the normative feeling rules (Hochschild 1983) that keep them apart. But leaders need to go first. Most of the teachers who had ventured uninvited into contentious emotional terrain had suffered additional shame. Only one teacher's daring had reaped the reward of a better relationship. Apologies from leaders and the ongoing sense of their openness to consultation and critique were respected and celebrated. Such leaders had engendered longstanding loyalty among staff members, some of whom would be happy to follow leaders to their new schools when they were reassigned.

In the context of policy reform toward greater accountability, the issue of mutual *emotional accountability* in the teacher–administrator relationship emerges as worthy of further consideration. The relationship among respect, care, support and the teacher's professional self, returns to the ability to hope, to remain optimistic. Leaders figured prominently in these teachers' ability to remain resourceful and effective.

> Remember the metaphorical lost cause, or Csikszentmihalyi's (1990) observation that "frustration is deeply woven into the fabric of life" (p. 7). This is the lot of teachers. The more they care, the more anxious they get. The more that they become emotionally detached, the poorer the decisions they make. Understanding the intimate two-way link between emotion and hope is a powerful insight. Hope is not a native, sunny view of life. It is the capacity not to panic in tight situations, to find ways and resources to address difficult problems.... Finding a way to reconcile positive and negative emotion is the key to releasing energy for change. The initiator or leader of change who combines hope and empathy, even in the face of seemingly lost causes, has a much greater chance for breakthrough (Fullan (in Hargreaves) 1997, pp. 221–223).

If the successful re-culturing to collaboration and connection is to be effectively addressed, the examination of assumptions about emotion's place is needed.

All of these stories from teachers who wanted to connect with their leaders, those who thrived in connection and those who feared contact and lived in a state of anxiety, made me wonder what their leaders were feeling too. How and why were the precious few of these leaders so open and connected and others so distant and threatening?

Giving voice to silenced selves was meaningful to the teachers who participated in the interviews. When they experienced a sense of having a supportive relationship with their leaders, as they explained, for example, "that's why you do more!" Creativity in their classroom endeavours had naturally followed. However, within their stories, there were further silences, which in the end spoke volumes. Hearing their stories was meaningful to me as I struggled to piece together this puzzle of emotions and leadership. This study of teachers' emotions primed my interest to know more about the emotions of the leaders. In the next section, I address this part of the puzzle. As you will see, we have only heard one side of the story.

Principals Explore the Emotions of Leadership

With a very good idea of some of teachers' emotional understandings of leaders, I turned to the leaders themselves for further insights. In an online forum conducted over seven months (the International Leadership Conversation or ILC), 35 principals and head teachers from England, Ireland, Canada, the United States, New Zealand and Australia convened to consider the emotions of school leadership. Topics ranged from policy pressures and the highly managed self, to issues of parental power, the joys and agonies around students and their own well-being, and of course, the teachers. Detailed discussions of these data appear elsewhere (Beatty 2002b, 2005). The following is a brief summary of some of the highlights from their discussions.

The online forum, far from the culture of isolation and loneliness to which these leaders were accustomed, was intensely personal and even intimate. For one principal, despite many good friends and close family ties, the ILC "virtual world" was "more powerful than the real version". Their references to "feeling known" by receiving a "response to me personally" online were held in stark contrast to not experiencing being responded to personally in the "real" world. For school principals, the personal self is "buried" under other roles and expectations. As well, emotional honesty was a "luxury" that most leaders had found they simply could not afford, not even with themselves. Online this was beginning to change.

Clear evidence of shifts in perspective and deepening of capacities for emotional meaning making processes or emotional epistemologies, as I call them, was evident from the leaders' retrospective comments. To explore this newly discovered potential for connection between them was decidedly counter-cultural at first. They noted that by sharing their emotional selves they were extending the definition of "professional". Reflections on the experience follow:

> It has made me reflect more on practice as a leader. My effects on other people....I am far more reflective as a leader now as a result of this conversation...than I was before having this kind of access to so many other colleagues. Headship is such a lonely position at times, it is also so busy that you don't necessarily have time to talk to colleagues down the road, but this makes that in-depth discussion accessible and possible away from the work place giving you time to reflect on issues. I realise now I need to give myself more breathing space before resolving issues, to stop jumping in and dealing with things in a "fire-fighting" way. I'm thinking much more about the emotional aspects of leadership—mainly the effects of my decisions on other people working with me. Before doing this I

> tended to think of headship in the U.K. in isolation. This has widened my perspective not just of leadership, but of education in general. It has been so valuable to be in conversation with other heads/principals in other parts of the world and to realise that their day-to-day issues are no different to my own. The context may be slightly different and the education system operated slightly differently but at the end of the day we are all dealing with young people's lives and our effects on them—that's the most awesome and powerful part of leadership.
>
> I was privileged to be part of just seeing and knowing how much we all react to the emotional dimension about our jobs and our lives…so often we don't see that when we are talking in groups/at meetings etc. I guess in those situations we tend to want to show that we are on top of all the situations thrown at us and we don't let people see how we really feel.
>
> The "emotions of leadership" has played an important part in my consciousness. …just knowing how angry, upset, happy, etc. other people get has allowed me to feel OK about the way I feel. I guess the privilege of being part of the conversations has been to legitimize MY feelings, and to go with them, rather than try to block them out. …We work with people and their emotions and their "emotional baggage" all day every day. Being able to talk on line about feelings was not only cathartic, it has helped me acknowledge the emotions of my staff members more openly.

In order to become and stay connected to their inner selves, school leaders need more than the usually efficient admin team relationships they have with their deputies and assistant principals. These data illustrate how, in the face of the isolation and emotional constrictions on their patterned interactions with others and themselves, there is tremendous value in the emotional support of a candid collaborative connection with other leaders. Emotionally grounded reflection in action began to affect both their inner and outer work, by assisting them in deepening their awareness of the emotional context in which they and others dwell.

> I know when I replay key emotional scenes with staff, and find myself wanting, it's often because I haven't allowed myself time to deal with the issues myself so my responses are borne more out of my needs, perceptions and immediate emotion rather than out of that empathy that develops with reflection and thought.

I concluded that the provision of support for leaders to consider themselves and others in such fully dimensional terms was a process that deserves serious attention in leadership preparation for a better future in schools.

Emotional Control and the Teacher–Leader Relationship

Like the problems noted by Starratt (1991) above, these leaders noted a definite distance between themselves and their teachers. They were keenly aware of the professional imperative to remain emotionally hidden, calm and rational at all times. Loath to appear weak or out of control, they could not afford to show or even to speak about their own fears to the faculty. While they tried always to take time to cool down when anger threatened to reveal them and harm others, when they had succumbed to the urge to burst out in anger, they were ashamed and regretful for having broken the smooth surface of their purely rational and detached personas.

In conversation online with their peers, they began to consider how teachers' emotional baggage presented challenges to them in their roles as authority figures: "Staff do forget you're human, and argue with the position not the person." Other colleagues echoed this experience.

> I sometimes feel that leaders are in a no win situation because no matter what your style, personality and knowledge of "the craft" people respond to you from their experiences of leadership in the last educational setting they were in, and this is often trapped in their emotions of how they interacted with the school principal when they were at school! I believe they take this emotional fear and weave it around an image of power, which many perceived as a child and often dump this on the educational leader they meet as a staff member.

These leaders were gatekeepers for the policies they had to get teachers to implement, a role which was taking an emotional toll.

> Confusion, exhaustion, exhilaration, the need to rebuild trust, realization that expectations must be realistic, identifying where individuals are and moving from there, building in personal time, empathy for others, designing support systems within your own building because that is where it is truly happening and the difference can be made. …As principal I feel I am somewhat of the gatekeeper, I have the responsibility to implement policy, however, I also have the power to manage and ensure that we don't totally drown in the policy shift.

After sharing some of the teacher study results with the online leaders, they began to consider the teachers' perspectives in their discussions. As they were recalling their own pleasure in seeing teachers thrive, they began making the connections between their treatment of teachers and teacher performance.

> Teachers are marvellous creatures. With my staff I feel the same. They achieve terrific things, especially if they are treated as trained, sensible adults who want to do a good job. It's important to let them get on with it. Giving a responsibility to a budding young teacher, and seeing him or her thrive and grow is just as satisfying and good fun as seeing students learn.

> I believe that creating an environment where teachers feel free to expand, take risks initiate projects is so important. The full issue of trust is front and centre. Knowing that they are valued, able to initiate the project or activity (always discussed prior to) inviting feedback is a powerful way to encourage teachers to grow.

However, these leaders seemed always to be giving something, whether their masked frustration and generated enthusiasm, or their encouragement, their concern, their patience. The giving was continuous and unrelenting. Along with caveats about the demands on teachers, the need to get out into the classrooms and the emotional rewards for leaders of enjoying teachers' successes, it was clear that teachers' needs can tax the already overloaded principal who sometimes finds it altogether too much to have to consider them too. For example,

> I respond with all my heart to the need for the principal to commend teachers for the daily job well done…and you can't do that if you don't know what is going on! All the rhetoric in the world about the importance of what is going on in classrooms is negated if no-one (i.e., the principal in particular) takes notice of what is going on in classrooms. The comment about why couldn't she do that every day? (I think in relation to feedback) made me mad. It is so easy for classroom teachers to say that. They want everything else done too. …Right now I feel that there is nothing left of me for anything else.

In the main, however, the online principals expressed a sense of duty to remain positive and cheerful to make up for the emotional baggage of teachers. If their own emotional needs deserved attention, they got none. Turning to teachers for support or companionship was considered unprofessional. Instead, their own emotional struggles would be waiting for them on the trip home.

The Leader's Self

One place to begin to understand the implicit and explicit emotional dimensions of the relationship between leaders and teachers is with the emotionality of leaders themselves. The capacity for connection with others depends heavily on the quality of connection one has with oneself as Ken Leithwood and I discuss in the last chapter of our book, *Leading with Teacher Emotions in Mind* (Leithwood and Beatty 2008). To extend trust and openness in communication, the leaders' own sense of inner security is essential (Blase and Blase 1997; Palmer 1998).

> Becoming a leader of that sort—one who opens, rather than occupies space—requires the same inner journey…beyond fear and into authentic selfhood,…toward respecting otherness and understanding how connected and resourceful we all are. As those inner qualities deepen, the leader becomes better able to open spaces in which people feel invited to create communities of mutual support,…of collegial discourse…more than support….—they could offer healing for the pain of disconnection from which many faculty suffer these days. (Palmer 1998, pp. 160–161)

The leader's relationship with her/himself will ultimately be involved in the in-depth exploration of relationships he or she may experience with others. All human relationships involve emotions. Echoing and reinforcing sentiments in earlier work by others (e.g. Noddings 1984, 1992; Sergiovanni 1992; Regan and Brooks 1995; Fullan 2001) we can see the connection between the ethics of caring, moral leadership and relationships. The ethical self is an emotionally connected self (Margolis 1998) and emotional understanding is critical to maintaining healthy relationships that engender trust in moral connection with one another.

> …leaders must be consummate relationship builders with diverse people and groups—especially with people different than themselves. Effective leaders constantly foster purposeful interaction and problem solving, and are wary of easy consensus. (Fullan 2001, p. 5)

Applying Emotional Ways of Knowing in Leadership Preparation

It has been exciting and rewarding to have had the opportunity in the United States and Australia to apply the implications of these prior studies in Masters level leadership preparation programming design and delivery. The emotional epistemologies framework (Beatty 2002a), which emerged from the reanalysis of all data from the teachers and leaders studies referenced above, reflects a progression of four stances. The first is a root position of literal and figurative "emotional silence" from which there is denial of emotions and their importance. The second stance reflects judgement of self and others from an "emotional absolutism" perspective, whereby emotions are considered right and wrong and rewarded or punished according to externally defined feeling rules and internal emotional knowledge authority is denied. The third stance, "transitional emotional relativism" sees emotions temporarily taking a position on the agenda. It is experienced when a deepening of emotional connectedness with self and other begins to occur. The proposed fourth stance, "resilient emotional relativity" depicts a deepened and integrated use of emotional knowledge as emotional meaning making is seamlessly integrated in the daily round. Problem solving and relationship building are enhanced as people learn to interpret and remain non-anxious yet fully present to others (Friedman 1985).

In the U.S. context, the framework was used as an advance organiser for part of a Masters level school leadership preparation course about understanding self. Students who participated in the study of the framework's utility indicated its powerful impact upon their reconceptualisation of their professional selves and leadership work (for a full report see Beatty and Brew 2004).

In Australia, first at Monash University and now at the University of Melbourne, I have been able to design Masters degrees with emotional meaning making and collaborative reflection positioned as foundational to the development of all educational leadership capabilities. The "Master in School Leadership" curriculum progresses through ever widening lenses, from a focus on *inner leadership* to *leading learning communities, understanding environments* and *leading change through professional action research.* Within this sequence of individual units, the concepts of the framework are embedded in the pedagogical, participatory and assessment protocols and thereby are applied more implicitly than explicitly. Discovery, challenge and explorations from the various emotional epistemological perspectives (Beatty 2002a) are inherent in this inductive design.

Breaking the silence on emotion occurs from the very first day when students who are aspirant and incumbent leaders and their mentors attend an orientation day on campus. Critical to the success of the course is the role of collaborative reflective practice which continues throughout the two years of part-time study. From the outset, students learn to embrace the pedagogy of discomfort (Boler 1999) by addressing the power of emotional wounding in their professional experience. The transformational effects of posting to an online reflection centre and giving feedback on these focused reflections are attributable to the deliberate and explicit integration of personal, professional, organisational and scholarly dimensions (Beatty 2000b). As budding scholars, their gleanings from the literature are considered in terms of personal and professional experience. This process helps to establish a practice for making sense of the tensions associated with increasing responsibilities in their school settings. Their engagement in collaborative reflection becomes a source of strength and protects them from the normative tendencies toward emotional numbness and interpersonal detachment. This collaboration with cohort colleagues continues beyond graduation providing ongoing support for long-term success in leading change in their schools. In addition to their intra-cohort collaborations, action research projects grounded in collaborative learning community building in their home schools, extends the application of these processes. Early results from studies of the efficacy of this approach indicated that it is highly successful in promoting leader preparedness for building collaborative cultures and accomplishing successful change agency along with maintaining leader well-being and resilience (Beatty 2006). Recently, I have been exploring the evidence of observable sustained impact—on leaders, colleagues and students—from these leaders' experiences in the course.

With ethics approval from the masters in school leadership (MSL) scholarship sponsoring government department, potential principal participants who were also graduates of the Monash masters course (grounded in the author's theoretical framework) were invited to participate in this follow-up study. In response to the initial call, from among a potential sample of 30 qualified participants, at the time of this writing 10 had consented to participate by granting an interview, and supporting the invitation to participate for their assistant principals, teachers and regional network leaders. All participants also granted access to school-level data through either direct provision or summaries. This study is in its earliest phase of data collection and preliminary analysis. A brief description of emerging patterns follows.

Looking Back on the MSL

Operationalising the author's theoretical framework of emotional epistemologies has informed the design of these purpose-built MSL courses, an intervention to promote a dramatic culture shift from traditionally distant hierarchical, command and control modalities, to more distributed and collaborative professional learning and leading cultures in Victoria's state school system. The MSL at Monash was in its seventh year at the time of writing. The new redesigned University of Melbourne MSL was in its first year. An earlier study, of student reflections, and interviews and surveys conducted upon completion of the MSL course, provided insights into a working set of "key elements" that reportedly had had a positive impact on their understanding of leadership and their preparedness to practice as collaborative culture builders (Beatty 2006).

Presently, I am exploring the lasting and flow-on effects from the course into the school system. Of interest to me are several research questions: What memories of the course experience might persist as having been significant and worthwhile, and of a high and lasting impact upon their personal and professional growth, their well-being, and their present leadership practices? What evidence of impact from this programmatic approach to leadership development might they be able to provide? How well might self-reported impacts be corroborated through interviews with subordinates, and super-ordinates? How might school-level data both formal and informal reflect these impacts? Of what lasting significance if any, have they found emotional meaning making or "em^2" in their practice?

The current impetus to reform school cultures and transform professional leadership practices includes the requirement to foster genuine inquiry into teaching and learning through ongoing collaboration in dynamic learning partnerships of various configurations. Empirically grounded programmatic approaches to leadership development that can support such a reform initiative are worth knowing. The identified course elements, the perceived impacts, and the flow-on effects into practice along with the potential triangulation of evidence of impact are all of interest in this large ongoing research project. Full results of this research will be reported on in detail in forthcoming publications. In this chapter, it is possible to report on some emerging themes in principal participants' self-report interview data. Interviews consider cutting edge culture reform-congruent leadership practices and the links participants have made between these practices and what I am calling "key elements" in the course.

Of particular note in this study's context are practices that participants report they would not have incorporated into their ways of leading had they not experienced them in the MSL. While this is not actually knowable, as other opportunities for similar learning could certainly have intervened and had similar effects, what these participants are reporting is that these elements did have these impacts upon them and that these practices are outside the traditional norms within the standard culture of leadership practices that they have observed or had implemented themselves, up to the point in their careers when they entered the course.

Preliminary Findings

From across a subsample of nine principal participants, emerging from the analysis of transcribed one-hour interviews is evidence of a definite departure from the standard fare. This notion of a "departure from the norm" has acted as a filter for inclusion in these preliminary data analysis stage.

Among the kinds of "course elements" that emerged in these initial interviews about participants' recollections of their key leadership-transforming learning experiences in the course are (1) readings; (2) pedagogy of discomfort; (3) modelling; (4) application of new learning:

1. Key readings acted as triggers to redefining leadership professionalism: broadening and deepening the definition to include the human, cultural, and symbolic along with the more traditional technical and educational domains (Sergiovanni 1984).
2. The requirement to move out of comfort zones, engage with discomfort in new ways, that involves reframing the discomfort itself as a catalyst for openness to new learning as well as a source of new understandings and ways of seeing and being.
3. Modelling of new leadership for learning practices by instructors.
4. The experience of applying the same concepts in collaborative reflective practices throughout the course—with cohort peers—and in professional action research "leading change" projects that were grounded in collaborative leadership principles applied in their schools.

All participants indicated the course had been personally and professionally transformational in a variety of ways, in particular in its influence upon their leadership style. Participants refer to the experience as (for example) "life changing". They consider themselves to be principals who have become far more:

- *Self-aware:* e.g. "more aware of how I operate particularly when under pressure [and] more aware of the impact I'm having on other people. [from] that first unit, 'Understanding yourself'... [In contrast to some of my principal colleagues] I treat everyone as equals and speak to everyone with the same amount of respect".
- *Courageous, open and willing to acknowledge their vulnerabilities:* finding this process freeing and strengthening, through the inner rebalancing effect this has on their own confidence, willingness to take risks, innovate and have the difficult conversations that honour their commitment to relational connectedness.
- *Collaboratively reflective:* new kinds of conversations occur in these principals' schools, conversations that illustrate the power of being able to reflect in action, with others, using emotional meaning making as a way of understanding and working with others.
- *Consciously and deliberately innovative and influential* upon others both subordinate and super-ordinate to their positions, within a vision of whole system reform.

Among the course elements to which they attribute some of these effects are those discussed in more detail below.

The Power of Print

Across the initial sub-sample of nine principal participants, all refer to key readings to which they attribute transformational impacts, including the following repeatedly mentioned: *The Wounded Leader* (Ackerman and Maslin-Ostrowski 2002), *Learning by Heart* (Barth 2004), *Leading with Teacher Emotions in Mind* (Leithwood and Beatty 2008). The reportedly transformational influence from these readings occurs by creating access to and legitimating the exploration of inner reflective spaces, including emotions, that were considered off limits in their prior professional perspectives on leadership in particular and education in general. In their principal roles, they were applying their learning, at their own schools and with their colleagues. One participant had shared *The Wounded Leader* with a fellow principal who was struggling.

> I gave her the wounded leader and said, "You've got to read this." She still says, "I wouldn't have made it had it not been for that."
> ...the one that I'll always get is a thing that always comes to my mind and that is Leading with Teacher Emotions in Mind. That is a throw away line. I think about that maybe once every couple of days or three days. Because we make a lot of decisions, and you'll hear, principals say it all the time, "It's about the kids." And that's a good way to justify anything. But I always now try and balance that against—think about the teacher—teacher emotions—and to me that's everything.

Embracing a Pedagogy of Discomfort—Working Through the Emotions

After an introductory day to acquaint mentors and mentorees, the course commences with a keynote lecture by one of the authors of a required text, *The Wounded Leader* (Ackerman and Maslin-Ostrowski 2002). Pat Maslin-Ostrowski invites her audience to consider their inner lived experiences, especially painful ones, as potential openings to new learning. Students then write and share their wounding stories, crafting them in final form as written reflections, which they post online for feedback from lecturers and peers. This is a confronting way to begin, deliberately so, and the desired effect is apparently quite memorable. Years after the experience, participants in this study still attribute this element with having promoted their openness to new learning and triggered a life altering journey of discovery.

> Pushing us out of our comfort zone from the very beginning got you over that big hurdle that you've got to get over—to then be able to be more open to learning.... Having that hurdle to jump at the beginning meant you're into that deep dip really quickly. Then you come out the other side and things start to feel good.
>
> The fact that we had to face up to the emotional side of this. And that there was one, and that was okay...just was the perfect beginning. And I think I've heard nearly all of them say that.
>
> The emotions stuff: I found that wounding, I think we might have touched down 5 times on the wounding. For me that was the best process. I've been through [pause] ever. I'm trying to think of something that would be remotely, other than some kind of physical challenge, like climbing a mountain somewhere or whatever, but looking at who you are as a...to go forward you need to really go back and look at our baggage and look at the things that did get us...for me it was certainly, it created a platform where I could go forward.

Seeing Is Believing

All participants noted in one way or another that they had had distinctive collaborative emotionally grounded leadership practices modelled for them in the course. This reportedly had led to their experiencing first hand, the feasibility of these practices, a kind of "seeing is believing" phenomenon. While readings, a traditional vehicle for knowledge transfer, were used to signal topics such as the relevance of emotions in leadership and learning, modelled by the instructors' in interactions with students, were ways of actually practising emotional meaning making (Beatty 2002b).

Applying Collaborative Reflective Practice: Creating Safe Spaces and Promoting Emotional and Cognitive Epistemological Shifts

Peer and connected knowing occurred regularly through the course, in face-to-face class discussions, preparation of group projects, virtual classroom and reflection centre online discussions.

> One of the things I probably didn't know going in to the MSL when I started it was that I learn through questioning and talking but need a safe space in which to do that because I haven't always had the confidence.
>
> Even if you didn't write that much into them, [the online forums] I just read everything I could get my hands on. I just felt that you just got this really great rounded picture of an idea.
>
> You had us [post online] our own [reflections] and reflect on three more? That's pretty simple but it made me really think about my own, and it made me think about other people's perspectives and other people's experiences. When you're doing it and are involved in that process, it was a pretty powerful process. I found that really outstanding. And to me, I was at a distance. I was a long way away most of the time, but that made me feel that it didn't matter where you were. You could have been in Siberia, but you were still getting a lot out of that. It was fantastic.

During the course students created collaborative teams in their schools to accomplish their action research projects, and participated in and initiated networks in ever-widening circles of potential influence on themselves and others. Implementation of emotional meaning making approaches were used to develop trust and foster relationships. These approaches were consistently aiding their pursuit of professional collaborative inquiry in the course, and change agency on the job.

> Really, the focus for the whole project for me has been the emotional side. The technical side is,…it's work, but it's not hard, or what I consider hard work.

Subsequent to the course, and in their capacity as leaders in the system, these principals are using readings to signal significance and model the integration of personal professional and organisational with scholarly dimensions of self (Beatty 2000b). Across the sample, it is apparent that they generate distinctly different kinds of conversations. Their use of these techniques is fostering the openness to collaborative inquiry and deeper professional learning in their schools and regions.

> I think what's happened in my principal group—there are nine of us—and our discussions are going through the roof. We met yesterday for three hours, and they get deeper and deeper and deeper and there are two of us on there that have completed your course which is probably a pretty high ratio for remote Victoria, and I reckon it has a real impact. And we had a person from Region there yesterday and they said they'd never seen a principals group discuss teaching and learning from the point of view of how it will affect their staff to such a degree. And I would—we sort of don't see it now, but I think on reflection that we would agree. It's pretty deep how we look at this stuff now, and I think that a lot of it's to do with what I experienced with you. Only yesterday, the topic was the ultranet which is basically an online portal…. Someone said, "We've got to support the teachers professionally" and someone else said "And personally because this stuff is 24/7 you know?"
>
> I let the conversation go longer now, with the staff. I let it go a bit longer than I would have and let it do its thing and often you get the good stuff—sometimes you don't there's no set rule for everything in the world….if you can keep that as a practice, people feel a bit safer, the next time a bit safer. I would imagine that if you had a principal that had done your course at a school, I reckon the staff there are going to get a better deal than a person that had not, quite simply. There you go.

Isolation, a perennial problem for principals, is less of a factor for these leaders, as they have been proactive in creating support groups of trusted colleagues with whom they can reflect and review their dilemmas and difficulties. The feeling of not being alone was assisting them in maintaining their well-being.

> I felt at the end of it that I didn't need to be isolated and that it was up to me whether I was or wasn't but it was a matter of finding people that could actually co-operate. And being able to be empathetic towards people is what allowed me to make that move.

There is evidence of a shift in perspective on knowledge and knowledge authority such that leadership was becoming synonymous with fostering adult learning.

> And it's really hard to find out where they're at so that then you can start to develop this understanding of partnership.
> Interviewer: So do you see that as a leader's role to try to find out where they're at and help them move along?
> And try **for them** to find out where they're at. Because...it's shifted now. It's all about how I can develop others. So I used to ask questions because I wanted the knowledge. Now I have to ask the questions because I want them to articulate where they think they're at. To actually build their own understanding of where they are. And even though I'm curious and I want to know, I don't really want to know for me anymore. I really want to know for them. [Emphatically] I want **them** to know **for them!**

Leading Change

In the course, students were required to lead whole school change in professional action research projects, developed and implemented over their two years of part-time study with a culminating assessment task in the final unit of writing a publishable research progress reporting article. Now, in their roles as principals and even further up the positional ladder, all participants have become focused and deliberate persons of influence. Self-efficacy to innovate, collaborate, network and reach out, challenge the system, do credible research, write and report, publish and present and assist others in achieving similar shifts in their knowledge authority indicate that these are learning leaders whose identities as change agents in the system are emerging strongly.

> The way I've learned to work is to be inclusive of people and say "We're all in this together and so let's design something that allows that partnership" and that whole sense...[getting] those connections between people in the best way that you can so that it will foster their learning.
> ...the other thing I think that's happened to me is I've got much more patient since your course. I reckon I'm just more patient. And you know your journey was quite long, and I know it seems like two years were quite short at times, but for me it was a long journey. I mean I went quite a long way.
> The biggest thing was that "leadership starts from within". The other thing was the building of networks and communities. That just gave me the confidence to be a systems thinker. And the other thing that I so value is the linking and triangulating of data and being able to have rigorous conversations with policy makers and people that look at my...and show that really my kids are doing really well. But having the confidence and not just accepting at face value what somebody says.

Further analysis will explore these themes and others that emerge from these and additional data to be gathered in the longitudinal project. Triangulation of evidence of impacts reported on by principal participants involves interviews with principals' super and subordinates, and system and school-level data both formal and informal.

At this first level of analysis, however, these principals have provided clear evidence of a turnaround leadership phenomenon, distinctive across the group. Extremely impressive school-level data; state-level learning team awards; high means in student performance, staff, student and parent opinion data; community engagement approaches; high-performing principal designations and successful innovative grant-funded initiatives: all signal that these are very effective leaders who are working in new ways.

Still, there are also emerging signs of a system in transition with some bothersome teething problems; for instance, between the departmental and regional levels of governance in hiring practices. Reportedly, the merits of learning-focused scholarly leadership that have been consistently promoted and scholarship-supported by the central department (and achieving impressive results) are not yet being acknowledged consistently at the regional level, especially in rural areas. There are signs that surveys, designed to confirm that performance and development cultures are in place, may not be fine tuned enough to capture what on the ground is clearly (according to an independent inspection team) a successful achievement of that objective. Even so, the leadership culture is shifting. Initial discomfort and corresponding push-back in opposition to a more professional learning-focused approach to leadership are gradually giving way to an increasingly enthusiastic embrace of collaborative learning among teachers in Victoria's schools. In response to initiatives of people like the principals interviewed in this study, outmoded hierarchical and even bullying ways of managing conflict are gradually being replaced by respectful, caring and supportive ways of working and learning together.

Conclusions

This chapter has provided a presentation and discussion of key findings from a decade of research into leadership practices, inner leader and teacher experiences, and the development of efficacious programmatic approaches to leadership development that supports leaders to become more confident and capable as supportive and facilitative change agents in their settings. Considered together, the findings from these studies suggest that the way *forward* and *out* into educational cultural reform, begins by journeying *back* and *in* to the dwelling places of personhood. The value of explicitly, consciously and consistently working through the integration of personal with professional, organisational and scholarly dimensions, and using emotional meaning making as professional practice, are emerging clearly as catalysts for this kind of system wide change. Cascading effects upon fellow principals and other leaders' colleagues through their new ways of working, are making a difference in teacher practices, parent involvement, and student engagement and performance. Principals in the most recent study report being highly engaged and even in flow (Csikszentmihalyi 1990) in their work. In these leaders, the signs of the highest level of commitment are clear. At the same time, they have learned not to be so hard on themselves.

> I think [before, I was leaning] more toward self-punishment. I'm a lot less harsh. I think I'm more reflective, but I think its' more beneficial because I'm trying to learn from it instead of beat myself up over it.

They don't hesitate to apologise, admit mistakes and forgive themselves and others. Able to stay the course in a purposeful direction, as they remain open and learning, these leaders have become more patient and yet they are still striving. A fine balance is their goal.

> No we don't get it right 100% of the time but you know, we're moving in the right direction.

Still there are indications of lingering threats to their well-being, with high blood pressure, exhaustion, and stress management issues emerging. The courage to act upon their commendable commitment to address others' needs and to influence a system to change is in evidence in these leaders' stories. However, the attention to their own needs continues to be an important part of their learning, something that every one of them is aware of and taking steps to address, some more successfully than others.

Is working through the lens of emotion a panacea to principal well-being and effectiveness? No. But from the early signs in these data, preparation programs that do open the door to these new kinds of socially and emotionally grounded learning, foster new perspectives on knowledge and knowing, the development of a broader and yet more relationally focused set of capabilities, as well as capacity building within individuals and across the system. As the job of school leader becomes more and more complex, just to survive, these principals need something practical. And there is nothing more practical than a good theory, not just espoused, but put to good use.

The theories and practices that these principals are employing need to become part of a global standard for leadership and leadership preparation. Without them, the work is too personally daunting and culturally prohibitive. With them the culture can change, one principal, one teacher, one parent, one student, and one school at a time.

In Victoria, the critical mass of people who are working in this way is building. The kinds of conversations that are occurring in classrooms, staff rooms, parent councils, principal networks, regional networks, and central offices are definitely different. Perhaps this phenomenon, of which this course is but one of many contributing factors, helps to explain some of the attention the Victoria state school system is currently receiving from the global community.[4] According to the principals, teachers, graduate students and Victoria state school principals who have been part of this decade of research, there is transformational power in reconsidering the role of emotions for its influence upon learning at all levels. The evidence is mounting that going through the emotions, can help school leaders get to the heart and soul of education.

---

[4] In 2007, the Victoria State School System became a case of note for educational leadership development according to the OECD. http://www.oecd.org/dataoecd/27/22/39883476.pdf. Accessed on June 18, 2010.

References

Ackerman, R., & Maslin-Ostrowski, P. (2002). *The wounded leader: How real leadership emerges in times of crisis.* San Francisco: Jossey Bass.

Ackerman, R., & Maslin-Ostrowski, P. (2004). The wounded leader and emotional learning in the schoolhouse. *School Leadership and Management, 24*(3), 311–328.

Barth, R. (2004). *Learning by heart.* San Francisco: Jossey-Bass. (Original work published 2001)

Baxter Magolda, M. (1992). *Knowing and reasoning in college. Gender-related patterns in students' intellectual development.* San Francisco: Jossey-Bass.

Beattie, M. (1995). *Constructing professional knowledge in teaching: A narrative of change in professional development.* New York: Teachers College Press, Columbia University and Toronto: Ontario Institute for Studies in Education Press.

Beatty, B. (2000a). The emotions of educational leadership: Breaking the silence. *International Journal of Leadership in Education, 3*(4), 331–357.

Beatty, B. (2000b). Teachers leading their own professional growth: Self-directed reflection and collaboration and changes in perception of self and work in secondary school teachers. *Journal of In-Service Education, 26*(1), 73–97.

Beatty, B. (2002a). *Emotional epistemologies and educational leadership: A conceptual framework.* Paper presented at the annual meeting of the American Educational Research Association, New Orleans, LA, 1–5 April 2002, ED468293.

Beatty, B. (2002b). *Emotion matters in educational leadership: Examining the unexamined.* Unpublished doctoral dissertation, Ontario Institute for Studies in Education, University of Toronto, Toronto Ontario.

Beatty, B. (2005). Emotional leadership. In B. Davies (Ed.), *The essentials of school leadership* (pp. 122–144). Thousand Oaks: Sage.

Beatty, B. (2006). Becoming emotionally prepared for leadership: Courage, counter-intuition and commitment to connectedness. *International Journal of Knowledge Culture and Change Management, 6*(5), 51–66.

Beatty, B., & Brew, C. (2004). Trusting relationships and emotional epistemologies: A foundational leadership issue. *School Leadership and Management, 24*(3), 329–356.

Beatty, B., & Brew, C. (2005). Measuring student sense of connectedness with school. The development of an instrument for use in secondary schools. *Leading and Managing, 11*(2), 103–118.

Belenky, M. F., Clinchy, B. M., Goldberger, N. R., & Tarule, J. M. (1986). *Women's ways of knowing: The development of self, voice and mind.* New York: Basic.

Belenky, M. F., Clinchy, B. M., Goldberger, N. R., & Tarule, J. M. (1997). *Women's ways of knowing: The development of self, voice and mind* (2nd ed.). New York: Basic.

Blase, J., & Anderson, G. (1995). *The micropolitics of educational leadership.* New York: Cassell.

Blase, J., & Blase, J. (1994). *Empowering teachers.* Thousand Oaks: Corwin.

Blase, J., & Blase, J. (1997). *The fire is back!: Principals sharing governance.* Thousand Oaks: Sage.

Blase, J., & Blase, J. (2001). *Empowering teachers: What successful principals do.* Thousand Oaks: Corwin.

Blase, J., & Blase, J. (2003). *Breaking the silence: Overcoming the problem of principal mistreatment of teachers.* Thousand Oaks: Corwin.

Boler, M. (1999). *Feeling power: Emotions in education.* New York: Routledge.

Brady, P. (2008). Working towards a model of secondary school culture. *Canadian Journal of Educational Administration and Policy, 73,* 1–26.

Bryk, A. S., & Schneider, B. (2002). *Trust in schools: A core resource for improvement.* New York: Russell Sage Foundation (The American Sociological Association's Rose Series in Sociology).

Collard, J. L. (2001). Leadership and gender: An Australian perspective. *The Journal of Educational Management and Administration, 29*(3), 343–355.

Coser, L. A. (1977). *Masters of sociological thought: Ideas in historical and social context* (2nd ed.). New York: Harcourt Brace Jovanovich.

Csikszentmihalyi, M. (1990). *Flow: The psychology of optimal experience.* New York: Harper & Row.
Dean, S., Beatty, B., & Brew, C. (2007). Creating safe and caring learning communities: Understanding school based development of social capital. In L. Smith & D. Riley (Eds.), *ACEL Yearbook, 2007: Blooming leadership* (pp. 25–50). Armidale: Australian Council for Educational Leaders.
Denzin, N. (1984). *On understanding emotion.* San Francisco: Jossey-Bass.
Dunlap, D. M., & Goldman, P. (1991). Rethinking power in schools. *Educational Administration Quarterly, 27*(1), 5–29.
Fineman, S. (1996). *Emotion in organizations* (2nd ed.). London: Sage.
Fink, D. (2005). Developing leaders for their future not our past. In M. Coles & G. Southworth (Eds.), *Developing leadership: Creating the schools of tomorrow* (pp. 1–20). Berkshire: Open University Press.
Friedman, E. H. (1985). *Generation to generation.* New York: Guilford.
Fullan, M. G. (1997). Emotion and hope: Constructive concepts for complex times. In A. Hargreaves (Ed.), *ASCD Yearbook: Rethinking educational change with heart and mind* (pp. 221–223). Alexandria: Association for Curriculum and Development.
Fullan, M. G. (1999). *Change forces: The sequel.* Bristol: Falmer.
Fullan, M. G. (2001). *Leading in a culture of change.* San Francisco: Jossey-Bass.
Fullan, M. G., & Hargreaves, A. (1996). *What's worth fighting for in your school?* (2nd ed.). New York: Teachers College Press, Columbia University.
Glickman, C., Gordon, S., & Ross-Gordon, J. (1998). *Supervision of instruction: A developmental approach.* Needham Heights: Allyn & Bacon.
Hargreaves, A. (1998a). The emotional practice of teaching. *Teaching and Teacher Education, 14*(8), 835–854.
Hargreaves, A. (1998b). The emotional politics of teaching and teacher development: With implications for educational leadership. *International Journal of Leadership in Education, 1*(4), 315–336.
Hargreaves, A. (2000). Mixed emotions: Teachers' perceptions of their interactions with students. *Teaching and Teacher Education, 16*(8), 811–826.
Hochschild, A. R. (1983). *The managed heart: The commercialization of human feeling.* Berkley: University of California Press.
Hoy, W. K., & Tschannen-Moran, M. (1999). Five faces of trust: An empirical confirmation in urban elementary schools. *Journal of School Leadership, 9*(3), 184–208.
Lasky, S. (2000). The cultural and emotional politics of parent-teacher interaction. *Teaching and Teacher Education, 16*(8), 843–860.
Leithwood, K., & Beatty, B. (2008). *Leading with teacher emotions in mind.* Thousand Oaks: Crowin and Sage.
Leithwood, K., Day, C., Sammons, P., Harris, A., & Hopkins, D. (2007). *Seven strong claims about successful school leadership.* London: National College for School Leadership Department for Education and Skills.
Lieberman, A. (1996). Networks and reform in American education. *Teachers College Record, 98*(1), 7–45.
Little, J. W. (1982). Norms of collegiality and experimentation: Workplace conditions of school success. *American Educational Research Journal, 19*(3), 325–340.
Mahn, H., & John-Steiner, V. (2002). The gift of confidence: A Vygotskian view of emotions. In G. Wells & G. Claxton (Eds.), *Learning for life in the 21st century: Sociocultural perspectives on the future of education* (pp. 46–58). Cambridge: Blackwell.
Malen, B., & Ogawa, R. T. (1988). Professional-patron influence on site-based governance councils: A confounding case study. *Educational Evaluation and Policy Analysis, 10*(4), 251–270.
Margolis, D. R. (1998). *The fabric of self: A theory of ethics and emotions.* New Haven: Yale University Press.
Maslow, A. (1954). *Motivation and personality.* New York: Harper & Row.
Maurer, R. (1996). *Beyond the wall of resistance.* Austin: Bard.

Nias, J., Southworth, G., & Yeomans, R. (1989). *Staff relationships in the primary school.* London: Cassell Education.

Noddings, N. (1984). *Caring: A feminine approach to ethics and moral education.* Berkley: University of California Press.

Noddings, N. (1992). *The challenge to care in schools.* New York: Teachers College Press.

Palmer, P. (1998). *The courage to teach.* San Francisco: Jossey-Bass.

Paterson, F., & West-Burnham, J. (2005). Developing beginning leadership. In M. Coles & G. Southworth (Eds.), *Developing leadership* (pp. 108–126). Berkshire: Open University Press.

Perry, W. G. (1970). *Forms of intellectual and ethical development in the college years: A scheme.* New York: Holt, Rinehart & Winston.

Peterson, K. D., Gok, K., & Warren, V. D. (1995). *Principals skills and knowledge for shared decision making.* Washington: U.S. Department of Education, Office of Educational Research and Improvement.

Regan, H., & Brooks, G. (1995). *Out of women's experience: Creating relational leadership.* Thousand Oaks: Corwin.

Schmidt, M. (2000). Role theory, emotions, and identity in the department headship of secondary schooling. *Teaching and Teacher Education, 16*(8), 827–842.

Sergiovanni, T. (1984). Leadership and excellence in schooling. *Educational Leadership, 41*(5), 4–3.

Sergiovanni, T. (1992). *Moral leadership.* San Francisco: Jossey-Bass.

Short, P., & Greer, J. (1997). *Leadership in empowered schools.* Upper Saddle River: Prentice Hall.

Silins, H., & Mulford, B. (2002). Organizational learning and school change. *Educational Administration Quarterly, 38*(5), 613–642.

Starratt, R. J. (1991). Building an ethical school: A theory for practice in educational leadership. *Educational Administration Quarterly, 27*(2), 185–202.

Vygotsky, L. S. (1978). *Mind in society.* Cambridge: Harvard University Press.

Author Index

C. Day, J. C.-K. Lee (eds.), *New Understandings of Teacher's Work*, Professional Learning and Development in Schools and Higher Education 6,
DOI 10.1007/978-94-007-0545-6, © Springer Science+Business Media B.V. 2011

Subject Index

C. Day, J. C.-K. Lee (eds.), *New Understandings of Teacher's Work,* Professional Learning and Development in Schools and Higher Education 6,
DOI 10.1007/978-94-007-0545-6,

CPSIA information can be obtained at www.ICGtesting.com
Printed in the USA
LVOW070250090113

314964LV00004B/72/P

9 789400 705463